SUPPLY CHAIN
RISK MANAGEMENT

SUPPLY CHAIN RISK MANAGEMENT

Vulnerability and Resilience in Logistics

Donald Waters

The Chartered Institute of
Logistics and Transport (UK)™

KOGAN PAGE

London and Philadelphia

Publisher's note

Every possible effort has been made to ensure that the information contained in this book is accurate at the time of going to press, and the publishers and author cannot accept responsibility for any errors or omissions, however caused. No responsibility for loss or damage occasioned to any person acting, or refraining from action, as a result of the material in this publication can be accepted by the editor, the publisher or the author.

First published in Great Britain and the United States in 2007 by Kogan Page Limited

120 Pentonville Road
London N1 9JN
United Kingdom
www.kogan-page.co.uk

525 South 4th Street, #241
Philadelphia PA 19147
USA

© Donald Waters, 2007

The right of Donald Waters to be identified as the author of this work has been asserted by him in accordance with the Copyright, Designs and Patents Act 1988.

ISBN-13   978 0 7494 4854 7

British Library Cataloguing-in-Publication Data

A CIP record for this book is available from the British Library.

Library of Congress Cataloging-in-Publication Data

Waters, C. D. J. (C. Donald J.), 1949–
    Supply chain risk management : vulnerability and resilience in logistics / Donald Waters.
        p. cm.
    Includes index.
    ISBN-13: 978-0-7494-4854-7
    ISBN-10: 0-7494-4854-7
1. Business logistics. 2. Risk management. I. Title.
  HD38.5.W3844 2007
  658.7--dc22

                                                                2007022711

Typeset by Saxon Graphics Ltd, Derby
Printed and bound in Great Britain by MPG Books Ltd, Bodmin, Cornwall

Contents

Preface

There is constant pressure on managers to improve the efficiency of their supply chains, allowing materials to move quickly and at low cost. This pressure has encouraged a stream of new initiatives and methods. But there is a growing realization that these new methods also bring unforeseen problems. In particular, they increase the supply chain's vulnerability to disruptions. By removing the slack that used to protect supply chains from unforeseen events, they create inflexible chains where even a small, unexpected event can bring everything to a standstill.

You only have to look at newspaper headlines to see evidence for this – with industrial action in US ports stopping deliveries of Chinese goods to Europe, an earthquake disrupting electronic supplies from Japan, a major supplier of components going out of business, a hurricane causing devastation in the Gulf of Mexico, a container ship losing its load in the Indian Ocean and a manufacturer moving its factories from Germany. Of course, not all risks affecting supply chains hit the headlines, and you rarely hear about late deliveries, price rises, road accidents, damaged goods, traffic congestion, and the host of other factors that supply chain managers have to worry about. But even the smallest risks can affect performance, and they need careful management. This probably seems obvious, but supply chain risk management is a surprisingly new concept and is at a very early stage of development.

A huge number of events can affect the operations of a long and complicated supply chain. These unexpected events define the risks, and supply chain risk management is the function responsible for managing them. The aim of this book is to introduce the principles of supply chain risk management, review current thinking, describe the methods that are most widely used in practice, and show where the subject is heading. We take a straightforward approach, developing ideas in a logical sequence without being diverted into philosophical discussion or getting lost in the latest jargon.

The book is aimed at anyone who wants to know about risk management and its growing impact on the supply chain. This includes people from many different backgrounds, so we cannot assume much common knowledge. To make sure that we are all moving in the same direction, the early chapters outline the importance of the subject, and review the core areas of risk and supply chain management. Then the book develops the principles of supply chain risk management, from the steps needed to introduce it, to the complexities of emergency planning.

Working with risk

Risk and management

Everyone is familiar with risk. We may not have a formal definition, but we generally think of risk in terms of unpleasant things that might happen. There is a risk that an investment will lose money, that a train will be delayed, that we will have a motor accident or that someone will become ill. For managers, risk is a threat that something might happen to disrupt normal activities or stop things happening as planned. For instance, there is a risk that a new product will not sell as well as expected, that a project will not be successful, that the costs of raw materials will rise, that a delivery to customers will be delayed, that a supplier will go bankrupt or that a warehouse will be destroyed by fire.

Risks occur because we can never know exactly what will happen in the future. We can use the best forecasts and do every possible analysis, but there is always uncertainty about future events. It is this uncertainty that brings risks. Alberta Highways can do everything possible to build a new road on schedule, but an unexpected snowstorm can cause delays; Mazda can carefully arrange a delivery of cars to Berlin, only to find their journey interrupted by industrial action; Dell can schedule its production of computers, and find that a typhoon in Taiwan hits the supply of chips.

The basic problem with discussing risks is that they come in so many different forms. They can appear at any point in a supply chain from initial suppliers through to final customers; they can interrupt the supply of materials or the demand for products; they can cause sudden peaks in demand or collapses; they can range in scope from a minor delay through to a natural disaster; their effects can range from short-term and lasting only a few minutes through to permanent damage; their effects might be localized in one part of a supply chain, or passed on to threaten the whole chain. And different risks can be linked, in the way that an outbreak of some disease can cause a spike in demand for surgical masks, vaccines and antiseptic wipes, but a drop in the availability of people to produce them.

In reality, most risks are fairly minor and have limited consequences. For instance, congestion on a motorway might make a delivery an hour late; although this is unfortunate, in the big scheme of things it is rarely a catastrophe. On the other hand, risks occasionally have enormous consequences. For instance, unexpected market conditions in 1997 left the clothing retailer Next with the wrong things in stock – and when it could not meet customer demand there was a dramatic drop in sales, followed by a fall in share price (Braithwaite and Hall, 1999a, 1999b). In 2001 over-optimistic forecasts encouraged the electronics manufacturer Cisco to build up stocks to meet customer demand that never materialized. It eventually wrote off $2.2 billion of excess stock. In 2006, the weaver Camillario lost 60 per cent of sales when its main customer moved operations to China, and it almost immediately went into liquidation. Toyota shut down 20 of its 40 assembly lines for six weeks following a fire at a valve supplier, with an estimated cost of $40 million a day (Nelson, Mayo and Moody, 1998).

Telefon AB LM Ericsson

On 17 March 2000 there were thunderstorms in New Mexico, and lightning hit an electric power line (Latour, 2001). This caused a surge in power, which started a small fire in Philips' chip-making factory in Albuquerque. The automatic sprinkler system put this out within 10 minutes, and fire damage to the building was slight. Unfortunately, thousands of chips that were being processed were destroyed. But more importantly, the sprinklers caused water damage throughout the factory and smoke particles got into the sterile area, contaminating millions of chips held in stock.

Four thousand miles away, Ericsson was Sweden's largest company with an annual revenue of $30 billion, 30 per cent of which came from mobile telephones. For many years, Ericsson had worked on the efficiency of its supply chains, and single sourcing was a key element in its drive towards lower costs and faster deliveries. Now the Philips plant was its sole source of many radio frequency chips, including those used in an important new product.

At first, Philips thought that the plant would return to normal working within a week, so Ericsson was not too concerned when it heard about the fire. However, it soon became clear that there was more extensive damage. Philips actually shut the factory completely for three weeks, it took six months for production to return to half the previous level, and some equipment took years to replace. Ericsson had no alternative suppliers, and at a time of booming sales it was short of millions of chips.

In 2001 Ericsson said that the drastic reductions in production and sales caused by the fire cost it more than $400 million. When this figure was published, its share price fell by 14 per cent in a few hours. For a variety of reasons, including problems with component supply, marketing mix, design, and the consequences of the fire, Ericsson's mobile phone division lost $1.7 billion that year. It decided to withdraw from handset production and outsource manufacturing to Flextronics International. It changed its approach to procurement, moving away from single sourcing and ensuring that there were always backup suppliers. It also introduced systems for risk management to avoid similar problems in the future (Norman and Jansson, 2004).

We can learn several lessons from Ericsson's experiences. First, it is surprising how vulnerable major corporations are to relatively small events. A 10-minute fire caused havoc, cost millions of dollars, and left Ericsson as 'an also-ran in an industry where it had once been a leader' (*Economist*, 2005). Second, organizations are affected by events that are far away, and over which they have no control. Here a Dutch company had a small fire in a US factory, and this had disastrous effects for a Swedish multinational. Most importantly, Ericsson had no mechanism for dealing with unforeseen events, and when something unexpected actually occurred it did not know what to do. This last point is important, as it suggests that the company had no plans for dealing with risks. Presumably it assumed that it would never be hit by risky events – or it would be able to deal with any events as they occurred. This policy clearly failed, suggesting that a better option is proactive, identifying potential problems before they occur and designing responses in advance. Then a company is prepared for any major incident and can immediately implement its previously designed response. At the time of the Albuquerque fire, this approach to risk management was already being used by one of Ericsson's rivals, the Finnish company Nokia.

Nokia

At the time of the 2000 fire in Albuquerque, Nokia was another leader in the communications industry, with revenues of $20 billion, more than 70 per cent of which came from mobile telephones. It also used the Philips factory as a source of chips, and between them Ericsson and Nokia bought 40 per cent of its production.

But Nokia's reaction to the problem was much faster and more positive than Ericsson's. In the 1990s Nokia had suffered from shortages of components that limited production and cost millions of dollars in lost sales. It took various measures to stop this happening again, including the appointment of a 'supply chain troubleshooter' who identified problems and sorted them out as quickly as possible. And it carefully avoided single-sourcing key components.

Its proactive risk management meant that Nokia did not have to wait until Philips told it about the fire, but its 'events management system' quickly noticed a hiccup. The company immediately contacted Philips, and within hours of hearing about the fire had assembled a team to assess problems, find ways around them, monitor conditions and offer technical support. More directly, it put pressure on Philips to divert capacity in other plants to maintain its supplies – and it negotiated with other suppliers, redesigned chips so that other companies could make them, and redesigned products to use slightly different chips. Nokia used its considerable influence to get everyone's cooperation. Alternative Japanese and US suppliers were delivering new chips within five days, and 10 million chips were supplied by other Philips factories in Eindhoven, the Netherlands and Shanghai, China. As a result of its actions, Nokia's production was hardly affected by the fire.

Need to manage risk

The differences between Ericsson and Nokia highlight the importance of managing risk. To put it simply, Nokia was prepared to deal with unforeseen events, and Ericsson was not. Peck (2004) says that Nokia got better results 'first because its supply chain was inherently more resilient than Ericsson's; second because its risk identification, control and mitigation procedures were much better; third because its operations were agile enough to respond to the unexpected'. This view suggests that three core elements of supply chain risk management are the design of a resilient chain, procedures to manage risk and agility. We develop these themes in later chapters, but it is interesting that even a leading company like Ericsson did not have procedures in place for managing risks in its supply chains.

The idea of managing risk is not new. You can see evidence for this when an insurance company charges a premium for taking on a risk, or banks charge higher interest rates for more risky loans. But in recent years risk management has expanded from its traditional home in finance and the view that it is a specialized function done by actuaries. Instead, it is becoming a broader function that is involved in most decisions, and is even becoming an intrinsic part of management. As Handy (1999) says, 'Risk management is not a separate activity from management, it is management.'

Perhaps the main reason for this expansion of risk management is the perception that business is becoming more risky. Hunt (2001) says that both the number of risks faced by organizations and their potential consequences are growing. This was confirmed by a survey from the Economist Intelligence Unit (2001), which found that 'Many companies perceive a rise in the number and severity of the risks they face.' To some extent, this growing concern is a response to well-publicized disasters – earthquakes, tsunamis, terrorist attacks, diseases, accidents, bankruptcies and so on. But it also recognizes that firms are vulnerable to small events. When heavy traffic delays deliveries, customers move to more reliable suppliers; when an internet service fails, users switch to other providers; when prices suddenly rise, customers look for alternative products; a late payment makes a supplier favour other customers. Even small events have a cumulative effect on an organization's performance – and eventually its long-term survival. Kleindorfer *et al* (2003) studied accidents in the chemical industry and found that huge economic and environmental damage was caused by not only major disasters like Bhopal and *Exxon Valdez*, but also the thousands of minor incidents that occur almost routinely. Then it becomes important for managers to recognize the risks in their normal work and take steps to manage them actively.

Growth of risk management

Governments have a long tradition of emergency planning for, say, terrorist attacks, riots, wars and natural disasters. But this is less clear in business, where companies tend to assume that they will not be hit by a major disaster. At first sight, this laissez-faire attitude makes sense. Why should they put effort into planning for events that will probably never happen? But you could ask the same thing about insurance. Why do you take out fire insurance when your house is very unlikely to burn down? And the answer is the same. Some events may be very unlikely, but when they do occur the consequences are catastrophic. If you do not have fire insurance and your house burns down, you face bankruptcy; if a company is hit by an unforeseen crisis, it may not have the resources to continue.

Unfortunately, it is easy to find examples of companies that are devastated by unexpected events. The Enron Corporation was widely praised as a model of good management – before its dramatic collapse due to accounting irregularities. This collapse also took along the auditors Arthur Andersen, which had been considered one of the world's leading firms of accountants. WorldCom followed in the United States, along with Barings Bank and Energis in the UK, the Dutch retailer Royal Ahold, the Italian dairy conglomerate Parmalat Finanziara, and a host of other major names.

It seems that even the biggest organizations are not immune from the effects of risk.

Following a spate of well-publicized problems, businesses came under growing pressure to improve corporate governance and, in particular, identify and manage risks. In 1992 the Cadbury Report said that company directors should establish and report on their systems for:

■ identifying significant risks;
■ considering the likelihood that the risks would materialize;
■ assessing consequences if the risks did materialize.

The London Stock Exchange soon insisted that listed companies adopt these guidelines, thereby reducing the chances of damage from unforeseen events and increasing financial stability. After the Cadbury Report came the Institute of Directors' (1995) *Standards for the Board*, Hempel's Committee on Corporate Governance (1998), the Turnbull Report (1999) and the Combined Code on Corporate Governance (2003). Governments were also looking more positively at corporate risk management, and they began introducing legislation – such as the German commercial code, which requires the early identification of risks that could threaten the existence of a company. In 2002 the United States passed the Sarbanes–Oxley Act, which requires chief executives and financial directors to make specific statements about risk in their annual reports. In particular, they have to disclose all significant risks to corporate well-being, including those that were previously considered outside their responsibilities. For instance, outsourcing agreements must be declared, together with statements that the third-party providers also use appropriate risk management. The Sarbanes–Oxley Act also extends the concept of senior management responsibility by removing their traditional defence of not knowing about the wrongdoing of other people within the organization.

Good corporate governance requires that companies use a formal approach to risk management, and as a minimum this should:

■ protect the interests of stakeholders;
■ ensure that senior managers properly discharge their duties of risk management;
■ safeguard the continuing operations of the organization by developing appropriate systems for risk management;
■ use formal procedures to identify and analyse the threats from risk;
■ have processes in place for dealing with risky events that actually occur and mitigating their effects;
■ monitor, review and control the whole risk management effort;
■ ensure the company's compliance with laws and regulations.

Risk in the supply chain

Supply chain management is responsible for the movement of materials all the way from initial suppliers through to final customers. Supply chain risk appears as any event that might affect this movement and disrupt the planned flow of materials.

> ■ There are risks in the supply chain when unexpected events might disrupt the flow of materials on their journey from initial suppliers through to final customers.

These risks might prevent deliveries, cause delays, damage goods or somehow affect smooth operations. But these initial effects are only a beginning, and the consequences are generally much broader. A late delivery of raw materials might halt production; it might raise costs by forcing a move to alternative transport, materials or operations; it might raise stocks of work in progress; it might make partners reconsider their trading relationships. An interruption to the supply chain can have widespread effects, with Hendricks and Singhal (2003) noting that shareholder return typically falls by 7–8 per cent on the day that a disruption is announced, operating income falls by 42 per cent and return on assets is down by 35 per cent.

There are basically two kinds of risk to a supply chain: 1) internal risks that appear in normal operations, such as late deliveries, excess stock, poor forecasts, financial risks, minor accidents, human error, faults in information technology systems, etc; and 2) external risks that come from outside the supply chain, such as earthquakes, hurricanes, industrial action, wars, terrorist attacks, outbreaks of disease, price rises, problems with trading partners, shortage of raw materials, crime, financial irregularities, etc.

External risks

The Sarbanes–Oxley Act acknowledges that supply chains are inherently risky. They move materials through a series of organizations, each with different operations, aims, cultures and structures, dispersed around the world and working in widely different conditions. And they move through regional instability, war zones, changing government policies, new trading regimes, inhospitable climates and every other problem that you can imagine. When you buy a toothbrush from the supermarket, it might have had a difficult journey starting from remote oil wells near the Arctic Circle or turbulent areas of the Middle East.

When we hear of things going wrong with supply chains, it is usually the dramatic effects of external risks – such as the 1995 earthquake in Kobe, the 1999 earthquake in Taiwan, the 2004 tsunami in the Indian Ocean, or

Hurricane Katrina in New Orleans in 2005. Each of these is certainly a major one-off incident – but when you add together all of the one-off incidents they form an ever-present background of external risk. We can illustrate this by the earthquake that damaged the Japanese city of Kobe. This was widely reported, because of the amount of damage – and because of concerns for a significant part of the world's electronics industry that was sited nearby. This earthquake was officially 'strong', registering 6.9 on the Richter scale, but we never hear about the 1,100 other earthquakes of equal size that occur around the world each year. With almost three strong earthquakes a day, it suddenly seems more likely that one of them might affect some part of a supply chain.

The key feature of these external risks is that they are outside managers' control. So managers cannot change the risk, but they can design operations that work as efficiently as possible within a risky environment. For instance, there is a continuing risk of hurricanes hitting the south-west coast of the United States. Managers cannot alter this risk, but they can design operations to reduce its effects, perhaps by having secure buildings, closing during the hurricane season or simply moving to another location.

Internal risks

Internal risks are generally less dramatic, but more widespread in their effects. These are the risks to operations that managers can control – such as delays and breakdowns – and there are traditional ways of dealing with them. For instance, risks from suppliers can be avoided by multiple sourcing, and when problems occur with one supplier it is easy to switch orders to another. Similarly, risks to the flow of materials are reduced by holding stocks throughout the supply chain to insulate the flows from unexpected variations.

The use of stocks to reduce the effects of risk illustrates a common pattern, where managers have to balance competing aims and risks. Stocks are expensive and there are clear incentives to reduce or even eliminate them. Then the initial balance seems to be between high stocks (which give low risk of disruption, but high costs) and low stocks (which give high risk of disruption and low costs). But a closer examination identifies other risks associated with high stock – such as obsolescence, deterioration, tied-up money, uncertain future demand, damage during storage and so on. So higher stocks increase some risks while reducing others, and managers have the more complex problem of balancing different types of risk and the associated costs.

UK fuel protests

In the 1990s the UK government was maintaining a policy of increasing fuel prices each year by 6 per cent more than the general rate of inflation. Between 1996 and 2000 the costs of fuel to road haulage companies typically rose from 28 per cent of total operating costs to 34 per cent, and up to 40 per cent for fleets doing high mileage. Other effects – such as the government's policy of charging high vehicle excise duty, and driver shortages that increased labour costs – gave UK freight operators significantly higher costs than operators in the rest of Europe. Transport operators from other EU countries, particularly Ireland and France, could work in the UK with distinct cost advantages over local operators, which saw their profit margins fall from 3.3 per cent in 1996 to 2.8 per cent in 1998 (*Commercial Motor*, 2000).

There were increasingly vocal concerns about unfair trading conditions, and the Road Haulage Association (2000) started a 'Fair Play on Fuel' campaign. Protest convoys were organized in several cities, and in September 2000 a combination of farmers and road hauliers started a blockade of oil refineries, which immediately interrupted fuel supplies. Two-thirds of transport companies said that they were affected, turning away business, giving priority to major customers, subcontracting out work, or lowering vehicle speeds to reduce fuel consumption. All customers could be affected by these measures, but particularly those that relied on small, frequent deliveries. Among these were just-in-time manufacturers who typically needed several deliveries a day – so they stopped production immediately the blockade started.

A continuing blockade would have caused immense damage to industry and the country as a whole, so the news that it would be lifted after a few days was warmly welcomed. There followed a 60-day period of consultation, during which the government's likely response remained uncertain. During this period, virtually all transport companies prepared for further disruptions, usually by installing bulk fuel tanks, but also by using more fuel suppliers and adjusting their terms of trade. In the event, there was no further industrial action.

In retrospect, very few transport operators actually ran out of fuel during the short blockade. But the widespread uncertainty and sense of impending chaos showed that few transport companies – or indeed their customers – had any plans to mitigate the effects of disruptions to fuel supplies.

Growing concern over supply chain risk

Logistics managers are under continuing pressure to improve the efficiency of their supply chains. For instance, they might remove stocks and use just-in-time (JIT) operations. But JIT illustrates the way that improving efficiency can also increase risks. In the past the effects of a minor event, such as a late delivery, could be absorbed by stocks – but now it can stop operations and bring an entire supply chain to a standstill. By removing slack from supply chains, managers are also making them more vulnerable – sometimes described as 'taut' or 'brittle'.

In 2005 the Chartered Management Institute surveyed 440 firms to see how their attitudes to risk had changed in the last six years and found that 'concern is almost universally higher across a broad range of threats'. The percentage of firms worried about disruption of the supply chain is clearly rising – even though the number that have actually experienced disruption is falling (see Table 1.1).

A dominant feature of supply chains is that all members are linked together, and a risk to one is automatically transferred to all other members. For instance, when one key supplier goes out of business, it is not just its immediate customers that are affected, but all other members of the chain. When a manufacturer stops production, all the upstream tiers of suppliers are affected back to the original suppliers. You can see the way that supply chain risks ripple around the world with the 2003 outbreak of SARS, or bird flu. This was largely contained to southern China and Hong Kong, but restrictions on travel disrupted business operations as far away as Toronto and London. Similarly, in 2005 hurricanes Katrina and Rita both hit oil refineries in the Gulf of Mexico, but the consequent fears of fuel shortages raised prices around the world.

Despite the obvious impact of supply chain risk, this is a new topic that has received very little attention. Christopher *et al* (2002) say that 'it appears from the available literature that the implementation of risk management in supply chains is still in its infancy'. In the past few years organizations have started making some progress in the area, largely motivated by the terrorist attack on New York's World Trade Center – now universally known as '9/11'. Suddenly it became clear that a single event can have catastrophic consequences. Although relatively few organizations were directly affected by the attack, the

Table 1.1 Firms and supply chain disruption

	2002	2003	2004	2005
Percentage of firms concerned with supply chain disruption	25	34	32	35
Percentage of firms experiencing supply chain disruption	19	11	12	10

raised awareness and new security at US borders had widespread effects. The Department of Homeland Security now coordinates the United States' strategy for terrorist threats and attacks, with similar organizations in other countries, such as the UK's Civil Contingencies Secretariat.

Responding to another terrorist attack, on the Abqaiq facility in Saudi Arabia through which 8 per cent of the world's oil supply passes, Karrenbauer says: 'The attack... is a compelling example of why [supply chain risk management] is so pressing. Every CEO/COO/CFO should be demanding a comprehensive supply chain risk audit and a corresponding set of mitigation strategies immediately, not waiting for a successful attack, pandemic, or another natural disaster' (www.insight-mss.com, 2006).

Clearly the main risks to supply chains do not come from terrorist attacks, but from the broad range of unforeseen events that might affect them (Sheffi, 2002). All supply chains face risks of many different kinds, and the flow of materials is much more likely to be disrupted by an unreliable supplier. Managers can control many of these risks, and the key point is that they should not wait to see what damaging events occur and then start thinking about their response. Instead, they should be proactive, identifying potential risks and planning their responses in advance. Then they are prepared and can take immediate action when an unexpected event actually occurs.

In summary

We generally view risk in terms of potential harm from unforeseen events. Because we cannot say exactly what will happen in the future, there are risks in all operations. These risks have to be properly managed. The alternative of ignoring them leaves organizations vulnerable to risky events (with consequences apparent from some major business failures).

The nature and broad complexity of supply chains makes them particularly vulnerable to risk. And the large number of links between disparate members mean that risks are transmitted throughout the chain, so that a small event in one remote area can grow into major consequences for other areas. Some of these risks are external to the chain and outside managers' control; others are internal and under managers' control.

A worrying trend has managers increasing the efficiency of supply chains by removing all the slack – and inadvertently increasing the risks. You can see this with JIT, which minimizes stocks but leaves the supply chain vulnerable to small disturbances.

Despite the growing concern for supply chain risk management, Christopher *et al* (2002) reported that 'Little research has been undertaken into supply chain vulnerabilities' and 'Awareness of the subject is poor.' This is changing, but progress is slow and most organizations have made little real progress.

The remainder of the book develops the theme of supply chain risk management. However, we have an immediate problem. If you collect any group of managers and ask them to discuss risk in the supply chain, they rarely agree about the meaning of either 'risk' or 'the supply chain'. So we have to ensure that we are all discussing the same things. For this reason, we start by reviewing the principles of risk in the next chapter, followed by a summary of supply chain management in Chapter 3.

2

Defining risk

Features of risk

The last chapter introduced the common view of risk, as the chance that an unexpected event can harm an organization. Risks occur because of uncertainty about the future – and, as we can never know exactly what will happen, there are always risks.

Specifically, risks to the supply chain are unforeseen events that might interrupt the smooth flow of materials. When a supplier delivers materials to a customer, there are always risks that the delivery will be later than promised, the goods will be damaged or lost, the wrong products will be delivered or the wrong amounts, the delivery will go to the wrong place, the invoice will have a mistake, the customer will not pay – or the many other things that can go wrong. These immediate symptoms can lead to more widespread effects throughout the chain.

Effects of risk

The main risk to a supply chain is disruption to the flow of materials. Other risks can be associated with this, and the UK's Security Service (2006) – commonly referred to as MI5 – lists the possible consequences from a major terrorist incident as:

- loss of staff through death or injury;
- damage to buildings;
- loss of IT systems, records, communications and other facilities;

- ■ unavailability of staff because of disrupted transport or their unwillingness to travel;
- ■ adverse psychological effects on staff, including stress and demoralization;
- ■ disruption to related organizations and businesses that are necessary for operations;
- ■ damage to reputation;
- ■ new business demands put on the organization.

The fundamental feature of risk is that unforeseen events may happen in the future – or, more properly, uncertainty about future events creates the risks.

- ■ Risk occurs because there is uncertainty about the future.
- ■ This uncertainty means that unexpected, risky events may occur.

Risks to the supply chain come in a huge variety. Some arise from external effects in the environment, while others come from internal operations; some are long-term that might strike at any point into the far future, and others are short-term and soon disappear; some have minor impact, while others destroy entire supply chains; some appear regularly in normal operations, and others are one-off disruptions such as natural disasters. But the risks only really materialize when some harmful events actually occur. You can see this in the following examples:

- ■ In 2002 a strike of fewer than 100 dock workers on the west coast of the United States disrupted the inward flow of consumer goods from Asia. It also disrupted the 'land bridge' that carries products from Asia, across the United States and on to Europe. Ships crossing the Pacific work to a monthly cycle, and it took almost six months for some containers to be delivered and for schedules to return to normal (Cavinato, 2004).
- ■ When Apple Computers released their first iPod, it was an instant success. In fact, it was so popular that the company had underestimated demand and could not deliver enough units for the important Christmas sales.
- ■ The retail chain Argos had a strategy of ambitious expansion, which it supported with large stocks of goods. When trading conditions changed it moved to a more limited expansion, but it already had excess stocks sitting in supply chains. The result was a write-down of stock value and a substantial fall in share price.
- ■ Coca-Cola had major problems with contamination in its bottling plant in Belgium, which it traced to a local supplier of carbon dioxide. Coca-Cola did not test the gas when it arrived, assuming that the supply was pure; the supplier did not test the gas, as it had never been asked to.

- A small agricultural company used child labour to pick crops. These crops moved through many intermediate stages in a complex supply chain, and eventually they arrived at a leading US food processor. The US company had never heard of the agricultural company and had no idea of the things that happened far upstream in one of its minor supply chains. However, publicity soon gave the impression that a major international corporation was exploiting child labour.
- Hurricane Floyd flooded DaimlerChrysler's plant in Greenville, North Carolina. The company makes many of its components there, and disrupted deliveries closed seven assembly plants across North America.

You can find other examples of supply chain risks in almost any newspaper, but the message is that when unpredicted events actually occur they can have severe consequences.

Reacting to risk

There are basically two ways of dealing with risk. The first – and almost the traditional approach – is to simply ignore it. For instance, an organization might depend on a key transport link, such as a container terminal; there may be no obvious way of continuing to work if this terminal hits problems – but, as this is very unlikely to happen, the easiest option is to simply ignore the risk. In the same way, managers might assume that deliveries from suppliers will always arrive when needed, that there is a steady demand for products, that customers pay their bills on time, that accidents never occur, that key people continue to work, and so on. This may seem naive or even foolish, but managers base their decisions on normal conditions, and risky events are, by definition, rare. As long as things continue to work normally there are no problems, and it is only when something unexpected actually happens that problems appear.

So ignoring a risk seems like a reasonable choice; as nothing generally goes wrong, so there are rarely problems. And preparing for events that are unlikely is a waste of time, which managers could spend on other jobs. And as a backup, when something does actually go wrong they will make appropriate responses to mitigate the effects.

But there are two problems with this approach. The first is the assumption that risky events are rare enough to ignore. Some are indeed very rare (such as earthquakes in New York) – but others are common (such as late payment of an invoice). Being risky is not the same as being rare. The second problem is that a reactive approach to problems – where managers wait to see what happens, then realize that they have to do something, design the response, implement it and wait for the recovery – is too slow. There can be considerable damage before the responses become effective, and managers will then be criticized with the cliché that they have done 'too little, too late'. You can imagine this with the Thames Barrier that stops London being flooded by exceptionally high tides. Building the barrier was a proactive policy that anticipated risks; a reactive policy would have been waiting until London actually flooded and then deciding what to do.

Clearly a reactive approach can be very expensive, and a far better option is to identify risks in advance and then prepare the best response. This response might avoid the risk, or reduce its effects, or do something else. Well-tried responses are holding stock to avoid risks to material flow, using multiple sourcing to overcome risks from suppliers, having spare capacity to avoid risks to operations, using long lead times to overcome variable demand, and so on. But you can see the difficulty that we have already mentioned, that these methods of avoiding risks often increase costs and reduce efficiency.

Georges Micheleau

Farmers have to supply very high-quality products to their customers, with any obvious faults meaning that they cannot sell their crop. Georges Micheleau grows a variety of soft fruits, which he sells to a local supermarket chain and a processing plant. Around August he employs seasonal pickers who take his annual crop to a packing shed, and from there a specialized transport company delivers it to supermarkets and the processor. In August 2006 the transport company's new IT system did not pay the fuel bill immediately but waited for a manual check of account details. The missing payment caused the fuel company to cancel its weekly delivery of diesel, and the transport company could not fill its trucks. It took three days to notice that something had gone wrong, sort out the problem and get more diesel – but then the transport company had a backlog of deliveries to make. Georges Micheleau is a small, irregular customer, and the transport company concentrated on reducing the backlog of its large, frequent customers. Georges did not realize anything was wrong until his customers began to ask about missing deliveries. Soft fruit can only be stored for a few hours before it begins to deteriorate, and by the time Georges's crop was delivered customers rejected 40 per cent of it as being in too poor condition.

In retrospect, simply improving the flows of information between Georges Micheleau, the transport company and the fuel company could have saved a lot of time, money and worry.

Decisions and risk

Risk management has largely evolved from the classic ideas of decision analysis, which considers the way that managers make – or should make –

decisions. It is based on the belief that a reasoned approach gives the best decisions, and managers should always use rational analyses for their decisions.

But you know that analytical methods do not really guarantee the best decisions. Managers make decisions in very complex circumstances – with rapidly changing conditions, uncertain goals, little information, tight deadlines, numerous constraints, diverse stakeholders, difficult relations with other organizations, political considerations, inherent uncertainty, varied opinions, limited resources and a whole range of other complications. The standard methods of analysis are too simplistic to deal with all of the complexities of real problems, so they cannot guarantee the best solutions (which is the reason they cannot say which shares will rise in value or which horse will win a race).

The need for judgement, as well as analysis, reinforces the view of 'management as an art' rather than 'management as a science'. This is an important point, as it suggests that managers can never guarantee to make the right decisions but only the ones that they think are best in the prevailing circumstances. And when a decision gives poor results, it may still have been the best option, as other decisions might have given even worse results. The problem, again, is uncertainty about the future – and risk. There is always a risk that events will not occur as expected, and when this happens even the best decisions can lead to poor results – and, on the other hand, managers might be lucky and make poor decisions that lead to surprisingly good results. As Merna and Al-Thani (2005) say, 'Uncertainty causes a rift between good decisions and good outcomes.'

Uncertainty and risk

So far we have been using the terms 'risk' and 'uncertainty', generally following Hetland's (2003) view that 'risk is an implication of a phenomenon being uncertain'. People often assume that the two terms mean the same (like Diekmann, Sewester and Taher, 1988), but technically there is an important difference.

■ Uncertainty means that we can list the events that might happen in the future, but have no idea about which will actually happen or their relative likelihoods.
■ Risk means that we can list the events that might happen in the future, and can give each a probability.

The key difference is that risk has some quantifiable measure for future events, and uncertainty does not. When you feel that a new product might sell well, you have uncertainty; when a market survey says that there is a 70 per cent chance of it selling well, you have risk. When suppliers say that a delivery of materials should arrive within three days, there is uncertainty; when they say that 90 per cent of deliveries will arrive within three days, there is risk.

Harm and benefit

Both risk and uncertainty deal with lack of knowledge about the future, and consider events that may or may not happen. But an important point is that they do not say whether the events are harmful or beneficial. The future price of oil is uncertain, but this does not say whether it will rise or fall – and we might be able to calculate a risk that it will rise, as well as a risk that it will fall. So Peck (2006) can describe risk as 'a measure of the possible upside and downside of a single rational and quantifiable decision'.

This goes against the general view of risk as being essentially harmful, appearing as lost deliveries, delays, supplier failure, shortages, accidents, falling demand, price rises, delays or any other damaging event. In this light, Stemmler (2006) says that 'Risk denotes the chance of danger, loss or injury.' The Royal Society (1983) describes risk as 'the probability that a particular adverse event occurs during a stated period of time', while March and Shapira (1987) consider the 'negative business impact'. This negative view probably originates from the overriding need to avoid catastrophes – as it does not matter how many good outcomes managers achieve, when a single bad outcome closes their organization. (During the English Civil war this view was summed up in the Roundhead saying, 'We can defeat Charles a thousand times and he is still the king; but if he defeats us once we shall all be hanged.') And the negative view is reinforced by the widespread publicity given to harmful events – and even managers' apparent belief that success is due to good management, but failure is due to unexpected events.

Managers certainly prefer to make decisions with more certainty, so they come to see all uncertainty as undesirable. By implication, the best option becomes the one with least risk. But to preserve a balance, we should not limit ourselves to the harmful effects of uncertainty and risk, but should also consider the things that might go well. For instance, we might consider deliveries arriving on schedule, lower costs, high customer demand, rising profits, smooth operations, accident-free periods and so on. Although it might seem odd, we can talk about 'the risk of higher profit' or 'uncertainty reducing the variability in demand' – and there is a risk of you winning the national lottery.

Many people go further and say that risk is positively beneficial. Apart from those who enjoy taking risks simply for the thrills, a classic principle of economics says that profit is a reward for taking risks, and the greater the risk the greater the profit (which is why banks charge higher interest rates to risky borrowers). Then some level of risk is beneficial – and even essential – for earning reasonable profits. The National Audit Office (2000) supports this view, saying that risk management 'offers the possibility for striking a judicious and systematically argued balance between risk and opportunity in the form of the contradictory pressures for greater entrepreneurialism on the one hand and limitation of downside risks on the other'.

So risk management should not necessarily try to eliminate or minimize risk, but it can also search for opportunities offered by uncertainty (Knight and Petty, 2001). This needs a balance, with managers setting the level of uncertainty that they are willing to work with. Some managers are natural risk takers and are happy to work with high levels of uncertainty, optimistically hoping for the best results; others are more conservative and prefer to avoid risk, pessimistically working to avoid potential harm (Figure 2.1).

Despite this advice, the reality is that managers rarely consider the potential benefits of risk and almost invariably concentrate on the threats (March and Shapira, 1987). Unfortunately, this makes a balanced view of events impossible (MacCrimmon and Wehrung, 1986). For instance, imagine a project with a 40 per cent chance of reducing profits and a 40 per cent chance of raising profits. All things being equal, you would expect managers to be fairly neutral about the project, but when they focus on the potential harm they only see the possibility of less profit and will reject it. This leads commentators to question managers' ability to take a balanced view, and suggests that they are more likely to be pessimistic and avoid risks. If the project had a 60 per cent

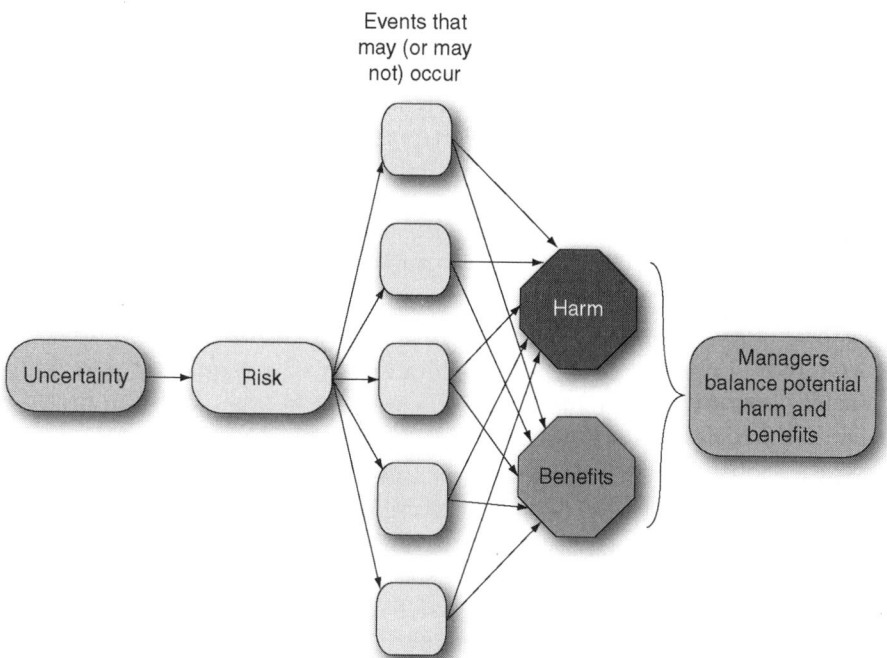

Figure 2.1 Balancing the potential harm and benefits from risky events

chance of making a profit, would the managers still focus on the possible loss and reject it?

Structure of decisions

To get a systematic approach to risk we have to look at its features in a bit more detail. We can start with a model that relates risk to management decisions, where all decisions follow a standard pattern with:

■ a decision maker – who is the manager;
■ an aim that the manager wants to achieve;
■ a number of alternative courses of action;
■ a decision of choosing the best alternative;
■ after the decision has been made, events occurring over which the manager has no control;
■ each combination of an alternative chosen being followed by an event happening, leading to an outcome that has some measurable consequence.

You can imagine this in a company that has identified a number of possible projects but only has enough resources to do one of them. The decision makers are the company managers, who have an objective of making the highest returns, the alternatives are the possible projects, and the decision is the project they will actually do. Then there are events over which the managers have no control and that determine whether the chosen project is a success or failure. The consequences give the value of choosing a project and having it succeed or fail.

North Face Industries

In 2004 managers at North Face Industries were considering a shortlist of four projects for developing ski slopes in the Canadian Rockies. (This identifies the decision makers, their likely aims and their alternatives.) After a lot of analysis, they chose to extend existing facilities at one of the resorts around Banff, Alberta (their decision). After two years of development and operation, it was clear that the new facilities were meeting customer needs and were judged a success (the event). At the end of 2006, the company sold their facilities to the neighbouring Foothills Resources Corporation, for a net profit of $11 million (the consequences).

Levels of uncertainty

Uncertainty can appear in every feature of a decision – who the real decision makers are, their real aims, the alternatives that are available, etc – but it is most obvious in the events. We can define different levels of uncertainty for the events as:

- *ignorance* – where we have no knowledge at all about what is going to happen in the future;
- *uncertainty* – where we can list the events that might happen but cannot give them probabilities;
- *risk* – where we can list the events that might happen and can give each a probability;
- *certainty* – where we know exactly what will happen in the future.

Each of these allows a different approach to decision making.

Decisions with certainty

The characteristic of certainty is that managers know, with certainty, which event will occur after their decision and what the consequences will be. If you put money into an investment that guarantees a return of 7 per cent, you know exactly what will happen. The obvious way of solving such problems is to list the alternatives, compare the outcome for each and choose the alternative that gives the best outcome. If you have a choice between four investments that guarantee returns of 5, 6, 7 and 8 per cent a year, you will obviously choose the one that gives 8 per cent.

This seems trivial, but in reality even decisions with certainty are difficult, and the best option is rarely obvious. For instance, would it be better for a health service to spend money on more kidney dialysis machines, higher wages for nurses, more open heart surgery, funding research into cancer, or building more parking spaces at hospitals? Most decisions contain subjectivity, and even when managers know all the circumstances they are still unlikely to agree about the best decision.

In reality, you will rarely meet certainty, as even the most assured conditions contain some doubt. In the investments mentioned above, there is the chance that the companies will go bankrupt, renegotiate conditions, be affected by new government legislation, be hit by criminal acts, and so on.

La Sociedad Camion

When the manager of La Sociedad Camion had a sudden booking to ship goods from Malaga, Spain to Moscow, Russia, she had several ways of providing drivers for the trucks. Each option had different costs, shown in Table 2.1. This table – called a pay-off matrix – gives a standard format for describing decisions, with alternatives listed down the left-hand side, events across the top and consequences in the body of the table.

Table 2.1 Pay-off matrix for ways of providing drivers

		Event
		Pay drivers
Alternatives	Pay full-time drivers for overtime	€5,600
	Hire current part-time drivers	€4,200
	Hire new temporary drivers	€5,000
	Use an agency	€6,700

Here the manager knows the costs, so there is only one event – to pay the drivers – and she is making a decision with certainty. Then she compares the consequences and chooses the best alternative of hiring current part-time drivers. In reality, her decision might also include some subjective factors (such as the quality of service offered by different options) and at least acknowledge uncertainty (perhaps reflecting the reliability of the options).

Decisions with uncertainty

Uncertainty means that several possible events might occur after a decision, but only one of them will actually happen. You can list all the events, but do not know in advance which one will occur, or even give them probabilities. For example, when you start a new job, a number of events can happen: you may not like the new job and start looking for another; you may get the sack; you may like the job and stay; you may be moved by the company. One event will occur, but they are largely outside your control and it is impossible even to give reliable probabilities.

Imagine that your company is about to launch a major new product. You have done all the market research, but customer reaction is still uncertain. It might be favourable, neutral or unfavourable – but you cannot put realistic probabilities to these. The profit from the product clearly depends on market conditions, so you might summarize these (in thousands of dollars a month) as follows:

Table 2.2 Pay-off matrix of customer reaction

	Customer reaction		
	Favourable	Neutral	Unfavourable
Launch product	19	5	–6

You cannot choose the event – or you would obviously choose a favourable response – but this is outside your control. The only thing that you can do is to launch the product and then sit back and see what happens. But what happens when you have a choice of launching three alternative versions of the product, with different profits, shown in Table 2.3?

Table 2.3 Pay-off matrix of customer reaction, with alternatives

		Events – customer reaction		
		Favourable	Neutral	Unfavourable
	One	19	5	–6
Alternatives	Two	11	8	–4
	Three	7	2	3

You clearly want to choose the best alternative, but it is by no means obvious which this is. If customer reaction is favourable, you would want to launch alternative One; if customer reaction is neutral you would want to launch alternative Two; and if customer reaction is unfavourable you would want to launch alternative Three. But the events occur after the decision, and you do not know in advance what the reaction will be. To solve such problems, managers use simple rules to suggest the alternative that achieves some goal. For example, they might treat all events as equally likely and choose the alternative with the best average outcome. Here the average outcomes are $6,000, $5,000 and $4,000 a month respectively, so managers would choose alternative One. Or they might have limited resources and want to avoid a big loss, so they might be pessimistic and find the worst outcome for each alternative and then choose the alternative with the best of these worst outcomes. Here, the worst outcomes for each alternative are –$6,000, –$4,000 and $3,000 a month respectively. Alternative Three is the only one that always makes a profit, so managers would be justified in choosing this.

Managers use many of these simple rules – called decision criteria – in different circumstances. For example, an ambitious manager might choose the alternative with the highest possible return; or a more cautions one might balance the best and worst outcomes for each event. The important point, though, is that these rules only give guidelines and they cannot identify any single 'best' decision.

Paco Menendes

Paco Menendes ran a computer store in the Mexican city of Guadalajara. In his spare time he did some system development, and in 2005 he designed a simple system for monitoring the movement of drivers and ensuring that they complied with legal requirements for working hours and rest periods. He had limited resources to market this system, and his main options were to market the system locally, sell nationally through a website, enter a partnership with an established software company, or sell the rights. His returns depended on demand, which he described as high, medium or low. Using this simple model he designed the pay-off matrix of potential annual gains (in thousands of dollars) shown in Table 2.4.

Table 2.4 Pay-off matrix of potential annual gains for Paco Menendes

| | | Demand | | | Calculation |
		High	Medium	Low	
Alternatives	Market locally	74	39	−30	11.6
	Use website	126	80	−15	41.4 Best
	Enter partnership	61	28	16	34
	Sell rights	38	41	28	33.2

He looked for a balance between the best and worst outcomes for each alternative, but put slightly more weight on the worst outcome by calculating:

$0.4 \times$ best outcome $+ 0.6 \times$ worst outcome

The results suggested that his best option was to sell through a website. However, when he explored the options more carefully, other considerations appeared and he decided to go into partnership with a national software supplier.

Decisions with risk

The characteristic of risk is that we can list the possible events, know that one of them will occur, and give each a probability. When you buy a lottery ticket you might not choose enough winning numbers to win any prize, or you might get some numbers right and win a small prize, or you might get more numbers and win a major prize – or you might get all the numbers right and win the jackpot. These are the events that might happen, and you can calculate the probability of each.

This description of risk was originally suggested by Knight (1921), when he explained, 'If you don't know for sure what will happen, but you know the odds, that's risk and if you don't even know the odds, that's uncertainty.' This distinction means that uncertainty remains 'the realm of judgement' – but for risk we can do some analyses.

Probability

The concept of risk is based on the probability of an event – where probability is a measure of likelihood, relative frequency or proportion of times an event occurs. When you toss a coin it comes down heads half the time and tails half the time, so you can say, 'The probability that a fair coin comes down heads is 0.5.' A pack of playing cards has 52 cards, 13 of which are hearts, so the probability that a card chosen at random is a heart (or any other suit) is $13/52 = 0.25$. As the probability of an event is the proportion of times that it occurs, it can only take a value in the range 0 to 1.

■ Probability = 0 means the event will never occur.
■ Probability = 1 means the event will always occur.
■ Probability between 0 and 1 gives the relative frequency or likelihood.
■ Probabilities outside the range 0 to 1 have no meaning.

An event with a probability of 0.9 is quite likely (it happens 9 times out of 10); an event with a probability of 0.5 is equally likely to happen as not; an event with a probability of 0.1 is quite unlikely (it happens once in 10 times).

There are three ways of finding probabilities for events:

1. *Calculation.* You can use your knowledge of a situation to calculate theoretical or a priori probabilities.

$$\text{Probability of an event} = \frac{\text{number of ways that the event can occur}}{\text{number of possible outcomes}}$$

The probability that two people share the same birthday is 1/365 (ignoring leap years). This is an a priori probability calculated by saying there are 365 days on which the second person can have a birthday and only one of these corresponds to the birthday of the first person.

2. *Observation.* You can use historical data to see how often an event actually happened in the past, and use this information to give an experimental or empirical probability.

$$\text{Probability of an event} = \frac{\text{number of times that the event occurred}}{\text{number of observations}}$$

In the last 100 deliveries from a supplier, 32 arrived more than a day late. This gives an empirical probability of 32/100 = 0.32 that deliveries are more than a day late.

A weakness of empirical probabilities is that the historical data may not be typical or relevant for the future. When a company has made a profit in each of the past 10 years, the empirical probability of it making a profit is 10/10 = 1.0. This may be accurate for the past, but changing conditions mean that it is not necessarily an accurate measure for next year.

3. *Subjective estimates.* This third approach is not really recommended, as it asks for people's opinions about the likelihood of an event. For instance, you might ask a finance department for a probability that a currency exchange rate will fall by more than 10 per cent next year. These personal estimates may be good enough to help with decisions, and they are the only option when there are no relevant data. Unfortunately, they are notoriously unreliable as they rely on people's judgement and opinions – as well as their ignorance, bias, lack of skills, prejudice and so on. You should always treat subjective estimates with caution.

Expected values

If the probability that a vehicle has an accident on a journey is 0.001, and an accident costs an average of €10,000 to repair, the expected cost of accidents on a journey is 0.001 × 10,000 = €10. Now suppose that you find generous sponsors who are foolish enough to pay you £20 every time you spin a coin and it comes down heads. On every spin of the coin there is a probability of 0.5 that it comes down heads, so your expected winnings are 0.5 × 20 = £10. But suppose the generous sponsors now want to recoup some of their losses and insist that you pay them £40 every time the coin comes down tails. Now on every spin of the coin you expect to win 0.5 × 20 = £10 for the heads, but lose 0.5 × 40 = £20 for the tails – giving a net loss of 20 – 10 = £10. This expected value is the average gain (or loss) that you would expect every time you spin the coin. Of course, it is not the amount you win or lose every spin, which is either a £20 win or a £40 loss – but it is the average return that you would expect from spinning the coin a large number of times.

■ Expected value = Σ (probability of event × value of outcome)

Suppose there is a probability of 0.5 that a project will make $2 million profit, a probability of 0.3 that it will make $1 million profit, or it will just break even. There are three events, one of which must occur, so the probabilities of the three events must add up to 1. Then the probability of breaking even is $1 - 0.5 - 0.3 = 0.2$. Now we can calculate the expected value as:

Expected value = 0.5×2 million + 0.3×1 million + $0.2 \times 0 = 1.3 million

This is the average profit you would expect to make when the decision is repeated a large number of times, and we can use this calculation to compare alternative decisions.

PJ Partridge Haulage Contractors

Last year PJ Partridge Haulage Contractors bid for a long-term contract to move newspapers from a printing works to wholesalers. When discussing its options, the company considered three tenders: a low one that assumed newspaper sales would increase and unit transport costs would fall; a medium one that gave a reasonable return if newspaper sales stayed the same; and a high one that assumed newspaper sales would decrease and unit transport costs would rise. The company estimated the probabilities for sales and profits (in thousands of euros) shown in Table 2.5.

Table 2.5 Probabilities for sales and profits

		Newspaper sales		
		Decrease P=0.4	Stay the same P=0.3	Increase P=0.3
	Low tender	20	30	32
Alternatives	Medium tender	10	40	20
	High tender	36	20	−10

The company calculated the expected value for each alternative:

Low tender	$0.4 \times 20 + 0.3 \times 30 + 0.3 \times 32$	$= 26.6$
Medium tender	$0.4 \times 10 + 0.3 \times 40 + 0.3 \times 20$	$= 22.0$
High tender	$0.4 \times 36 + 0.3 \times 20 - 0.3 \times 10$	$= 17.4$

As the low tender had the highest expected profit, this seems the best option.

Utilities

The expected value is widely used for comparing alternatives with risk, but it does not always reflect real preferences. For instance, consider the pay-off matrix of returns from an investment shown in Table 2.6.

Table 2.6 Pay-off matrix of returns from an investment

		Events	
		Gain P=0.1	Lose P=0.9
Alternatives	Invest	£500,000	–£50,000
	Do not invest	£0	$0

There is clearly a 90 per cent chance of making a loss, so most people would think this is too risky and not invest. But the expected values are:

Invest	$0.1 \times 500{,}000 - 0.9 \times 50{,}000$	$= £5{,}000$
Do not invest	$0.1 \times 0 + 0.9 \times 0$	$= £0$

These clearly show that investing is the better decision. The problem is that the expected values show the average return when a decision is repeated a large number of times – but it does not show the value for a single decision. Here, repeating the decision many times would give an average gain of £5,000 a time, but if you only make the decision once you are likely to lose £50,000.

Another weakness with expected value is that it assumes a linear relationship between the amount of money and its value. In other words, €1,000 has a value exactly 1,000 times greater than €1, and 1,000 times less than €1 million. At first sight this seems reasonable, but the rigid linear relationship is not really accurate. Imagine that you have no money at all, not even enough to buy food for the week. If you could suddenly get some extra money it would make a lot of difference, and even €10 would have a very high value. On the other hand, if you already have €10 million sitting in your bank account you would not notice an extra €10 and it would have virtually no value at all.

The message is that the same amount of money can have widely different values in different circumstances. We can describe this effect by a 'utility', which gives a more accurate view of the value of money. Figure 2.2 shows a graph of a typical utility curve. At the top of the curve, near point A, the utility is rising slowly with the amount of money. A decision maker in this region already has a lot of money and would not put a high value on even more. However, the decision maker would certainly not like to lose money and move nearer to point B where the utility falls quickly. Gaining more money is not very attractive, but losing it is very unattractive – so this suggests a conservative decision maker who does not take risks.

Region B on the graph has the utility of money almost linear, which is the assumption of expected values. A decision maker here is likely to look for a balance of risk and benefit. Finally, a decision maker at point C has little money, so losing some would not appreciably affect the utility, but gaining money and moving nearer to B would be very attractive. A decision maker here is keen to make a gain and does not unduly mind a loss – which suggests a risk taker.

In principle, we can establish a utility function like Figure 2.2 and then calculate expected utilities in the same way as expected values, but replacing the amount of money by its utility. Unfortunately, we usually hit problems in

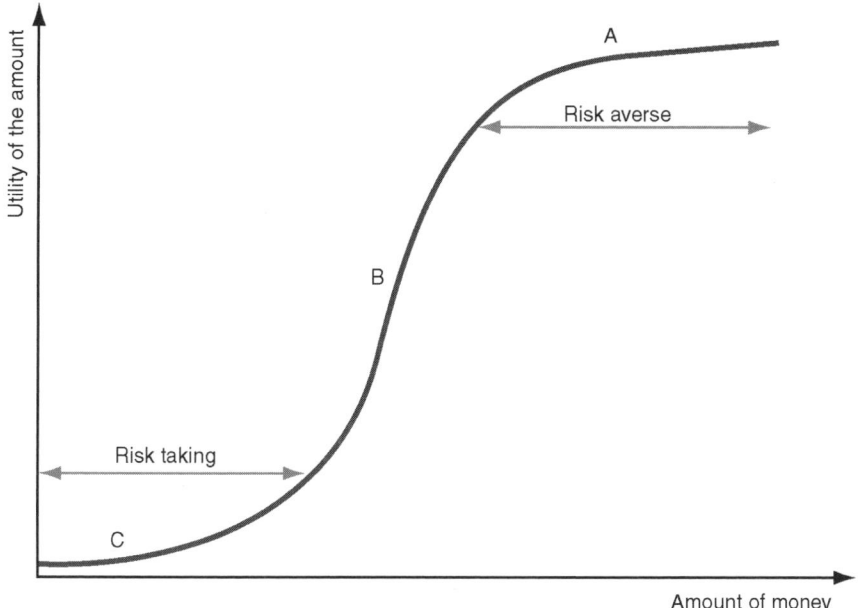

Figure 2.2 Utility curve showing the value of money

defining a convincing utility function. Each individual or organization has a different view of the value of money, and works with a different utility function. And to make things more difficult, these curves can change quickly – in the way that you might feel confident and risk-taking in the morning and conservative and risk-averse in the afternoon. However, these are really problems with the calculations and not with the underlying principle. People and organizations clearly put different values to money, and this affects their attitude to risk.

Decisions with ignorance

Uncertainty and risk mean that we do not have complete knowledge of future events – but they are both a long way from ignorance. We know the alternatives available, the events that might happen, the consequences that might occur – and with risk we can give probabilities to events. But the characteristic of ignorance is that we genuinely know nothing about a situation. In reality, this is very unusual – almost as rare as certainty – so we generally take a much more limited view and assume 'ignorance' means that we cannot identify all the possible events.

Usually, we know something about future conditions. We know that the sun will probably rise tomorrow – and in business we use forecasts and available knowledge to provide a lot of information. But we are still surprised by unforeseen events – and ignorance is based on the notion that we cannot really know what will happen in the future, and real circumstances are so complex that we cannot really identify every feasible event. Some people develop this view and say that all decisions are really made in ignorance, and any analyses are trying to impose an artificial structure on inherently unknowable conditions. For instance, managers may not know the probabilities of certain events, so they will tend to omit them from analyses – but this omits some events and effectively gives decisions with ignorance.

Earthquakes illustrate an interesting type of event, as they are always unexpected – suggesting that they are real risks, but are inherently unforeseeable or unknowable in advance. This suggests decisions with uncertainty, but realistically earthquakes are so rare that it is better to ignore them – and the myriad of similar risks – rather than consider them any further. Other examples of unknowable risks are an unidentified competitor entering a market, new technology making a product obsolete, a military coup, a trade union taking industrial action, a hurricane disrupting transport, the failure of a transport link, a supplier going out of business, and so on. Such events are essentially invisible and do not even exist until they actually happen.

It might seem that there is no way of dealing with unknowable risks except to wait until they occur and then make an appropriate response, effectively returning to reactive policies. However, an alternative is to design emergency plans that can be used in many different circumstances. For example, a company might install a backup power supply that it can use when any event disrupts the normal supply; or it can keep vehicles in reserve to cover any event that affects part of the normal fleet. These emergency plans act in the same way as the United Nations' emergency relief coordinator, who prepares plans to deal with general emergencies and then tailors them to meet any specific crisis that arises.

Managing risk

The essential feature of risk is a quantifiable analysis, principally involving events with known probabilities. Then risk management becomes the broad function for dealing with risks. But most tools for managing any level of doubt really assume risk, so we should repeat the warning that people use terms here rather loosely. For instance, you might hear someone say that 'There is a small risk of making a loss', suggesting that risk is a chance or probability. Or someone might say, 'The risk in this project is the $100,000 invested', using 'risk' to mean the value of the outcome. Or someone might consider risk in terms of the expected value – perhaps saying, 'With a 20 per cent chance of losing the €1 million deposit, our total risk is €200,000.' And people often talk about 'risk' in much vaguer ways, referring to any situation where there is doubt about the events or outcomes.

The broad function that considers any doubts about future events has become known as 'risk management' – even when it deals with other levels of uncertainty. Then risk management includes all the activities for dealing with situations of uncertainty, and it fits into our general model of decisions (shown in Figure 2.3) with:

■ *a decision maker* – the risk manager;
■ *an aim* – of dealing with uncertainty and risk;
■ *a number of alternatives* – the available responses to risk;
■ *a decision* – choosing the most appropriate response;
■ *events* – the risky events that actually occur;
■ *consequences* – of the event and response.

Much of risk management focuses on the three core activities of identifying risks, analysing their consequences and designing appropriate responses. We develop this theme in the following chapters. However, it is important to recognize that our knowledge of a situation changes over time. We might have very little information about events a year in advance, and be working with virtual ignorance; then as time passes we learn more and move through uncertainty, and then on to risk. We might even be approaching certainty for events a few days in advance. So another classification of events defines them as:

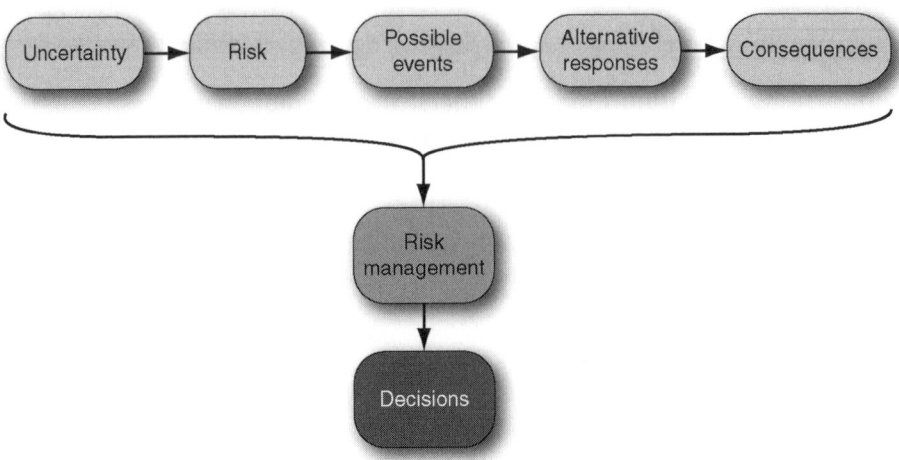

Figure 2.3 The basic process of risk management

1. known some time in advance, and certainly far enough in advance to be useful for decision making;
2. emerging over time, so that we can identify events and consequences as they get closer;
3. depending on progress, with events appearing when we move in a given direction, but not appearing when we move in a different direction;
4. inherently unknowable, where we work in ignorance and do not recognize events until they actually occur.

The importance of this classification is its suggestion that risks are not constant but emerge and change over time. This, in turn, means that risk management is never completed but is a continuing process. You can imagine this with a supplier who quotes delivery lead time of 72 hours; if a series of deliveries takes 75 hours, is this a normal variation or a sign that the lead time is getting longer and increasing the risk from late deliveries? To answer such questions, managers clearly need to monitor conditions, note how conditions change, and revise their plans for mitigating the effects.

In summary

Risk is generally viewed as the chance that an unexpected event can harm an organization. In practice, there are many types of risk to the supply chain, ranging from minor inconveniences of, say, a late payment through to the complete destruction of the chain in a natural disaster.

The idea of positively managing these risks is new, even though logistics managers have traditionally used standard methods to mitigate the most obvious effects (such as high stocks and spare capacity). More usually, managers tend to ignore risks to the supply chain and make a reactive response when an unforeseen event actually occurs. The problem is that this reactive approach is too slow, and a lot of harm can be done before it begins to have an effect. A better approach to risk management is proactive, analysing likely events before they occur and planning steps to mitigate their effects. In principle, managers should take a balanced view of risk, but they tend to be pessimistic and focus on the negative impact.

As we do not know exactly what will happen in the future, there is always risk to operations. We can develop analyses for this based on the standard features of decisions. In particular, we can categorize the doubts about future events as certainty, uncertainty, risk and ignorance. With certainty we know exactly which event will occur; with uncertainty we can list possible events but not give them probabilities; with risk we can add probabilities; with ignorance we cannot even list the possible events.

Different analyses deal with each level of uncertainty, but the most common use expected values to deal with risk. Then 'risk management' has become the general term for dealing with any level of uncertainty. The approach of risk management fits into our general model for decision making, but it focuses on the three core tasks of identifying risks, analysing the consequences and designing appropriate responses.

Now we can begin to consider risk management in the supply chain, but before we can do this we have to review the key ideas of supply chain management. This is done in the following chapter.

3

Supply chain management

Definitions

A problem when discussing any aspect of supply chain management is that people use different terms, or give the same terms different meanings. This is because the function now called 'supply chain management' emerged from a combination of formerly distinct disciplines, and each of these disciplines brought its own legacy of terms and ideas. As a result, terms still tend to mean – or at least imply – different things to different people. As a basic step, everyone probably agrees that supply chain management is responsible for the flow of materials through supply chains – but we still have to ask what they mean by materials, and what exactly is a supply chain?

Materials

When we talk about materials moving through an organization, it is easy to imagine this movement for tangible goods – such as a power station collecting coal from a mine, a farmer moving wheat to a wholesaler, or a computer manufacturer delivering PCs to a warehouse. But this movement is often less obvious, particularly when the materials are intangible – such as a television company delivering entertainment to viewers, a telephone company providing a communications service, or a research company creating new knowledge. Taking a broad view, we can consider everything that an organization 'moves' as material, whether it is raw materials, components, finished products, people, information, paperwork, messages, knowledge, consumables, energy, money, software or anything else.

> ■ Materials include everything that an organization moves.
> ■ These materials are both tangible goods and intangible (such as information).

All organizations move materials. Manufacturers collect raw materials from suppliers and deliver finished goods to customers; wholesalers move different types of product to retail shops; a courier delivers a book you ordered from a website. Every time a company buys, sells, rents, leases, hires, lends or borrows anything at all, someone has to make sure that materials are collected and delivered to their destination.

Supply chain

Logistics is the management function responsible for all movements of materials. Moving materials into an organization from suppliers is called inbound or inward logistics; moving materials out of an organization and on to customers is called outbound or outward logistics; moving materials within the organization is generally described as materials management (shown in Figure 3.1).

But organizations do not work in isolation, and each acts as a customer when it buys materials from its own suppliers, and then it acts as a supplier when it delivers materials to its own customers. So a wholesaler is a customer when buying goods from manufacturers, and is then a supplier when selling them to retail shops: a component maker buys raw materials from its suppliers, assembles these into components, and passes the results to other manufacturers. Products move through a series of organizations as they travel from the original suppliers of raw materials, through intermediate organizations, and on to the final customers. For instance, milk is a basic commodity

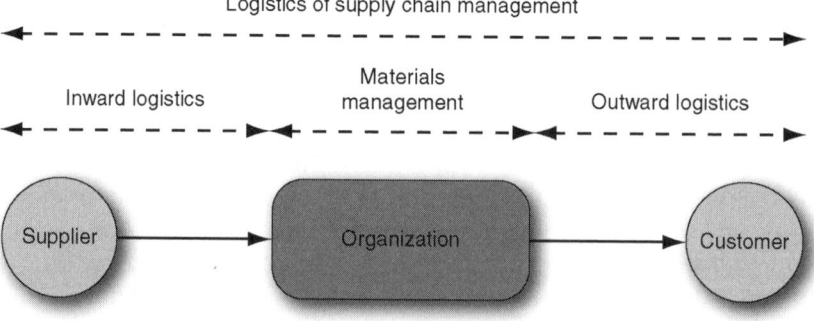

Figure 3.1 Logistics and material movement

that moves from a farm, through tanker collection, dairy, bottling plant, distributor and supermarket before we buy it. This chain of linked organizations and activities forms its supply chain.

■ A supply chain consists of the series of activities and organizations that materials move through on their journey from initial suppliers to final customers.

The Institute of Logistics (1998) described a supply chain as 'a sequence of events intended to satisfy a customer', giving a view so broad that it could include virtually anything. Other views are more focused, such as Peck's (2006) description of the 'flow of materials, goods and information (including money), that pass within and between organisations, linked by a range of tangible and intangible facilitators, including relationships, processes, activities, and integrated information systems'. Christopher (1998) focused on value to define a supply chain as 'the network of organisations that are linked through upstream and downstream relationships in the different processes and activities that produce value in the form of products and services in the hands of the ultimate customer'.

Every product has its own unique supply chain, and these can be both long and complicated. The supply chain for Cadbury's starts with cocoa beans growing on farms and ends with a hungry customer buying a bar of chocolate; the supply chain for Diesel jeans starts with cotton growing in a field and ends when someone buys them in a shop. The supply chain describes the total journey of materials as they move 'from dirt to dirt' (Cooper, Lambert and Pagh, 1997). Along this journey, materials might move through raw material extractors or growers, raw materials merchants, shippers, processors, transport companies, manufacturers, finishing operations, distributors, logistics centres, warehouses, wholesalers, retailers – and a whole range of others. Increasingly, the supply chain extends beyond the final customer to add recycling, recovery of materials and reuse.

From the point of view of risk, the significance of this arrangement of linked organizations is that a risk appearing to one can be transferred to all other parts of the chain.

Pharmaceutical supply

The demand for vaccines can vary widely in response to seasons, epidemics, scares, population movements – or military hostilities. In March 2003, the US led an invasion of Iraq, involving more than 300,000 troops. All of these needed various vaccinations, and world demand rose sharply. One of the world's largest pharmaceuticals companies raised production to meet the demand, but it was constrained by limited capacity. The constraint was not its own capacity to produce vaccines, but a supplier's ability to provide enough packaging. In particular, vaccines were put into glass vials, and the supplier of these high-quality vials was working at full capacity and could not meet the increased demand. Despite the severe shortage, the supplier of the glass vials was reluctant to transfer production away from other products destined for regular customers, predominantly the huge quantities of bottles used by breweries for their beer.

Supply chain management

Since the 1980s the term 'supply chain management' (SCM) has been used increasingly by people who argue that 'logistics' does not give a broad enough feel for the subject. Their feeling is that logistics is a somewhat narrower subject, concerned with movements within a single organization, while supply chain management takes a broader view of movement through all the related organizations that form the supply chain (Larson and Halldorsson, 2004). Then Handfield and Nichols (1999) describe supply chain management as a 'holistic management approach to integrating and co-ordinating the material, information and financial flows along a supply chain'.

In reality, SCM might emphasize the importance of integrating activities, but this has been a developing theme of logistics for decades (Forrester, 1958). The choice of terms is largely a matter of semantics, and here we stick to the convention that the two terms refer to exactly the same function. This is supported by the Chartered Institute of Logistics and Transport (www.ciltuk.org.uk, 2007), which says that 'Logistics is the time-related positioning of resources, or the strategic management of the total supply-chain.'

■ Logistics – or supply chain management – is the function responsible for the transport and storage of materials on their journey from original suppliers, through intermediate operations, and on to final customers.

Structure of a supply chain

The simplest view of a supply chain has a single product moving through a series of organizations, each of which adds value to the product. Taking one organization's point of view – the focus organization – activities in front of it (moving materials inwards) are called upstream; those after the organization (moving materials outwards) are called downstream (as shown in Figure 3.2).

The upstream activities are divided into tiers of suppliers. A supplier that sends materials directly to the organization is a first-tier supplier; one that sends materials to a first-tier supplier is a second-tier supplier, and so on back to the original sources. Customers are also divided into tiers. One that gets a product directly from the organization is a first-tier customer; one that gets a product from a first-tier customer is a second-tier customer, and so on to final customers. Then a manufacturer might see sub-assembly constructors as first-tier suppliers, component makers as second-tier suppliers, materials providers as third-tier suppliers, and so on; and it might see wholesalers as first-tier customers, retailers as second-tier customers, and end-users as third-tier customers.

There are a huge number of different configurations for supply chains. Some are very short and simple – such as a restaurant buying vegetables directly from a farmer. Others are long and complicated, like a shirt moving from a cotton farmer through to the final customer. Most organizations collect materials from many different suppliers, so supply chains tend to converge on the focus organization as raw materials move through the tiers of suppliers; then they tend to diverge as products move out to meet demands from different types of customer.

This picture of supply chains is getting more complicated, and the reality can be enormously complex. The complete supply chain for a car contains thousands of different organizations, and each organization can work with many – often thousands of – different products. The French company Carrefour is Europe's largest retailer, and comes at the end of tens of thousands of supply chains; the Anglo-Dutch company Corus makes steel that is in countless final products. And although we concentrate on the flow of materials, there are at least three flows through a supply chain – materials, information and money. So a computer company like Dell can be on many supply chains through its manufacturing of PCs, and many other chains through its information processing.

The reality is that supply chains consist of entwined sets of interacting entities of almost unimaginable complexity. Because of this intrinsic complexity, many people argue that the term 'supply chain' gives too simple a view and we should really talk about supply networks, supply/demand networks or supply webs. Other terms refer to a logistics channel to emphasize marketing, a process to emphasize operations, a value chain to emphasize value added (Porter, 1985) and a demand chain to emphasize customer satisfaction. Again, such differences reduce to semantics rather than content, and we will stick to the usual name – but recognize that a supply chain really includes a very complex pattern of movements between connected members.

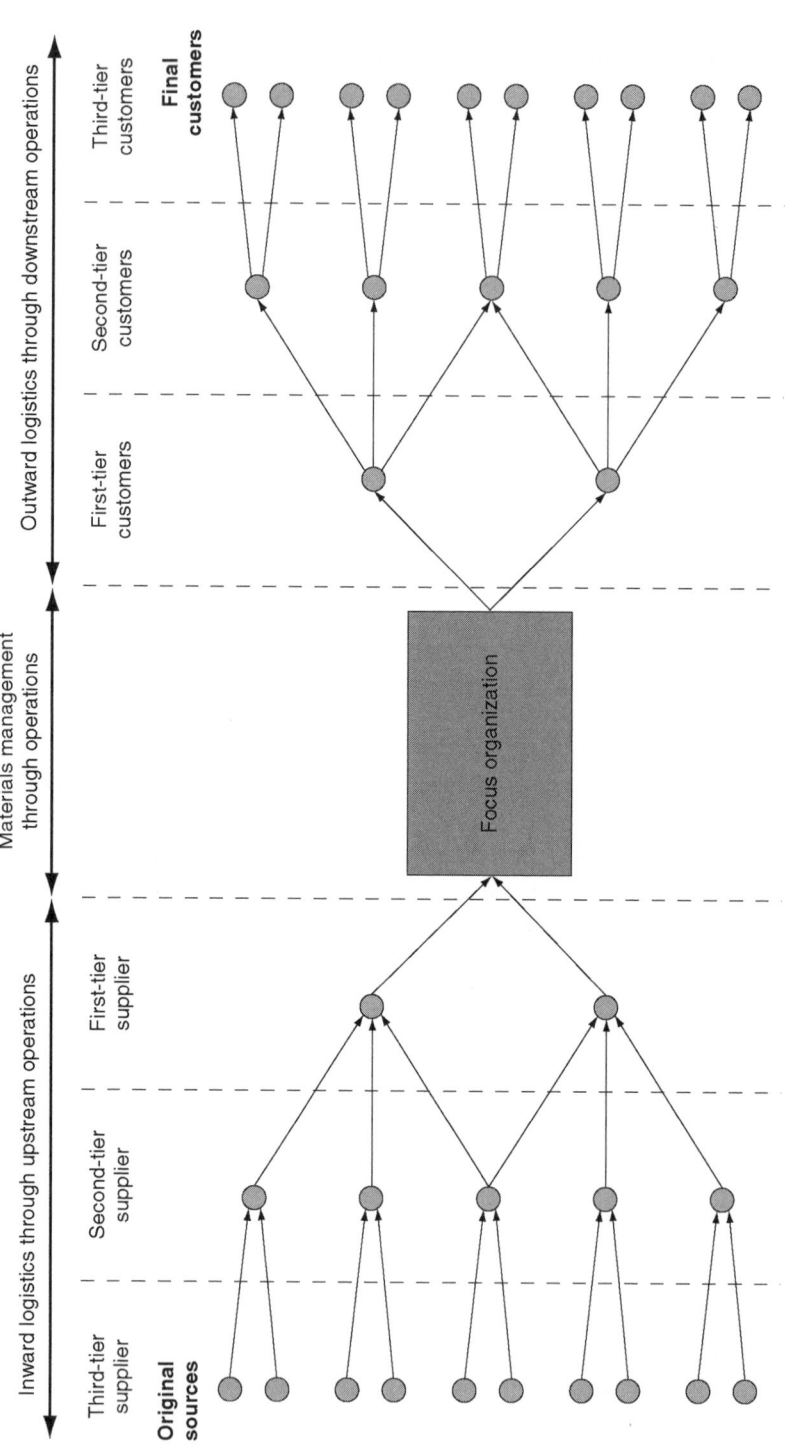

Figure 3.2 Structure of a typical supply chain

MoktoPol

The process for making paper essentially consists of forming a slurry of water and fibres, putting this in layers, and then removing water to leave flat sheets of dry fibres. MoktoPol is a small supplier of paper in Central and Eastern Europe, which summarizes the main elements in its supply chain as follows:

■ Subcontract the felling of trees in sustainable forests in Northern Europe, cut these into logs and ship them to a chipping plant.
■ Collect recycled paper and material from major cities in Poland.
■ Assemble the wood chips, recycled material and other necessary items at a paper mill outside Gdansk.
■ Move the materials through the production process of digesting, screening and blowing to give brown stock.
■ Treat the brown stock with bleaching, washing, beating, 'defibring' and screening to give white stock.
■ Move the stock to a Fourdrinier paper-making machine, followed by drying to give large rolls of paper.
■ Move the rolls to a paper cutter to make the required sizes and packages.
■ Distribute the packages through logistics centres, wholesalers and retailers to final customers.

This seems like a straightforward supply chain, but it involves a lot of movement between the forests and final customers' desks. And there are associated movements of chemicals, other fibres, equipment, consumables, energy, information, services, money and all the other resources used by members of the paper supply chain. The result is a surprisingly complex network that links several hundred organizations.

Aims of supply chain management

Supply chains exist to overcome the separation between suppliers and customers; they allow for operations that are best done, or can only be done, at locations that are distant from customers or sources of materials. For example, coffee beans grow in South America, but the main customers are in Europe and North America; and the best locations for power stations are far away from both their main customers in cities and their fuel supplies.

As well as moving materials between geographically separate operations, supply chains allow for mismatches between supply and demand. The demand for sugar is more or less constant throughout the year, but the supply varies with the harvesting of sugar cane and beet. During the harvest there is excess supply, which accumulates as stock in the supply chain, and this stock is used to meet demand after the harvests finish.

Then the overriding aim of supply chain managers is to look after the movement and storage of materials. Specifically, they have a narrow responsibility for the movement of materials into, through and out of their own organization – and then they have a broader responsibility for the flow of materials through the whole supply chain. Traditionally, managers concentrate on the first of these, focusing on those parts of the supply chain that they directly control. Hopefully, if each organization looks after its own logistics properly, materials move efficiently through the whole chain, so achieving the broader aim. To some extent this is true, but it is by no means inevitable, and an action that benefits a single member may harm the broader chain. For instance, when one company decides to raise its prices its own profit might increase – but the other members have a choice of absorbing the extra costs and reducing their own profits, or passing the price rise on and risking a fall in final customer demand.

So each organization sometimes has to set aside its pure self-interest to achieve better performance for the chain as a whole. This is a fundamental principle of logistics, that trading partners do not work in isolation but they genuinely cooperate to improve overall results. In reality, this also provides one of the key challenges of supply chain management, as most organizations still focus on their own performance with little regard for other members of their chains.

Customer service

Considering the primary role of logistics within an organization, its aim is to help the organization succeed. An organization can only succeed through its ability to satisfy customers – and when it does not satisfy its customers it cannot expect to survive, let alone make a profit, have high return on assets, add shareholder value or achieve any other measure of success. But an overriding problem with achieving customer satisfaction is that each customer wants different things and judges products by a whole series of factors. For example, when you buy a DVD, you judge its contents, appearance, how easy it is to buy, how long you have to wait, how much it costs, whether the right DVD was delivered, whether it was damaged, how courteously you were treated by sales staff, and a whole range of other factors. But your neighbour will have different requirements and want different performance in each factor.

However, one common element with customer satisfaction is that it always depends to a large extent on logistics. With the DVD, its availability depends on stocks; the delivery time depends on transport; damage is prevented by good material handling; the price is affected by logistics costs, and so on. So a fundamental aim of logistics managers is to organize the flow of materials in such a way as to help achieve customer satisfaction.

But customer satisfaction is not the end of the story, as any organization can give outstanding customer service if it is prepared to allocate enough resources. Customers will only pay a certain amount for a product, and this limits the resources that can be used to deliver it. So a realistic aim for logistics is to help achieve customer satisfaction, while using available resources efficiently and giving acceptable costs. This is the view implied by Christopher (1998) in his definition of SCM as 'the management of upstream and downstream relationships with suppliers and customers to deliver superior customer value at less cost to the supply chain as a whole'.

> ■ The overall aim of SCM or logistics is to manage the flow of materials through the supply chain, helping to achieve high customer satisfaction and using resources efficiently to give low costs.

When companies were asked to list their top three objectives for logistics, a survey (IBM, 2005) found the most common answer from 83 per cent of respondents was cost reduction, with 78 per cent wanting improved customer responsiveness. Related answers mentioned improvements to working capital efficiency (25 per cent) and shorter cycle times (21 per cent).

People often summarize the aims of SCM in terms of getting 'the right materials, to the right place, at the right time, from the right source, with the right quality, at the right price'. This may be broadly correct, but it clearly depends on the definition of 'right'. In different circumstances, customers value different types of performance, so logistics managers might aim at fast deliveries, low costs, little wastage, quick response, high productivity, low stocks, no damage, few mistakes, high staff morale or a host of other objectives. These are all worthy goals, but they only really suggest the route for achieving the overriding aims of high customer service and low costs.

Activities of logistics

There are essentially two types of decision about a supply chain. The first is largely strategic, and designs the best structure for a chain. The second is about execution, and finds the most efficient ways of moving materials through the chain.

Harrington (1996) summarizes this double role by saying that 'logistics is both the glue that holds the materials/product pipeline together and the grease that speeds product flow along it'. To achieve this, logistics brings together a series of functions that are responsible for different aspects of the movement of materials. It is usually based on the following core activities:

- *Supply chain design*: the strategic function that finds the best structure for the supply chain, the number of members, its length, breadth, locations, systems used, relationships and so on.
- *Procurement or purchasing*: initiates the flow of materials into an organization by sending purchase orders to suppliers, developing the major links with upstream operations.
- *Inward transport or traffic*: moves materials from suppliers to the organization's receiving area.
- *Receiving*: does the necessary checks and accepts deliveries into the organization.
- *Warehousing or stores*: moves materials into storage, takes care of them and makes sure that they are readily available when needed.
- *Stock control*: sets the policies for inventory, including stock levels, procedures and patterns of purchases.
- *Material handling*: the general term for moving materials within an organization.
- *Order picking*: removes materials from stores and assembles them at departure areas ready for loading on to delivery vehicles.
- *Outward transport*: takes materials from departure areas and delivers them to customers.
- *Physical distribution management*: the general term for the delivery of finished products to customers, developing the major link with downstream operations.
- *Recycling, returns and waste disposal*: often referred to as reverse logistics or reverse distribution, this brings various types of materials back from customers.
- *Communication*. Alongside the flow of materials are the associated flows of money and information. Coordinating the flow of information is increasingly complicated, and logistics managers often describe themselves as processing information rather than moving goods.

In different circumstances, many other activities can be included in SCM, such as outsourcing, leasing, sales forecasting, production scheduling, customer service management, overseas liaison, third-party operations and so on. The important point is not to draw arbitrary boundaries between functions, but to recognize that they must all work together to get an efficient flow of materials.

Jahan Brothers

Jahan Brothers manufacture garments for sale in the United States and Europe. Production starts when their development centre in India has an idea for a new product. This is sent to major markets for testing and to finalize the design. Results are sent back to manufacturing operations in Bangladesh, with parts of the process done in Pakistan, Indonesia, the Philippines and Vietnam. Manufacturing brings material from India, Indonesia and 12 other countries; buttons, zips and fastenings come from China and 10 other countries; other parts are brought in from countries throughout South-East Asia. Then the finished garments are sent to 48 different countries, with customer reaction analysed and returned to the development centre.

Jahan Brothers' supply chains stretch around the world, and this can give long lead times before products reach final customers. This means that they can only make standard items with longer life cycles rather than short-lived fashion items. The main supply chain for a typical product has the following elements, from the start of a supply chain, with fibre available on the open commodity market, to the end of the supply chain, when the customer buys the garment from a shop:

- Store fibre in commodity warehouses   107 days
- Sell fibre and move to spinners   11 days
- At spinners:
  - store raw fibre   27 days
  - spin to form yarn   9 days
  - store yarn as finished goods   23 days
- Sell yarn and move to knitters   14 days
- At knitters:
  - store yarn   21 days
  - knit to form fabric   7 days
  - store work in progress as grey stock   14 days
  - dye standard colour and finish fabric   7 days
  - store fabrics as finished goods   10 days
- Sell fabric and move to manufacturing   7 days
- At manufacturing:
  - store fabric   13 days
  - cut to form components   6 days
  - store components   9 days
  - sew components to form garments   8 days
  - store garments as finished goods   20 days
- Export to market and store in regional distribution centre 53 days

■ Deliver to local wholesaler and store	13 days
■ Deliver to retail shop and store	11 days

It takes an average of 390 days for materials to move through the supply chain. The main operations of spinning, knitting, dyeing, cutting and sewing take 37 days, and various aspects of logistics fill the rest.

Importance of logistics

Logistics is essential for every organization. Christopher (1986) says that 'Logistics has always been a central and essential feature of all economic activity.' Shapiro and Heskett (1985) agree, saying that 'There are few aspects of human activity that do not ultimately depend on the flow of goods from point of origin to point of consumption.' Without logistics, no materials move, no operations are done, no products are delivered and no customers are served.

Not only is logistics essential, but it is also expensive. Unfortunately, it is difficult to say exactly how expensive, as there is a good deal of uncertainty in the area. Normal accounting conventions do not separate logistics' costs from other operating costs, and there is some disagreement about the activities to include. Surveys often give surprising results, such as the findings by *Supply Chain Digest* (2006) that only 32 per cent of their respondents include the cost of carrying stock in their logistics, while 21 per cent include customer service. A more detailed view from Computer Sciences Corporation (2004) suggests that most companies include transport and warehousing in logistics costs (85 per cent), procurement (77 per cent), inventory and materials management (68 per cent), forecasting, planning and scheduling (52 per cent) and supply chain software and technology (51 per cent). But there were still some surprises, with 37 per cent of companies including manufacturing and 22 per cent including marketing, sales and customer service.

Because of these variations, very few organizations can put a precise figure on their logistics expenditure, and many have almost no idea of the costs (Hill, 1994). A rule of thumb suggests a figure of around 15–20 per cent of turnover, but this clearly varies across industries. Building materials, such as sand and gravel, have very high logistics costs compared with, say, jewellery, pharmaceuticals and cosmetics. The UK government says that 12 per cent of the GDP comes from wholesale and retail trades and 5 per cent comes from transport and storage (Office of National Statistics, 2006). These figures suggest that overall logistics' costs are considerably higher than expected, perhaps supporting an earlier estimate by Childerley (1980) that logistics accounted for 32.5 per cent of the GDP.

Although we may not know the precise cost of logistics, we know that it can be very high. Whether it is getting more expensive is open to debate. Some people say that fuel, land, safety, environmental protection and employee costs are all rising, and these are making logistics more expensive. An opposing view says that improved practices are more than compensating for price rises, and the overall cost is falling. The true picture depends on circumstances, with the survey by Computer Sciences Corporation (2004) finding that logistics costs in 47 per cent of companies had remained about the same over the past three years, in 20 per cent they had risen somewhat, and in 20 per cent they had fallen somewhat.

Reviewing the importance

Logistics has the awkward combination of being both essential and expensive – and it directly affects an organization's competitiveness, performance, customer satisfaction, operating costs and profit, the perceived value of its products, and just about everything else. No organization can expect to succeed if it ignores logistics, and on the other hand efficient logistics can give a huge competitive advantage. So we can summarize the importance of logistics by saying that it:

- is essential, as all organizations rely on the movement of materials, even those offering intangible services;
- is expensive and often forms the largest part of costs;
- directly affects profits and other measures of organizational performance;
- has strategic importance with decisions having significant effects over the long term;
- is a major point of contact with suppliers and defines relationships with upstream operations;
- is a major point of contact with customers and defines relationships with downstream operations;
- affects customer service through lead time, reliability, etc;
- determines the best size and location of facilities;
- is risky, because of safety, health and environmental concerns;
- prohibits some operations, such as moving excessive loads or dangerous goods;
- encourages the growth of related organizations, such as third-party service suppliers;
- gives public exposure, with visible locations, advertising on trucks, etc.

The overall message is that poor logistics management can lead to poor performance of the organization. But not all mistakes about the supply chain are a result of poor management, and we saw in the last chapter that risk can mean that good decisions give poor outcomes, and occasionally bad decisions give good outcomes. These two factors – the importance of logistics, and the vulnerability of supply chains to risky events – have encouraged managers to look more closely at the broad area of supply chain risk.

International logistics

During the 1960s the Japanese economy became more industrialized and grew at an unprecedented rate until it became the world's second-largest economy. It was followed by the 'tiger economies' of Taiwan, Singapore, Hong Kong and South Korea. Now China is growing into a major economic force, with its GDP growing by almost 10 per cent a year since the economic reforms of 1978. It is already the world's fourth-largest economy, and is moving quickly towards the size of Germany and Japan.

These surges in economic growth – and particularly China's move to become 'the world's factory' – cannot be driven by internal growth, but they depend on exports. And for this China must meet two requirements. The first is the obvious need for manufacturers to design and make products that customers around the world want, at prices they are willing to pay. But there is no point in being an outstanding manufacturer if products cannot be delivered to customers. So the second requirement is a network of efficient supply chains that can move products through to final customers.

The main supply chains for China are the shipping lanes across the Pacific to the United States, and through the Indian Ocean to the Middle East and Europe. Without sophisticated supply chains and efficient management, China could not be achieving its current economic growth, and the rest of the world would not be benefiting from its products.

In November 2006 the Swedish-owned MV *Emma Maersk* finished its maiden voyage from China and Malaysia to the UK. This ship weighs 170,000 tonnes, is 400 metres long and is powered by the biggest diesel engine ever built. It carries 11,000 containers, and unloaded 50,400 tonnes of goods in Felixstowe, before moving on to mainland Europe.

When supply chains are this long and complicated, they become very vulnerable to disruption. In this case, any problems with a single ship could cause immense difficulties for traders.

Risk in the supply chain

SCM is a very complex function that faces an enormous range of inherent risks, ranging from the minor irritation of delays through to the destruction of an entire chain. But a more worrying trend is for logistics managers to change operations to give better service and efficiency, without considering the consequences on risk. As a result, supply chains are becoming more efficient, but at a cost of increasing vulnerability. This means that organizations are facing greater disruption to an essential function, not because of positive decisions, but because managers are not aware of the full consequences of their actions. And a problem with any single member of a chain expands to give consequences for all the other members. This sets the scene for supply chain risk, where each member not only is susceptible to its own risks, but also can be hit by risky events affecting other members.

Even when the individual risk to each member of a chain is small, the cumulative effect over the hundreds or thousands of members in a large chain becomes very significant. You can see this effect in the survey by the Aberdeen Group that found that 82 per cent of managers reported disruptions to supply chains within the preceding two years (Minahan, 2005). The main causes were:

Poor quality or damaged goods	50%
Missed or late deliveries	49%
Unexpected increases in supply costs	47%
Longer lead times	33%
Supply capacity constraints	32%

Even a relatively minor problem with a supply chain can have broad consequences – in the way that a delayed delivery can affect operations, with effects to company reputation, perception of brands, ability to win orders, quality, prices, profit margins, lead times and a host of basic performance measures. This recognition of the high costs of problems in the supply chain has encouraged managers to consider formal methods of supply chain risk management (SCRM). But it is not only costs that are driving an increased awareness of SCRM, but also the need to comply with new legislation and regulations for improving corporate governance. Other incentives include growing demands from customers to provide evidence of risk management procedures (so that their supplies are not disrupted), desire to avoid any repetition of actual harm from risky events, new trading patterns encouraging an examination of logistics activities, and broader recognition of the potential harm from vulnerable supply chains.

But the principle incentive for developing SCRM is the empirical evidence that suggests that organizations with well-defined policies for SCRM tend to perform better than those with no such policies. This observation is based on the important principle that SCRM is not an extra burden that adds work and costs, but is a way of reducing overall costs and improving performance. For instance, reducing the risk of late deliveries from suppliers allows a firm to reduce its stock of raw materials, with the savings more than compensating for the increased effort of SCRM. By using such methods, Hewlett-Packard's procurement risk management programme is estimated to have saved the company $100 million over five years.

Despite the obvious benefits of SCRM, managers are only just starting to recognize its importance, and most are at a very early stage of development. However, things are changing, and the Aberdeen Group's survey 'strongly suggests that supply risk management will emerge as a major business discipline and measure of competitiveness within the next five years' (Minahan, 2005). It will take a long time for SCRM to be universally implemented, with obvious hurdles being the lack of knowledge about risk management in general, lack of senior management leadership, divided responsibilities for risk, absence of systems for measuring risks and their impact, limited information flows in the supply chain, limited cooperation with trading partners, reactive rather than proactive management style, and a whole host of other problems. Overcoming these will not be easy – but it is becoming increasingly important to try.

Supplies of oil

Oil prices have an effect on world trade and the consequent movement of goods. When prices become too high, economies suffer and they tend to move towards stagnation and even recession.

In 1990 the Gulf War led to record high oil prices. To mitigate their effects, OPEC increased its production, the United States released some of its strategic reserve, production was increased in Alaska, and there were widespread calls for reduced consumption. There was enough slack in the system to limit the economic impact of the prices.

In 2003 the invasion of Iraq again raised oil prices to record levels, but now circumstances were different:

■ Oil supply chains were working with much lower stocks, largely as a way of reducing costs.
■ The economy of China (in particular) was growing quickly and using much more oil.
■ Cold weather in the United States caused a sharp increase in demand.
■ Closure of a nuclear power station in Japan raised demand from electricity generators.

- A strike affected exports from Venezuela.
- Supplies from the North Sea were declining and replacements from Russia seemed vulnerable.

The supply chains for oil were clearly stretched, with the *Wall Street Journal* (2003) saying that 'even modest missteps can trip up the oil industry's delicate dance'. Lee Raymond, chief executive of Exxon Mobil, said that, 'If a couple of suppliers get into trouble, there's a problem.'

In summary

Logistics, or supply chain management, is responsible for the movement and storage of materials in supply chains. Here we take a broad view, with materials as everything that moves, including both tangible goods and intangible services; and a supply chain as a series of activities and organizations that materials move through on their way from initial suppliers through to final customers. Each product has its own supply chain, and these can form very long and complicated webs of interacting parts.

The overall aim of SCM is to move materials along the supply chain efficiently enough to give high customer satisfaction and low costs. To achieve these, managers must design both the structure of the supply chain and the methods of controlling the flow of materials.

The broad function of SCM integrates several different activities, ranging from procurement through to physical distribution. In most organizations, the cost of these activities is unclear, but is typically around 15–20 per cent of revenue. So SCM is in the awkward position of being both essential and expensive. This means that any disruption can be very damaging, not only to logistics but also to the whole organization and even the broader supply chain. This recognition is encouraging more logistics managers to consider formal methods for supply chain risk management (SCRM). However, there has been limited progress, and new types of operations are continuing to increase levels of risk. We explore this effect in the next chapter.

4

Trends affecting the supply chain

Increasing risk

The last chapter developed the theme that logistics is an essential function in every organization, and when it is disrupted there can be serious consequences for the whole organization and broader supply chain. Although managers are giving more attention to supply chain risk management, we know that 'the implementation of risk management in supply chains is still in its infancy' (Christopher *et al*, 2002). The problem is that, when no one pays attention to risks, they go unnoticed and inevitably begin to rise – and greater risk means that the supply chain becomes more vulnerable to disruption.

- Vulnerability reflects the susceptibility of a supply chain to disruption.
- It is a consequence of the risks to the chain.

The nature of supply chains and their complexity make them vulnerable to different kinds of internal and external risk. These risks expand when managers ignore them and do not pay the necessary attention, so levels of risk have tended to drift upwards. One more positive contributor to this effect arises from the efforts of logistics managers to make their supply chains more efficient by simultaneously raising customer service and lowering costs. They have made considerable progress here, but it is increasingly clear that this progress has unwittingly raised levels of risk and vulnerability. You can see this effect with stocks, where managers have spent years introducing

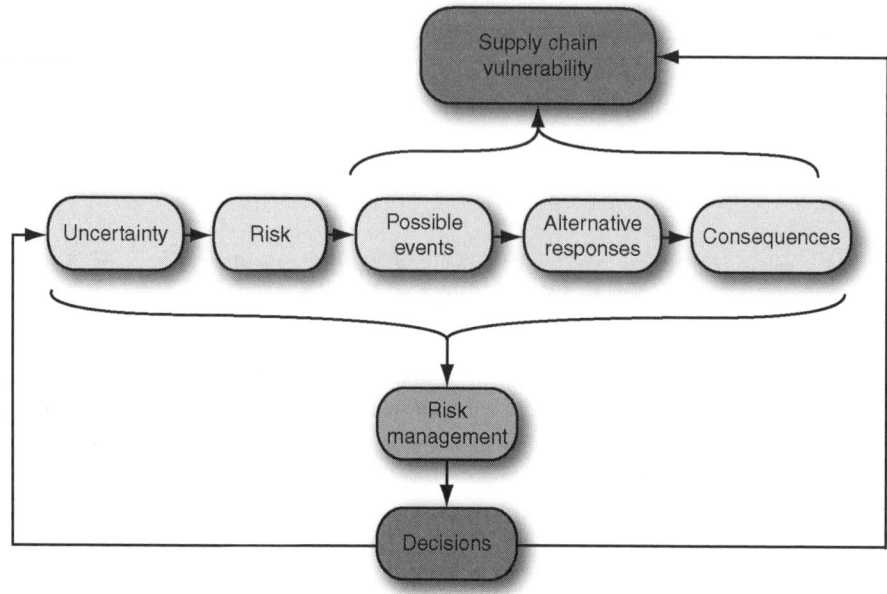

Figure 4.1 Vulnerability of the supply chain

methods that lower – and preferably eliminate – all stocks. Their belief is that stocks are an expensive waste of resources. But the reality is that stocks can serve a genuine purpose, giving a buffer between variable and uncertain supply and demand. Without this cushion, supply chains become more vulnerable to unforeseen events, and even a small disturbance that would have been absorbed by stocks can now cause severe disruptions. This partly accounts for the observation by Hendricks and Singhal (2003) that there has been a significant increase in both the number and the costliness of supply chain disruptions.

The problem of new logistics methods increasing supply chain risk is that this does not happen because managers are positively deciding to work with higher levels of risk, but because they are simply not considering the risks and including them in their calculations. To be fair, managers usually do include risk in their decisions, but they take a superficial view and do not include all aspects of risk. For instance, looking at stocks again, managers say that lower stocks actually reduce risk as there is less chance of unsold stock, obsolescence, damage, deterioration and all the other risks of accumulated stock. This is undoubtedly true, so there is an apparent paradox, with methods designed to reduce some risks actually increasing others. Ideally, risk management would balance such risks – but the limited development of SCRM means that many logistics managers are simply unaware of key risk areas. Then their decisions do not balance all risks, but only the ones they are familiar with – and they completely miss risks that are outside their direct experience. And we could argue that managers are more familiar with minor risks, and rarely have direct experience of more severe ones, so the drive for efficient logistics is reducing exposure to ordinary, minor risks, but at the expense of increasing exposure to less frequent, more severe ones.

A survey by the Aberdeen Group (Minahan, 2005) found that more than 80 per cent of companies had experienced supply disruption in the preceding two years and almost the same proportion expected risks to supplies to increase over the next three years. There are many reasons for this, but we cannot escape the underlying notion that current trends in logistics are inadvertently increasing levels of risk.

- Current trends in logistics are increasing risks to supply chains.
- This is not a result of planned change, but is an unintentional side effect.

Trends in supply chain management

For many years logistics was seen as an operational problem that did not deserve much attention, with Drucker (1962) describing it as 'the economy's dark continent' and saying that it formed 'the most sadly neglected, most promising area of... business'. But we have come a long way since then and SCM is now going through a period of immense change. People buy more things from websites rather than visiting shops; many products that were made locally are shipped from China; mobile communications ease the transfer of information; European logistics centres are replacing local warehouses; many industries are dominated by a few multinationals; RFID (radio frequency identification) and GPS (global positioning systems) track the movement of materials; free trade areas such as the European Union have greater impact. Supply chains are clearly changing – but what are the drivers causing the changes? There are many different ones, but some of the most important are:

- recognition that logistics is an essential function that needs careful management;
- recognition that decisions about the supply chain have a strategic impact on the organization;
- realization that logistics is expensive and gives opportunities for substantial savings;
- emphasis on customer satisfaction and its dependence on logistics;

- new operations with different demands on the supply chain – such as virtual organizations, just-in-time, agility, mass customization, lean operations, time compression, etc;
- globalization and growing international trade, encouraged by free trade areas such as the European Union, the North American Free Trade Area and the Association of South East Asian Nations;
- improved communications, particularly through e-business;
- other technology, including vehicle telematics, intermodal systems, tracking systems, automated handling, etc;
- increasing competition, with distant suppliers competing directly with local ones;
- integration of activities in the supply chain, particularly through strategic alliances and partnerships;
- changing patterns of power in the supply chain, with the growth of a few dominant members;
- organizations focusing on core activities and outsourcing logistics to third parties;
- growing concern about environmental damage, and changing attitudes towards pollution, waste, traffic congestion, road building, etc;
- changing government policies on the ownership, regulation, use, responsibilities and cost of transport.

This list suggests the scale of the pressures, and in response logistics managers continually introduce new methods and procedures. By the 1990s over 90 per cent of organizations were actively making improvements to their supply chain or planning improvements in the near future (Factor, 1996). A more recent survey found that 57 per cent of companies were currently planning new initiatives in transport and warehousing, 53 per cent in procurement, and 42 per cent in inventory and materials management (Computer Sciences Corporation, 2004). The same survey found that new supply chain methods had reduced costs in 72 per cent of companies and increased revenues in 57 per cent. These improvements seem like good news, but you have to remember that they rarely take into account all of the risks – and the damage from extra risks might offset the gains in operational efficiency.

Unfortunately, as soon as managers make one set of changes to their supply chains, circumstances again alter and they have to start looking for new arrangements. The result puts logistics in a continuing state of flux. Most logistics managers accept this as inevitable and believe that supply chains are too volatile ever to become mature and stable.

Jüttner (2005) found that the factors likely to increase supply chain vulnerability are globalization (reported by 52 per cent of managers), reducing stock levels (51 per cent), smaller supply base (38 per cent) and outsourcing (30 per cent). In the next sections we can look at these effects with:

- integration of supply chains;
- cost reduction;
- agile logistics;
- e-business;
- globalization;
- outsourcing;
- changing practices in logistics.

Integration of supply chains

When managers began looking for improvements to logistics, they started with the separate activities – procurement, inventory control, transport, warehousing, materials handling, packaging and so on. However, it soon becomes clear that these are not distinct activities that can be handled in isolation, and any change to one inevitably affects the others. Improvements to procurement have consequences for stock levels; changes to transport affect warehousing; changes to material handling put new demands on packaging. Overall improvements only appear when all aspects of material movement are considered as part of a single, integrated function.

It can be difficult to achieve this integration, but a common approach progressively merges activities over time. Then one department might eventually take over all responsibility for the inward flow of materials (materials handling), while another department delivers finished products (physical distribution). But this still leaves an artificial break in an essentially continuous function, and the next step completes the internal integration by forming a single function that is responsible for all material movement into, through and out of the organization.

Internal integration means that each organization can make its own logistics as efficient as possible, but there are still boundaries between members of the supply chain. These boundaries break up the smooth flow of materials, making it more difficult and expensive – which prompted Christopher (1999) to comment, 'Most opportunities for cost reduction and/or value enhancement lie at the interface between supply chain partners.' And there is always the problem that actions by any one member working in isolation can harm all the other members and reduce overall performance. The next step is clearly external integration, which merges logistics along the supply chain and removes the boundaries between members.

This last step is notoriously difficult, as each member of the chain is owned and managed by a different legal entity and has its own interests, aims, operations, culture and so on. An initial step has partners align their interests, recognizing that they all share the same overall aim of satisfying final customers. If there are any problems with the chain of activities for achieving this, then all members suffer. The essential aim of external integration is to make products more attractive to final customers – thereby selling more and giving extra benefits that can be shared by members of the chain. This can only be achieved through cooperation and closer working relationships.

We now have three levels of integration – the first has logistics as separate activities within an organization; the second has internal integration to bring them together into a single function; the third has external integration, where organizations look beyond their own operations and integrate more of the supply chain. The lowest levels are characterized by arm's length relationships between supply chain partners, while the highest levels are formalized in strategic alliances or partnerships. You can imagine this integration as progressively coordinating physical movements, information, control and then infrastructure (Decker and van Goor, 1998).

It seems that the move towards greater integration is inevitable, but this is not always the best model, and neither integration nor arm's length relationships are intrinsically best. And it is often better to have elements of both, in the way that Dell has strong single-supplier relationships with Intel for its processors and Microsoft for operating systems, but more distant relations with vendors of other components.

External integration

Although difficult to achieve, the benefits from external integration include:

■ common aims for all parts of the supply chain, emphasizing higher customer service and lower costs;
■ joint working and cooperation to achieve these aims;
■ sharing information throughout the supply chain, allowing informed and coordinated decisions;
■ easier planning with less uncertainty, fewer errors and more stable conditions;
■ coordinated operations, giving greater efficiency and productivity, with lower stocks, faster movement, less investment in assets, etc;
■ faster and more flexible responses to changing circumstances;
■ new methods of control, such as efficient customer response;
■ removal of duplicated effort, information, planning, stocks, etc;
■ elimination of activities that add no value for customers.

From a risk perspective, the benefits of external integration can be summarized as lower risk, achieved through transparency. Here transparency, or visibility, means that one part of a supply chain can see what is happening in other parts. This is achieved when all members share information and have a clear view of activities throughout the chain. Then a manufacturer can monitor sales at retailers and plan production from actual sales rather than forecasts, and raw materials suppliers can see manufacturers' production schedules and use these to plan their own operations. The result is less uncertainty and lower risks.

The free exchange of information is formalized in different types of operations, especially efficient customer response (ECR), where a final customer purchase automatically sends a message back through the chain and triggers responses from upstream suppliers. When you buy a pair of jeans in a clothes shop, the electronic point of sales system (EPOS) sends a message back to the wholesaler and logistics centres to say that stock needs replenishing; and then the message goes back to the manufacturer to say that it is time to make another pair of jeans; and then it goes further back to suppliers to say that they should deliver materials to the manufacturer, and so on. The result is 'a focus on the consumer, the development of partnership relationships between retailers and their suppliers and an increased integration of the components of the supply-chain' (Szymankiewicz, 1997).

The clear benefits from ECR – and visibility in general – have encouraged organizations to move in this direction, and by 1997 P-E Consulting found that 57 per cent of companies had some form of integrated supply chain, and more than 90 per cent expected more integration in the near future. Unfortunately, we have to ask if these ambitious goals have actually materialized. Szymankiewicz (1997) noted that 'In the grocery sector ECR is often regarded as an established way of doing business... [but] overall there is more talk than action.' And by 2003 Poirier and Quinn noted that most organizations were still working on internal integration, and although they were moving towards external integration only 10 per cent had made any significant progress. Christopher *et al* (2002) found that 'upstream and downstream visibility was poor' and 'all interviewees agreed that end-to-end management of an organisation's complex and unstable supply chain network, (particularly up-stream into the supplier base), would be an improbable if not impossible task'.

Integration and risk

Broad supply chain integration – with all members working together to give more efficient flows of material and lower levels of risk – seems to be an ideal rather than a reality. And one reason is that each member still has to search for individual benefits, even when these come at the expense of their trading partners. We know that one member can raise prices to increase its own profits, but perhaps at the cost of lower demand for all of the chain. Similarly, one firm might reduce its own risk from, say, high stocks by transferring them to other organizations – perhaps through vendor-managed inventory (VMI) or collaborative planning, forecasting and replenishment (CPFR). But now we see the familiar pattern with risk, where reducing one type (the risk of holding too much stock) increases another type (the risk from transferred or outsourced operations). And as well as changing the nature of the risk, this move affects the options available for dealing with it. When managers feel that internal stock levels are too low, they can easily adjust them upwards – but they cannot do this when they have outsourced inventory management to a third party.

We can conclude that external integration is likely to reduce some risks (say, from surprise actions of trading partners) but increase others. Among the increasing risks are those inherent to sharing information. When information is distributed more widely, there is a greater threat to its security and greater chance that it is passed on to unwanted bodies. This alone encourages some members to withhold information for competitive and commercial self-interest, while others are never completely candid – so the information flows are never perfect. These effects are particularly noticeable when one organization sees itself as already owning most knowledge in the supply chain, and any exchange would be unbalanced.

No amount of cooperation can overcome the underlying reality that each member of a supply chain can only make a profit by paying less for materials bought from one partner, and charging more for materials sold to another partner. So each must try – at least to some extent – to gain an advantage over its trading partners. And the concept of shared benefits is unconvincing when a dominant organization decides to flex its muscles and attract more benefit to itself, but at the expense of smaller, more vulnerable partners.

A fundamental principle of external integration is that firms reduce the number of suppliers they work with. Traditionally, each organization uses many suppliers to make sure they get the best deals, encourage competition and guarantee continuing supply if one runs into difficulties. However, external integration encourages long-term relationships, with each organization finding the best supplier for a product, developing a relationship and then working largely – or even exclusively – with it. This was the reasoning that made Rank Xerox reduce its suppliers from 5,000 to 300, while Ford moved from 4,000 to 350 (Lamming, 1993).

So external integration encourages single sourcing, which has the advantages of (Waters, 2003b):

- a stronger relationship between customers and suppliers, often formalized in alliances or partnerships;
- the commitment of all parties to the success of the relationship, developing joint systems and procedures;
- economies of scales and price discounts with larger orders;
- easier communications, reduced administration and simpler procedures for orders;
- less variation in materials and their supply;
- easier – or joint – forecasting, planning, scheduling, etc;
- greater confidentiality of operations, requirements, conditions, etc.

But again these advantages come at higher risk, as we ask: what happens when the sole source hits problems? With single sourcing there are, at least in the short term, no alternative suppliers – but, with multiple sourcing, when one supplier hits problems it is disappointing but not a major problem. Some benefits of multiple sourcing include (Waters, 2003b):

- less chance of disrupted supplies, as problems can be avoided by switching suppliers;
- reductions in prices through competition between suppliers;
- varying demand being easier to deal with;
- access to wider knowledge and information through the involvement of more organizations;
- a greater likelihood of innovation and improvement;
- the avoidance of relying on one external organization.

Problems with single sourcing

Land Rover

Land Rover is a subsidiary of Ford, and makes its well-known multi-terrain vehicles. In common with all car makers, the company actively reduced its supply base, and UPF-Thompson became the sole source of chassis frames for its best-selling model, the Discovery. Unfortunately, UPF lost money on other ventures into foreign markets and went bankrupt at the end of 2001. To find a new supplier would take Land Rover up to nine months, during which it would lay off its 1,400 workers at Solihull, UK – with a further 10,000 people working for suppliers also losing their jobs.

KPMG were appointed receivers for UPF and demanded a payment of £35 million from Land Rover to continue supplies. They justified this claim by saying that they were legally obliged to recover money for creditors, and the sole supplier agreement was a valuable asset. Land Rover refused to pay, questioning the legality of the claim and saying that the demand would make customers liable for suppliers' debts.

Eventually, Land Rover paid £10–20 million of UPF's debt and took effective control of the company. This gave a continuing supply of chassis frames, and allowed Land Rover time to review its longer-term options.

British Airways

British Airways reduced its operating costs by outsourcing virtually all catering, with in-flight meals at Heathrow provided by Gate Gourmet.

This company has its headquarters in Switzerland, and generates an annual turnover approaching $2 billion by producing more than half a million meals a day for major airlines. But in 2005 the company had a dispute with staff over working conditions at Heathrow, and it sacked a number of people – variously reported to be between 350 and 600. BA lost its sole source of in-flight meals at Heathrow, and its problems increased when 650 of its own ground staff – who had close associations with Gate Gourmet staff, including many family members – staged a four-day sympathy strike. Such secondary strikes had been unknown in the UK for decades and were technically illegal. But the results for BA were hundreds of cancelled flights, 70,000 stranded passengers, and additional costs of £40 million.

Delphi Corporation

In 1999 General Motors (GM) spun off its component-making units to form Delphi Corporation. This remained its sole supplier of many parts, with business amounting to $30 billion a year. But Delphi could not compete with increasingly efficient competitors, and its problems were compounded by GM's falling sales. In 2006 it went bankrupt, and GM risked losing its only supplier of a wide range of parts. Chapter 11 bankruptcy meant that Delphi continued trading, but its survival plans included cutting 23,000 jobs, closing 25 plants and cutting employee benefits, as well as renegotiating contracts for parts with GM and passing some of its employee pension liabilities back to GM.

Cost reduction

A firm's logistics strategy consists of all the long-term goals, plans, policies, culture, resources, decisions and actions that relate to the supply chain. This strategy gives the context for all other decisions about an organization's supply chain, and should balance the competing demands of:

■ *higher strategies* – including the mission and corporate and business strategies;
■ *the business environment*, which includes all external factors that affect logistics, but which managers cannot control – such as customers, market conditions, available technology, economic conditions, legal restraints, competitors, shareholders, interest groups, social conditions and political conditions;
■ *internal features*, which are factors within the organization that managers can control – such as employee skills, finances, products, facilities, technology used, customer relations, choice of suppliers, resources available, etc.

Defining a logistics strategy means that managers design the internal features that work best within the fixed environment. When they do this well, there is good 'strategic fit', and to achieve this organizations build on their strengths to develop 'strategic competencies' (Prahalad and Hamel, 1990). Strategic competencies are the things that an organization does particularly well, and their importance is that success only comes by doing key activities better than competitors or by doing completely different activities (Porter, 1996).

Doing operations better than competitors suggests a generic strategy of cost leadership, which gives the same, or comparable, products at a lower price. In logistics terms, this uses efficient, lean operations to give low costs. Doing different operations contributes to a generic strategy of product differentiation, which gives products that customers cannot find anywhere else. In logistics terms, this uses flexible or agile operations to improve customer service.

A lean strategy gives low-cost logistics, and managers achieve this by designing efficient operations to minimize stocks, reduce lead times, use fewer resources, employ fewer people, remove duplicated effort, eliminate non-value-adding operations and generally remove all waste from the supply chain. This can be achieved by specific methods, such as just-in-time (which makes sure that each activity is done at exactly the time it is needed), continuous improvement (which searches for a continuing stream of small improvements), time compression (which eliminates wasted time from the chain), stockless production (which removes stocks of work in progress) and total quality management (which removes the effects of defective materials).

The benefits of leanness are obvious, as there is no point in wasting resources, and any cost reductions appear as more attractive products or higher profit margins. But we have already suggested that more efficient operations invariably come with increased risk. We can illustrate this with just-in-time operations (JIT), which are at the heart of leanness. JIT reduces waste by making sure that activities are done at exactly the time they are needed. They are not done too early (which would waste resources that would then wait until used) or too late (which would cause delays and reduce service). The result is efficient flows of materials, no stocks of work in progress – and lower risks from waste, interruptions, delays, obsolescence, loss and so on. But the real picture is more complicated, as JIT removes slack from operations and makes them vulnerable to the slightest hiccup. If there is even a small delay, breakdown, accident, surge in demand, new product or any change, there is no cushion and the whole supply chain comes to a halt. So the real picture is that JIT reduces some risks, while increasing others. In the same way, other lean measures reduce costs and some risks – but they also tend to increase other risks. Managers often focus on the benefits, but do not consider (or are not even aware of) the increasing supply chain vulnerability.

Agile logistics

Lean logistics can be criticized for putting too much emphasis on costs, and removing the flexibility to deal with unexpected events. An alternative strategy puts more emphasis on customer satisfaction by responding quickly to changing conditions – giving agile logistics. The ultimate aim of agility, which clearly remains a theoretical ideal, is to have production batches of one and zero lead time.

An agile strategy allows the supply chain to react to all kinds of unforeseen conditions, both internal and in the environment, and ranging from short delays in delivery, through changing customer demand, and on to natural disasters. The essential aim of agility is high customer service, but this can be measured in many different ways. Lennox (1995) gives some examples, starting with the proportion of items supplied at first demand, the number of order-pick errors, the availability of back orders, the proportion of orders satisfied in full, the amount of damage, the costs as a percentage of price – and continuing down to lead time, courtesy of staff, ease of ordering, etc. When managers choose a measure of performance, it must clearly relate to significant factors in operations, so there is no point in, say, an insurance company including the efficiency of rail freight.

From a supply chain perspective a common problem is separating the performance of logistics from other factors. For instance, a late delivery to a customer might be caused by poor logistics – but it might also be caused by poor demand forecasts, production problems, roadworks, traffic congestion, ferry operators on strike, or a whole range of other factors. Logistics provides the final link between suppliers and customers, so it often gets blamed for faults in other parts of the system.

Agility is becoming more important, as product cycles are getting shorter, market requirements change quickly, and demand is becoming more volatile. It is also the best way of satisfying more demanding customers, who are looking for more choice, better products, lower prices, shorter lead times and better value – and can use websites to access suppliers in any part of the world, giving a transparent market where they can compare products, deals and conditions. Logistics managers respond by designing agile operations that deliver materials in the best ways – thereby reducing the risks from unsatisfied customers, lost orders, and slow response in general.

But agility brings its own risks. For instance, it generally needs spare capacity to allow flexible operations, but this reduces productivity and increases costs. So there is more risk that customers who are primarily interested in low prices will move to other suppliers – confirming the point that you cannot satisfy all the customers all the time – and there is more risk of underused resources, higher overheads and so on.

In their different ways, both lean and agile logistics affect the vulnerability of supply chains, but they seem to adopt almost opposing policies. At first sight it seems difficult to reconcile their differing aims, with one minimizing costs and seeing customer service as a constraint, and the other maximizing customer service and seeing costs as a constraint. In practice, the two policies are not necessarily distinct. For instance, a supplier that improves its electronic data interchange (EDI) links with customers can both reduce costs and increase customer service – becoming both leaner and more agile. Evans and Powell (2000) conclude that 'lean and agile are not mutually exclusive; they both have their merits, but also limitations, especially if an individual aspect is taken, in isolation, to the extreme'.

E-business

Procurement is a complex activity. It starts with an identified need for materials, and then someone has to generate a description of the material, search for suppliers, request a price and conditions, issue a purchase order, negotiate details, organize transport, discuss special conditions, organize finance, arrange payment – and potentially many other activities. In the past, this needed a lot of paperwork, but now automated systems largely replace the onerous manual ones. EDI appeared in the 1990s, and now electronic purchasing – through intranet, extranet or the internet – allows instant access to suppliers, irrespective of their location, with a transparent market, low entry costs and low transaction costs.

Electronic trading, under the general umbrella of e-business, has developed in three main directions – B2B (business-to-business, where one business buys materials from another business), B2C (business-to-customer, where a business sells directly to a final customer) and C2C (the electronic car boot sale where no formal business is involved). In the UK, 83 per cent of suppliers used B2B by 2000 (MRO, 2001), with worldwide trade now valued at over US$2 trillion (Gartner, 2006). However, it is difficult to put a reliable value on e-business as there are so many variations. Is it a transaction where every stage is completed through the internet, one that is initiated by a website or one where even a single activity is done electronically? With this warning, Figure 4.2 gives an idea of the growth of global electronic trade in recent years.

E-business does not just improve purchasing, but allows completely new types of logistics, with the emphasis moved away from physical materials to information. For instance, organizations that traditionally held stocks to allow for uncertain demand can now wait until actual demand is known and then use agile operations to quickly meet it – moving the emphasis from inventory to information.

As well as improving routine administration, other aspects of communications track movements using bar codes, magnetic stripes and radio frequency identification (RFID); they monitor vehicles through telematics; they control warehouses with automatically guided vehicles; they monitor transactions,

The millennium bug

In the 1990s it was widely thought that a computer BIOS (basic input–output system) was only programmed to deal with dates up to 1999. The story grew that when the internal clocks clicked up to 2000 they would not be able to cope and there would be widespread disruption of computer systems. Most organizations were aware of this and took action to check that their systems were 'Y2K compliant', but it was difficult to get guarantees that networked systems would actually continue to work into 2000.

In practice, most firms thought that their own systems were all right, but they feared problems with their suppliers' systems or others in the supply chain, and there were particular concerns that utility companies could not guarantee uninterrupted service (Wilding and Bernon, 1999). And if anything did go wrong, the problems would appear during a holiday period when few people were around to solve them. Faced with the perceived risk, organizations took steps to mitigate their effects, typically holding extra stocks. But these stocks had knock-on effects that included the following:

- There was pressure on limited warehousing space.
- The cost of pre-emptive purchases strained cash flows.
- Financial pressure increased as customers looked for extended credit to cover their own financial difficulties.
- The strain on finances increased the risk of business failures.
- Pre-emptive purchases were interpreted as genuinely increasing demand, with demand amplification in upstream suppliers.
- Rising demand gave an apparent boom in some industries in 1999, followed by a recession in 2000 as excess stocks were used.
- Customers transferred business from smaller suppliers to larger ones that they considered more able to cope with any problems.
- Customers moved from suppliers in the third world to those in industrialized countries that might be more able to cope with problems.

In practice, very few problems actually appeared with the millennium bug. Systems were perfectly able to deal with the new date, and more harm was done by actions taken to avoid problems than by the problems themselves.

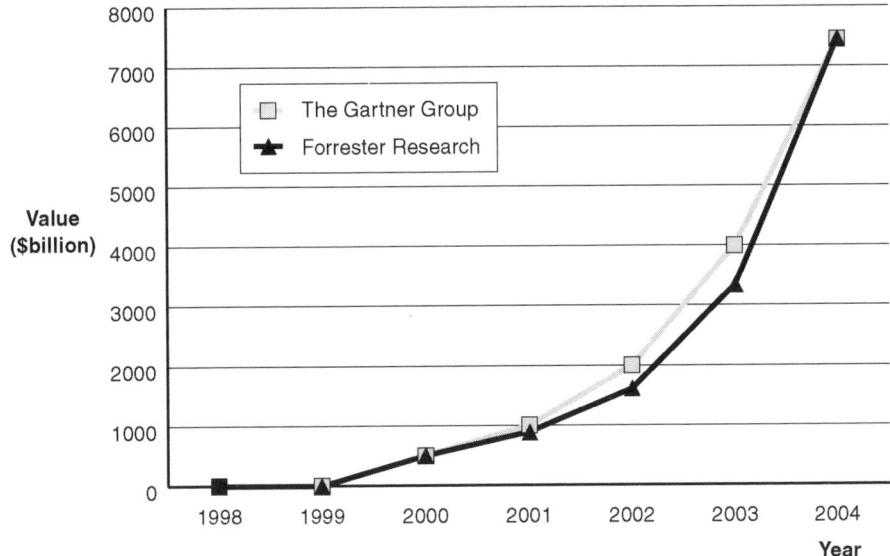

Figure 4.2 Estimates of the value of global electronic trade

plan operations – and a host of other functions. Externally, they allow vendor-managed inventory (VMI), collaborative planning, forecasting and replenishment (CPFR), synchronized material movement throughout the supply chain, payments by electronic fund transfer (EFT), roadside detectors to monitor congestion, and a host of other methods. Realistically, it is difficult to find any area of logistics that is not affected by improved communications.

But as usual the news is not entirely good, as logistics has come to rely on a complex network of integrated systems. When any one of these develops a glitch, not only is it inconvenient, but it can bring the whole supply chain to a standstill. When a new virus enters one computer it can quickly travel to all the connected systems throughout the supply chain. So systems in the supply chains are as vulnerable as the weakest links – and this is particularly worrying when it comes to data security. If one system has access to all your banking information, what is to prevent someone hacking in from another system? The reliance on new – perhaps only partially tested – systems introduces new types of risk, as demonstrated by the Y2K 'millennium bug'.

Experience from the millennium bug can be interpreted in two ways. The first says that organizations overreacted and wasted a lot of time and money doing things that were completely unnecessary; there was never any real risk from the millennium bug, so there was no reason to spend time combating it. As Peck (2004) says, 'Y2K made everyone aware of how IT dependent our societies had become, but its legacy was to leave managers sceptical about the need to spend scarce time and resources warding off supply chain disruptions that might never occur.' The second interpretation says that there was a real risk, with genuine and severe consequences. By taking appropriate actions, firms managed the risks, avoided potential problems and learned valuable lessons. Which of these two interpretations is 'correct' depends on your viewpoint – which is a common feature of risk management.

Globalization

Improved communications – particularly through the internet – allow organizations around the world to communicate as if they are physically close. Then they become global in outlook, broadening their supplier and customer bases to buy, transport, store, manufacture, sell and distribute products in a single worldwide market. Factors that encourage global operations include:

- *lower costs* – from moving operations to cheaper locations, such as manufacturing in China and call centres in India;
- *economies of scale* – the optimal size for manufacturing, say, is often larger than demand in any single market;
- *risk reduction* – by moving to safer locations (ie those that are remote from identified risks);
- *availability of skills and knowledge* – that are scarce in one market but readily available in another;
- *closeness of raw materials* – with operations close to original suppliers;
- *removal of trade barriers* – particularly in free trade areas, such as the European Union, the North American Free Trade Area and the Association of South East Asian Nations;
- *growing demand in new markets* – particularly developing regions that are becoming increasingly prosperous;
- *increasing knowledge of consumers* – that are familiar with products from outside their immediate region;
- *more demanding customers* – aware that local suppliers may not be able to meet their needs, and willing to look further afield for better sources;
- *convergence of market demands* – with different markets increasingly accepting the same products, or products with minor differences (which Ohmae, 1985, called 'Californianization');
- *improved communications* – linking businesses around the world as easily as those in the next town;
- *efficient logistics* – with tools such as containerization, satellite tracking and intermodal transport;
- *growth of support services* – that can be supplied by firms remote from the host country;
- *cross-border mergers and acquisitions* – with new operations spread over many countries.

Leontiades (1985) says that 'One of the most important phenomena of the 20th century has been the international expansion of industry. Today, virtually all major firms have a significant and growing presence in business outside their country of origin.' Perhaps half of the trade between industrialized countries is accounted for by transfers between subsidiaries of the same company (Julius, 1990). In the United States a third of exports are sent by US companies to their overseas subsidiaries, and another third are sent by foreign manufacturers based in the United States back to their home market. By 2004 around $9 trillion of merchandise was moved around the world each year, with $21 trillion of commercial services (World Trade Organization, 2005).

Risks of international operations

Global operations bring obvious benefits, but there are also risks in extended journeys around the world, including earthquakes and tsunamis, hurricanes and other extreme weather conditions, wars and terrorist attacks, outbreaks of disease, problems with supply chain partners, fire and other accidental damage, loss of information technology systems, financial risks, crime and financial irregularities, industrial action, human error, different languages and culture, and a whole host of others. Increasingly global operations mean that a problem in one part of the world can seriously disrupt business in other areas. For instance, a flood in DaimlerChrysler's plant in Greenville, North Carolina, caused seven of the company's other plants to close for a week; a strike in US ports caused car manufacturers to halt production in Japan; an earthquake in Kobi, Japan, disrupted computer production in Europe. Three obvious sources of risk with globalization are:

1. Risks from working in a region that is less familiar and more distant from the organization's usual operations. These include reduced control over remote sites, cultural differences, variable levels of skills, language problems, legal systems, political instability, unstable economic conditions, changing costs, rapidly changing conditions, different levels of commitment to quality, and so on.
2. Risks of moving materials through longer supply chains. These include the inherent risks of extended journeys, crossing international borders, meeting different cultures, extended lead times, more stock in transit, more handling, the need for bigger order quantities, greater chance of loss, obsolescence of products with short life cycles, and so on.
3. Unexpected barriers to trade, such as:
   - product design limiting demand, with different regions demanding different types of product, a product not lending itself to global operations, or customers simply not liking products;

– practical difficulties making it impossible to meet demand – such as protectionist government policies, problems at national frontiers, inadequate infrastructure, missing technical skills, or other cultural and economic differences.

Another source of risk comes with centralization, as firms moving to new locations normally look for the economies of scale from large facilities. For instance, a single European logistics centre might be more efficient than a number of separate national warehouses. In practice, such moves rarely go as smoothly as hoped, and the resulting facilities tend to be less flexible and more vulnerable to change. And there is always the risk that the relative transport and manufacturing costs will change, reducing the cost advantages of concentration.

To protect themselves from such risks, organizations adopt various structures, with the main choices of working nationally, internationally, multinationally or globally. Essentially, a national company only works within its home market and exports to foreign countries; an international company has a centre in one country, from which it controls the activities of subsidiary divisions in other countries; a multinational consists of connected, but largely independent, companies in different countries; a global company sees the world as a single market and works in the locations that are most effective and efficient. These descriptions suggest rigid structures, but companies are usually much more responsive to local conditions.

MV *Xin Qing Dao*

On 27 October 2004 the 66,433-tonne container ship *Xin Qing Dao* was sailing from Valletta, Malta, to Felixstowe, UK, when it ran into storm force 11 weather off Brittany. The ship rolled by 30 degrees as it moved through 30-metre seas and winds of 65 knots. When it reached the container port of Felixstowe, it was clear that 31 full 40-foot containers had been lost overboard and another 29 had been severely damaged.

These 60 lost or damaged containers were filled with everything from computers to sportswear, and each had a value somewhere between $50,000 and several million dollars. Each lost container led to insurance claims and legal disputes about whether this was an 'act of God' or someone was to blame for not taking enough care of the cargo.

Each year an estimated 10,000 containers are lost over the side of container ships, generally the result of high seas, improper stowage, fire or even pirates. The cost of these losses runs into billions of dollars.

Damage to shipping is relatively common, and reports for a typical month, December 2006, list 132 significant incidents reported for commercial shipping (Countryman and McDaniel, 2007). These incidents included collisions, fire, losing power and drifting, running aground, losing cargo overboard, piracy and taking on water.

Outsourcing

Organizations are most successful when they focus on core competencies that differentiate them from competitors – and peripheral areas where they are less competent are best handled by other, specialized organizations. This is the principle behind outsourcing, which is used for activities as diverse as cleaning and catering through to accounting, legal services and information processing. It is increasingly common to outsource logistics, with specialist service providers taking over some, or all, of the activities. In the United States, around three-quarters of firms outsource some logistics (Eye for Transport, 2005; Logistics Institute, 2006). In the EU the outsourced logistics market was valued at €176 billion by 2004, and forecast to rise to 45 per cent of all logistics expenditure by 2008 (Datamonitor, 2004).

Outsourced logistics – or third-party logistics (3PL) – has the benefits of lower fixed costs, expert services, combined work giving economies of scale, matching capacity to demand, ability to deal with changing demand, increased geographical coverage and guaranteed service levels. These clearly reduce some risks, which are passed on to the service providers. A common way of reducing risk even further is to outsource some – but not all – logistics. Then a firm might combine third-party transport with its own fleet, so there is backup when problems appear with either.

But, again, a decrease in some risks comes at the cost of increases to others, particularly loss of control and too much reliance on a single partner. And outsourcing needs an organization to switch to new types of operations – thereby replacing a set of relatively familiar and well-known risks with new ones that are less clearly understood. One surprising risk is that outsourcing does not work as well as expected (Manktelow, 2006; Richards, 2006). Almost half of 3PL does not give the service level needed or the expected reductions in cost, and more than a quarter of firms find that outsourcing does not reduce the internal time and effort spent on logistics (Logistics Institute, 2006). This gives increased risk of poor performance, more complex chains, uncontrollable costs, 'price creep', unsatisfactory working relationships, and so on. Another less obvious risk comes when problems in one chain encourage the service provider to move resources away from other customers – so that one supply chain becomes susceptible to problems in a completely different chain.

At the heart of 3PL is the problem of deciding which activities are peripheral enough to pass to someone else. Some managers become so enthusiastic for outsourcing that they discard core activities, leaving themselves in the awkward position of transferring risk to a third party but still retaining the operational consequences of failure. When a manufacturer hires a transport company to bring in raw materials, the transport company may be responsible for a lost delivery, but it is the manufacturer's operations that are disrupted. And once 3PL is introduced it is difficult to reverse and move activities back in-house, as the necessary skills, experience and infrastructure have been lost.

Changing practices in logistics

The trends outlined above indicate some of the trends in logistics and the effects on risk. There are actually so many trends at the moment that we cannot give anything like a full list, but it is worth mentioning a few more that have significant effects:

■ *Increasing environmental concerns* – about global warming, air and water pollution, energy consumption, urban development, waste disposal and other aspects of environmental damage. It is fair to say that SCM does not have a good reputation for environmental protection – demonstrated by the emissions from heavy lorries, noisy and inefficient vehicles, use of greenfield sites for warehouses, demands for new road building, use of extensive packaging, oil spillage from tankers, and so on. But it is moving towards greener practices, and there is a growing recognition that careful management can bring both environmental protection and better logistics.
■ *Concentration of ownership* – with large companies getting economies of scale and growing at the expense of smaller rivals. The result is a concentration of ownership, with a few large companies dominating many supply chains.
■ *Movement of power to retailers.* Historically, most power in the supply chain has been with manufacturers, but power has tended to drift towards retailers because of their direct links to final customers.
■ *Changes in manufacturing processes* – with SCM inevitably affected by JIT, ECR, shorter product life cycles, common components, mass customization, e-business and so on.
■ *Economies of scale* – encouraging firms to concentrate operations into fewer, larger facilities. But this increases risk, as there are now fewer facilities in the supply chain, and a problem with any one has more severe conse-

quences for the whole network. Interestingly, this seems at odds with the view that increasing supply chain complexity automatically gives greater risk. The answer comes from the design of the chain and the way that members are linked (as we shall see in Chapter 10) – and it confirms the view that reducing some risks inevitably increases others.

▪ *Postponement* – which moves almost-finished products into the supply chain, and delays completion until the last possible moment. For instance, a manufacturer of electrical equipment keeps stocks of standard products and only adds the transformers, cables and instructions needed for a particular market when the products are about to be shipped.

▪ *Factory gate pricing.* A way of coordinating the flow of materials in a supply chain is to have one key player – such as a dominant retailer or manufacturer – taking over responsibility for all logistics. Factory gate pricing allows this by quoting a price delivered to some specific point in the supply chain (not necessarily the factory gate), and then the dominant player becomes responsible for all remaining movements through to final customers.

▪ *Cross-docking* – which coordinates the supply and delivery of materials in a warehouse, so that goods arrive at the receiving area and are immediately transferred to the loading area and put on to delivery vehicles. There may be some sorting, breaking bulk, merging and consolidation of materials at the warehouse – but no storage. Related practices avoid the use of the warehouse completely by transfer points (where the transfer is arranged at some intermediate point rather than a warehouse) and delivery coordination (where the warehouse coordinates the movement of materials directly from upstream suppliers to downstream customers).

▪ *Direct delivery* – with 'disintermediation' allowing more customers to buy from earlier tiers of the supply chain – even directly from manufacturers – using websites, mail order or catalogues.

▪ *Small deliveries.* Some methods – such as JIT, agility and direct delivery – inevitably lead to smaller, more frequent deliveries. This gives a move away from large trucks towards smaller, less efficient delivery vehicles. This has also spurred the growth of parcel delivery services such as FedEx, UPS and DHL – and it has encouraged operators to look for efficiencies, such as round-the-clock deliveries to unattended destinations.

▪ *Increasing vehicle utilization.* For a variety of reasons – such as unbalanced demand, composition of the vehicle fleet, characteristics of the vehicles and loads, poor coordination, etc – vehicles spend a proportion of their time travelling empty or with partial loads. After almost half a century of continuous improvement, productivity of the UK's transport fleet peaked in 1999 and is now stable or even falling (Department for Transport, 2005). Methods for improving productivity include backhauls (where delivery vehicles find loads for their return journeys), reverse logistics (returning goods for repair, reuse or recycling), freight forwarding (where loads from several companies are combined) and more efficient schedules (perhaps including out-of-hours delivery) (McKinnon, 2006).

In summary

SCM is evolving quickly, with managers under continuing pressure to find better ways of organizing their logistics. These improvements are changing both the activities that are done in logistics and the way that they are done. Managers generally aim at lower costs (with leanness corresponding to a strategy of cost leadership) or better customer service (with agility corresponding to a strategy of product differentiation).

Supply chain risk management is at an early stage of development, and when managers try to improve operational efficiency they rarely consider all of the risks. Typically they focus on some of the more obvious risks, but they do not take a balanced view of them all. This inadvertently increases overall levels of risk and supply chain vulnerability. The disturbing point is that this increase in risk is not a deliberate decision, but an unplanned side effect of related decisions.

We can illustrate this effect with several trends. For instance, organizations are moving toward greater integration of their supply chains. This brings many benefits, but it also increases some risks through, say, greater reliance on fewer trading partners and single sourcing. In the same way, an emphasis on cost reduction can remove all slack from the supply chain, increasing vulnerability to unexpected events; agility emphasizes customer service, but increases the risks of reduced financial and operational performance; improved communications are essential, but they make the supply chain vulnerable to any problem in the network of systems; globalization continues to grow, but increases risks from working in distant and unfamiliar locations; outsourcing should improve performance, but increases the risks from lost control and reliance on external partners.

The message seems clear that SCM is an inherently risky function, and the risks are inadvertently drifting upwards. Logistics managers are increasingly aware of this problem and are looking more seriously at risk management. We discuss the principles of risk management in the following chapter.

5

Approaches to risk management

Definition

In Chapter 2 we reviewed the concept of risk, which arises from the uncertainty about future events. All operations involve risks of some kind, and these have to be carefully managed. This is the function of risk management.

> ■ Risk management is the process for systematically identifying, analysing and responding to risks throughout an organization.

Imagine an organization with no risk management. Managers are happy to sit back and wait to see what risky events occur; then they analyse the problems, design their response and implement it. But this purely reactive approach is too slow, and considerable harm is done before the response starts to work. For instance, when a sole supplier goes out of business, operations have to stop until a replacement is found, and this might take weeks or even months. And when managers make hurried decisions to deal with pressing problems, they are prone to make mistakes. For instance, when procurement managers hear rumours of possible shortages of some material, they suddenly place large extra orders to safeguard their own supplies – thereby artificially increasing demand and creating a real shortage. So a reactive approach has managers who:

■ do not recognize that there is a need to do anything until it is too late;

- only respond to events that have actually happened, rather than look for ways of preventing them or mitigating their effects;
- have to work quickly to get things sorted out, and can be rushed into making the wrong response;
- may imagine some response is needed and make unnecessary changes when there is no real risk.

In contrast, risk management takes proactive measures to identify risks, analyse them and design appropriate responses. The responses might avoid risks, prevent them from actually appearing, reduce their effects or generally do whatever is needed to mitigate their effects.

In the last two chapters we developed the theme that risk to a supply chain is anything that threatens the smooth flow of materials. Supply chains are inherently vulnerable to risks, and the levels seem to be rising. Logistics managers need ways of dealing with these risks, and this is the role of supply chain risk management (SCRM).

- Supply chain risk management (SCRM) is the process of systematically identifying, analysing and dealing with risks to supply chains.

R4 Project Management Inc

Logistics managers do a lot of work that can be described as projects, where the four main areas of risk are to scope, schedule, budget and quality. R4 Project Management Inc recommend the following procedure for managing project risk:

1. *Identify risk.* At any point during the project, any member of the project team can identify a risk. This risk originator describes the nature of the risk and passes it to the project manager.
2. *Register risk.* The project manager reviews each identified risk and decides whether it really affects the project. If the risk does affect the project, the project manager assigns an initial view of its likelihood and possible consequences, and enters these into a risk register.
3. *Analyse risk.* A project review group systematically analyses each risk in the register and decides on the appropriate response. This might be to take no further action, make minor adjustments to the project or make more significant changes.
4. *Implement actions.* This is to turn the decisions of the project review group into positive actions. The project manager presents the

findings, communicates requirements, and assigns responsibilities, resources, schedules and funds.

5. *Monitor and control.* The project team then performs the project – including the latest changes. The project manager continues to monitor and control operations to see if risky events materialize, or whether the risk can eventually be 'retired'.

Development of risk management

Early work on risk looked at gambling, and by the eighteenth century insurance companies were using their methods to assess the risk of a venture and calculate an appropriate fee for taking over some of this risk. Lloyd's of London was established in 1771 to insure against losses at sea.

The insurance-based view of risk uses a standard procedure to analyse historical records and find the probability of an event, estimate the potential damage, calculate an expected value and use this to set a reasonable premium. However, there are some weaknesses with this approach. For instance, it concentrates on the types of events that occur fairly often and can be predicted, but is less useful for events that are rare or essentially unknowable in advance. It is also based on compensation for damage that might happen, but does not automatically look for ways of avoiding the damage or reducing its effect. A more fundamental weakness is that it encourages organizations to focus on the costs of risk and avoidance of harmful effects, inevitably encouraging a risk-averse, conservative style of management. This last point is consistent with other pressures on managers, who feel that they are more likely to be punished for a wrong decision than rewarded for a right one – so they look for the safest option.

Three factors counteract the pressures for a risk-averse management style:

1. A more balanced view of risk, accepting that it can also bring opportunities. Then managers should not try to avoid risk, but to analyse it and work with it.
2. The irrational optimism that makes managers ignore serious threats under the belief that 'It can't happen to us.' Unfortunately, the fact that something is unlikely, or potentially embarrassing, does not mean that it will never happen – and disasters really can appear out of the blue.
3. The rather negative observation that managers simply do not recognize or analyse risks – so their ignorance prevents any steps to avoid risks.

The third point is important, as there were clear signs in the 1990s that even major companies were not using any systematic approach to risk management. This made them vulnerable to risks, and well-known examples – such as the Enron Corporation and Barings Bank – showed that their lack of preparation could have serious consequences. We saw in Chapter 1 that subsequent calls for improved corporate governance led to the Turnbull Report of 1999, which gave 'Guidance for directors on internal controls for risk management'. The central message was that risk management should be an essential element of every organization, and embedded in its corporate culture. In particular, there should be a move away from the old view that risk management is an additional burden that increases workload without giving appreciable benefits, and instead it should be seen as an essential element of good management. Unfortunately, it seems that few organizations have really been successful at embedding risk management within their corporate culture (Buehler and Pritsch, 2003). It may be essential – and in many cases a legal requirement – but there is still a lot more progress to be made.

Having said this, many organizations have made progress with risk management, expanding it beyond the narrow confines of insurance against financial loss and into new areas. We can illustrate this with procurement, which is always an area of high risk (typically emerging from disagreements over the interpretation and implementation of contracts). In the 1980s, firms moved away from insuring against these risks, and formed strategic alliances to make sure that harmful events never actually materialized. Similarly, total quality management (TQM) moved away from methods to insure against the effects of poor quality to methods that guaranteed poor quality was eliminated. Such methods allow the positive management of risk, rather than its passive acceptance.

In practice, managers are encouraged to take more interest in risk for four main reasons:

1. They recognize that risk management can give benefits – including smoother and more reliable operations, fewer disruptions, lower overall costs and increased added value – and they use it to gain a competitive advantage.
2. They recognize that risk management is growing into a more central issue that they cannot afford to ignore.
3. Other organizations are introducing risk management and insisting that their trading partners also use appropriate procedures.
4. Regulations and legislation are making risk management compulsory in an increasing number of areas.

k-Tech Research

James Borrows and Wellford Cheng left university in 2000 after doing research into high-storage memory devices. They developed a commercial version of a concept they had been researching, which gives parallel processors faster access to data and is used in high-performance systems. They marketed their idea through a new company, k-Tech Research, and as they do not have resources to manufacture the product they license the technology to major hardware companies.

The problem for k-Tech is that, despite further developments, they only really have one product and this will quickly become outdated. They are still leading research in the area, but the results are always risky and do not necessarily lead to usable new ideas. In 2006 they asked a firm of consultants to give advice on their options. The consultants compared the total expected profit for k-Tech over the next five years with four levels of research. A summary of their figures shows:

■ *No research:*
  – expected profit from continuing product is $15 million.
■ *Sponsored research:*
  – with a 50 per cent chance of new products making an additional contribution of $5 million to profit;
  – expected profit $(15 + 0.5 \times 5) = \$17.5$ million.
■ *Continuing their own research:*
  – with a 20 per cent chance of new products raising profits by $25 million, a 40 per cent chance of raising profits by $2 million, and a 40 per cent chance of losing the $5 million research budget;
  – expected profit $(15 + 0.2 \times 25 + 0.4 \times 2 - 0.4 \times 5) = \$18.8$ million.
■ *Doubling research expenditure:*
  – with 10 per cent chance of raising profits by $30 million, a 10 per cent chance of raising profits by $20 million, a 20 per cent chance of raising profits by $10 million, a 30 per cent chance of covering the research budget, and a 30 per cent chance of losing the $10 million research budget;
  – expected value $(15 + 0.1 \times 30 + 0.1 \times 20 + 0.2 \times 10 + 0.3 \times 0 - 0.3 \times 10) = \$19$ million.

Obviously these figures only summarize one part of the analyses, but the interesting point is that more risky options have higher expected returns. Managers using the expected returns would not avoid the risk, but would actively choose the most risky options.

Risk strategy

Managers may feel that risk management is generally 'a good thing' and even recognize that its benefits are greater than its costs, but its introduction still needs some positive trigger. This might come from the appearance of a particularly risky event, but it is more likely to emerge from individual managers including risk assessments in their normal decisions. One manager might become a 'risk champion' or risk manager who leads, encourages, coordinates, controls and generally organizes risk management within the organization. Then, to be formal, we can draw a distinction between the risk manager who is responsible for risk management and the risk owner who is responsible for the operations containing the risk. But some people argue that this distinction suggests too much transfer of authority to someone who is remote from the actual risk, and the best person to manage risks is a knowledgeable and skilled risk owner.

It soon becomes clear that any risk can have widespread effects on the organization, so its management needs a holistic approach – typically led by a risk committee. This is a group of managers (probably working under a different title, like 'risk management team') who design and agree overall policies for dealing with risk. As the strategic impact of their work becomes increasingly clear, this committee tends to move up the organizational hierarchy – moving from a technical or actuarial committee making operational decisions to a senior committee making strategic ones. Then the senior managers involved can access all the necessary information and resources, and they have the authority to get things done.

Not only is this involvement of top managers the best approach in principle – with Fraser (2003) agreeing that successful risk management must start with top-level support and executive-level leadership – but it is also a statutory requirement in many areas. Based on the Turnbull Report, the Companies Act of 2006 requires the board of directors of public companies to accept overall responsibility for and ownership of risks. So the board of directors should, at the very least:

■ define the organization's attitude towards risk, its philosophy and the strategic direction of risk management;
■ create an appropriate environment for risk management, with necessary systems and resources;
■ publish risk management policies defining attitudes, approaches and responsibilities;
■ know about significant risks that the organization faces;
■ understand the potential consequences of these risks for stakeholders;
■ ensure that appropriate processes are in place for identifying, analysing and dealing with risks, and that these work effectively;

■ communicate with stakeholders to ensure that everyone is aware of their responsibilities for risk management;
■ know how the organization will manage a crisis;
■ assess the performance of risk management.

Below the broad principles established by senior managers, the management of risk is devolved throughout the organization. In particular, each function has an inherent responsibility for its own risk management, and this is described as 'operations risk management'. In our context, logistics managers are responsible for risk in the supply chain – and hence supply chain risk management (SCRM).

Operations risk management gives a mechanism for passing the aims of senior managers down to the rest of the organization. For instance, when senior managers are risk-averse, this attitude is spelled out in their broad strategies and is transferred to the supply chain through SCRM. Within logistics and every other function, departments and then individuals have their own devolved responsibilities for risk. So the mechanism moves risk management down from corporate ambitions to actual operations – and with widespread acceptance it becomes a part of corporate culture. And unless risk management really becomes a part of corporate culture, there will be a lot of lip-service to the ideas but no real commitment.

Risk management may be devolved to separate functions, but it is usually supported by a specialized risk management group. Depending on the size of the organization, this specialized group can range from a single part-time manager through to a full department. Whatever its size, its aim is to coordinate the efforts of different functions, offer specialized knowledge and manage the areas that would otherwise be missed. It gives a focal point within the organization, and might define procedures and standards, increase awareness, develop a culture, educate, train, design and review internal processes.

Supply chain risk management

SCRM is responsible for all aspects of risk to the supply chain. Specifically, it ensures that principles established by senior managers are applied to logistics risk. So a reasonable starting point for SCRM has senior logistics managers analysing the organization's overall risk strategy and identifying its requirements from logistics. Then they start designing their own long-term plans for risk in the supply chain – included in a supply chain risk strategy, which contains all the long-term goals, plans, policies, culture, resources, decisions and actions that relate to risks within a supply chain. The main elements of this strategy are usually presented in a written document, which is called a risk policy, strategic plan, management plan or some equivalent title.

A strategic plan does not consider specific risks, but it describes a general view of supply chain risk and how managers will approach risky events. The contents of this plan vary widely, but typically include:

■ statements of who is responsible for the strategic management of risk within the supply chain, the work of a risk committee, its membership, and other details of the management structure;
■ a review of the organization's attitude towards risk, extracted from its broad strategies and consequent objectives for SCRM;
■ a summary of policies for supply chain risk and the scope of risk management;
■ a review of the resources, systems, tools and facilities available for SCRM;
■ procedures, methods and tools for assembling a list of risks and their causes, likelihoods and consequences;
■ procedures, methods and tools for analysing the impact of risks and their significance;
■ procedures, methods and tools for designing alternative responses to the risks and selecting the most appropriate;
■ policies for allocating and sharing risk among stakeholders;
■ methods for monitoring risk, maintaining the risk management process, updating procedures, communicating results, measuring performance and achieving continuous improvement.

The existence of a supply chain risk strategy suggests some high-level commitment to SCRM, and it sets the context for progressively more detailed decisions and actions at lower levels, where the strategic aims are translated into operational terms and implemented. But not all decisions are devolved, and some are so important that senior managers remain directly involved. In particular, they should take responsibility for the relatively few – say around a dozen – serious risks that could have a significant impact on the whole supply chain. For example, the financial insecurity of a major supplier, a move to offshore sourcing, outsourcing non-core operations, or a new type of product could all raise issues of long-term vulnerability and would need a holistic response coordinated by senior managers.

Saunders-Brody

Saunders-Brody is a leading consultant in risk management, which defines six essential requirements from senior risk managers:

1. Have enough responsibility and authority to lead risk management.

2. Work independently with all internal and external risk stakeholders to understand and discuss their objectives and needs.
3. Create and maintain effective policies and procedures for managing risk.
4. Deliver accurate, timely and relevant information about risks to those concerned.
5. Embed risk management in the corporate culture.
6. Ensure that risk management is included in all significant company decisions.

Bottom-up risk management

The approach to SCRM that we have outlined is essentially top-down, with the board of directors and corporate managers designing broad strategies that set the overall direction for risk, followed by senior logistics managers designing their own strategy, with decisions and actions passed progressively down through the supply chain hierarchy. One problem with this approach is that surprisingly few organizations have logistics managers in the most senior positions – so the top risk committee might have no logistics managers. Then there is a missing link between corporate and logistics risk, and it becomes difficult to move ideas either up or down. But the top-down approach has a more fundamental flaw, which is that senior managers who design policies can never have enough knowledge of the effects of their decisions at lower levels. For instance, a logistics director will rarely know the effects of a particular policy on drivers' schedules. Then the strategic directions might be good in principle, but completely unworkable.

The way around this is to recognize that everyone is involved – at least to some extent – in the management of risk. And people at lower levels often have a clearer understanding of the risks and ways of dealing with them. For instance, if you want to know how to improve delivery schedules to avoid delays, you would ask vehicle drivers for their ideas rather than logistics directors. So an alternative approach to supply chain risk strategy is bottom-up – with people lower down the organization identifying risks in their normal work and suggesting ways of dealing with them. Initially, this will probably bring a series of disjointed and uncoordinated suggestions of variable value, so the role of more senior managers is to review, analyse, evaluate, consolidate and formalize the best into a strategy.

In reality, both top-down and bottom-up approaches are needed to give a comprehensive view of risks, so there is a mixture of the two rather than a choice. Then some factors that contribute to a successful logistics risk strategy include:

- senior managers who are aware of the consequences of risks in the supply chain and support the concept of SCRM;
- risk management as an integral part of supply chain management – reinforced by a risk culture;
- an understanding of the role and requirements of SCRM among everyone working in the supply chain;
- formal procedures for identifying and dealing with risks;
- acceptance that supply chain risks continually change and need monitoring, with updating of risk management procedures.

Al-Misra Risk Auditors

Al-Misra Risk Auditors are a specialized group of management consultants in Cairo, Egypt. They routinely advise companies on supply chain risks, and always start with an audit to find the current state of SCRM. This audit asks a series of related questions, such as the following list. The answers to these questions give an overall view of SCRM within the company:

- *Plans:*
  - Do you have formal plans for risk management, or do you think that these are unnecessary?
  - Do you define protocols and procedures to deal with risks, or rely on ad hoc procedures to solve problems as they occur?
- *Approach:*
  - Do you consider risk as an inevitable fact and even an opportunity to differentiate your firm, or do you try to avoid it or pass it to someone else?
  - Do you consider risk to have a strategic role, or is it a more limited task for functional staff?
  - Do you consider risk as a part of the business culture and a part of normal decisions, or should it be left to actuarial specialists?
  - Do you plan for risks in advance, or start planning a response when events actually occur?
  - Do you routinely test risk management procedures, or assume that they will work properly when needed?
  - Do you see risk as an expensive overhead, or an integral part of management?
- *Span:*
  - Do you consider risks to the whole logistics function, or those affecting each logistics function separately?
  - Do you limit risks to those affecting your own operations, or do you include risks to your immediate trading partners?

- – Do you consider risks in remote tiers of suppliers and customers, as well as those to your immediate trading partners?
- ■ *Staff:*
  - – Do you train staff to recognize the importance of risk management, or assume that this is obvious?
  - – Do you train staff to identify and deal with risk, or assume that they will know what to do when something goes wrong?
- ■ *Suppliers:*
  - – Do you work with other members of the supply chain to manage risks, or work in isolation?
  - – Do you cooperate with suppliers to reduce risks and audit their operations, or assume that they are doing appropriate management on their own?
  - – Do you identify alternative supplies, or assume that your current supplies are safe?
- ■ *Customers:*
  - – Do you work to identify alternative routes to customers, or do you assume that your current routes are secure?
  - – Do you work with customers to consider joint risks, or assume that their risks are their own concern?
  - – Do you see risks as a burden, or an opportunity for differentiation?
- ■ *Technology:*
  - – Do you analyse the risks of using new technology, or avoid new ideas until they have been proved?
  - – Do you monitor and control systems, or assume that they continue to work normally?

Integrated supply chains

The last chapter discussed the major trend towards integration along supply chains. This is particularly significant for SCRM, as a risk might appear within an individual organization, but the links between organizations automatically transmit its effects to other members of the chain. One supplier might hit financial problems, but if it fails there is a knock-on effect on all other members of the chain. The reliability of the whole supply chain depends on its weakest link, and there is no point in one organization – or even most of them – increasing their ability to deal with risks, when one link remains vulnerable. So again, all members of a chain should work together for their mutual benefit, reducing the overall vulnerability. We mentioned different levels of integration within a supply chain, and can use the same approach to suggest five levels of integration for SCRM:

- *Level 1.* No significant risk management is done anywhere in the supply chain.
- *Level 2.* Some basic risk management is done within the separate activities of logistics within some organizations.
- *Level 3.* Risk management is done for the broad logistics function, but is contained within separate organizations.
- *Level 4.* Risk management is extended and coordinated along the supply chain to include first-tier suppliers and customers.
- *Level 5.* Risk management is extended to the broader supply chain.

In reality, most SCRM is still at an early stage of development, with a survey (Christopher *et al*, 2002) reporting that 'Managers were conscious that supply chain vulnerability and indeed resilience were important issues, but not ones that they were explicitly required to address.' Realistically, most firms still work at level 1 or 2 and are contemplating moves to level 3. Optimistically, an increasing number are working at level 3, but very few have reached level 4, and none seem to be really working at level 5.

In principle the approach of SCRM is the same for all levels, but there are differences in detail. Bearing in mind the limited progress in the area, we start by describing the approach of a firm aspiring to work at level 3, and then will move on to discuss the requirements of higher levels.

Aims of SCRM

We have developed a view of supply chain risk management as dealing with all possible threats to the smooth flow of materials through supply chains.

> ■ The overall aim of supply chain risk management is to ensure that supply chains continue to work as planned, with smooth and uninterrupted flows of materials from initial suppliers through to final customers.

We can phrase this aim in terms of decreasing the vulnerability of a supply chain, increasing its ability to withstand unexpected events, improving sustainability or increasing resilience. Vulnerability describes how likely a supply chain is to be affected by risky events. The idea of resilience is somewhat different, as it suggests the speed with which a chain can return to normal working after some kind of damage. So in different circumstances SCRM might either try to prevent risky events from occurring (reducing vulnerability) or accept that they will occur and then return the chain to normal working as quickly as possible (increasing resilience).

To support its underlying aim of uninterrupted material flows, SCRM has a series of more immediate goals that include:

- designing a supply chain risk strategy that fits in with higher organizational risk strategies and sets the context for SCRM;
- meeting any legal, regulatory, contractual or societal requirements for risks;
- embedding risk management within the function of supply chain management;
- ensuring appropriate resources, systems, facilities and infrastructure for SCRM;
- identifying best practices for supply chain risk management, with relevant procedures, technology, information and planning;
- using these practices to identify, analyse and plan responses to risks that are relevant to SCM;
- implementing the planned responses to risks when necessary, and controlling the subsequent actions;
- monitoring performance and continually developing and improving methods;
- cooperating with other parts of the organization and members of the supply chain to give a coherent attitude towards risk.

Notice that these aims say nothing about reducing risks. Most managers do not like risk, as it involves uncertainty that they cannot control, so their preference is to reduce and preferably eliminate risk. But it is unrealistic to aim for conditions of certainty, and it may not even be sensible. The Turnbull Report (1999) clearly states that 'risk management is about mitigating, not eliminating risk'. And Merna and Al-Thani (2005) say, 'The task of risk management is not to create a project or business that is totally free of risks... but to make the stakeholders aware of the risks, both negative and positive, help them to take well-calculated risks and to manage risks efficiently.' We know that, in a competitive economy, profit can be viewed as a reward for taking risk, so firms should be looking for the best balance of costs and benefits. The message, then, is that effective SCRM does not eliminate risks, but manages them – and tilts the balance towards the opportunities and away from the threats.

Benefits of SCRM

Achieving these aims gives various benefits, based on improved decisions and uninterrupted operations. Whenever some unexpected shock hits a supply chain or there is a significant divergence from plans, managers tend to over-react, causing dramatic fluctuations. For instance, fears about the availability of some material encourage companies to buy excess stocks, add warehouse space, extend delivery times, switch suppliers and so on. These are often irrational responses that 'cost money, alienate customers, put companies at risk for financial loss, and create misleading distortions throughout the entire supply chain' (Christopher and Lee, 2004). Such problems are avoided by proper SCRM, with other benefits including the following:

■ Issues surrounding risks are considered early, and as part of normal management practice.
■ Balanced decisions are possible, including reference to risks.
■ Operations that are too risky or financially unsound are avoided.
■ Responsibility for risk is devolved to the most appropriate people.
■ Management performance can be measured, drawing a distinction between good luck and good management.
■ Risks are identified before events actually occur and create a crisis.
■ Early assessment of risks allows better planning, prioritization and allocation of resources.
■ Alternative responses to risks can be designed, evaluated, compared and planned.
■ Imaginative responses can be developed when there is enough time and no urgent need to respond to actual events.
■ Plans and contingencies can be implemented quickly when risky events actually materialize.
■ Operations have less disruption and volatility.
■ Uninterrupted operations improve financial performance, customer service, corporate image, etc.
■ Operations are constantly monitored to identify emerging problems.
■ Profiles of historical risks are built into a register that improves responses to future risks.
■ Improved communications about risk give common involvement and understanding.
■ The analytical skills of people are developed and they are allowed to give attention to the most important issues.

Steps in risk management

Having described the context of SCRM and listed its aims and benefits, the next job is clearly to describe how these can be achieved. In other words, we need a formal process for identifying, prioritizing and planning for risks – with results that are communicated to everyone concerned (Fraser, 2003).

The Turnbull Report advises companies to consider the nature and extent of the risks they face, the risks they are responsible for, the likelihood of a risk actually occurring, possibilities for reducing risks, opportunities for minimizing the impact on operations, and evaluation of the costs of managing these risks. In line with this, we have already suggested that three core elements of SCRM are:

1. *Identify risks to the supply chain.* This examines the supply chain, defining the separate activities and their relationships, and systematically studying these to find areas of risk.

   The output from this first step is a list of risks facing the supply chain.
2. *Analyse the risks.* Having identified the risks, the next stage is to consider their potential impact. The impact depends on two factors – the probability that a risky event will occur, and the severity of consequences when it does occur. Then managers can prioritize risks according to the impact and decide where to concentrate resources. Clearly they should focus on risks with the highest impact, but should consider other factors, such as the likelihood that they can actually reduce the impact.

   The output from this second step is a prioritized list of risks and their expected consequences.
3. *Design appropriate responses to the risk.* Here managers know the seriousness of risks and consider different ways of dealing with them. There are many types of response, but three common ones are prevention (to reduce the probability of a risky event occurring), mitigation (to reduce the consequences) and response (waiting to evaluate actual events before deciding on a response).

   The output from this third step is a planned response to each risk.

These three steps are characterized as identification (which we discuss in Chapter 6), analysis (described in Chapter 7) and response (considered in Chapter 8).

Expanding the core activities

The three core activities focus on important steps, but they clearly do not give the whole picture. In reality, there are additional steps beforehand to prepare and set the scene – and there are steps afterwards to maintain the systems, monitor events and control the risks. The Project Management Body of Knowledge (Project Management Institute, 2004) describes these extra steps as planning at the start, with monitoring and control afterwards. There are many other views of the steps involved, such as Chapman and Ward's (1997) eight steps of 'define, focus, identify, structure, ownership, estimate, evaluate and plan'.

Presumably the preparatory steps really start with an acknowledgement that there are actually risks to manage. This seems an obvious step, as risk is an inevitable part of all decisions, but someone has to recognize that work is needed and then initiate it (Smith, 1995). But this implies that someone in authority has the foresight and incentive to look at SCRM – so the first real

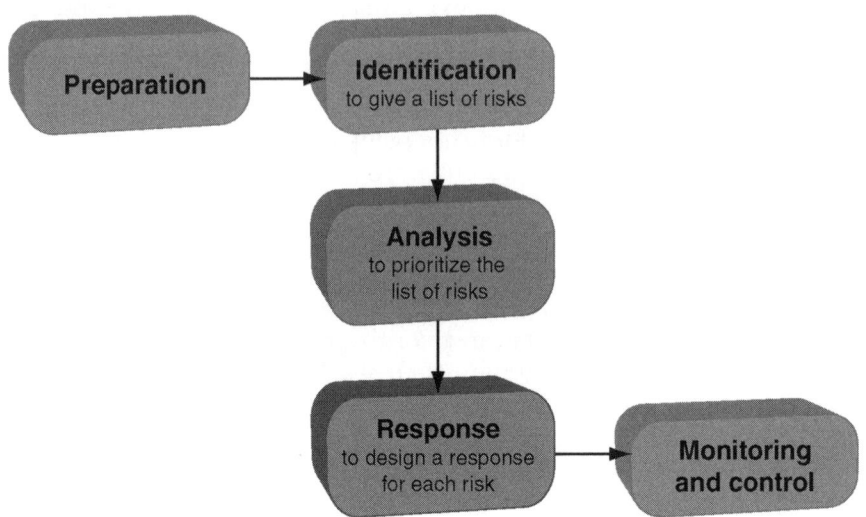

Figure 5.1 Three core steps in supply chain risk management

step is to acknowledge the importance of risk and get senior management involvement.

After the three core activities come the detailed activities to implement plans as necessary, monitor operations to see if things are turning out as planned, report, make statutory reviews, and so on. And as circumstances continuously change, managers have to control their responses – which means making periodic reviews to check for new risks, adjust plans and improve procedures. This is an important point, as risks are constantly changing, so managers have to monitor and control their decisions – with SCRM as a continuing cycle rather than a single procedure.

Adding these extra activities allows us to suggest the following fuller list of steps for SCRM:

1. Acknowledge the importance of risk management, get senior management understanding and approval, and set up the necessary organizational infrastructure.
2. Analyse the organization's risk strategy, attitude towards risk and policies – and review the consequences for SCRM.
3. Define a supply chain risk strategy to give the context for all other decisions, including attitudes towards risk, aims, methods and procedures.
4. Do an audit to describe the details of the supply chain, and define the scope of supply chain risk management (particularly whether this refers to the whole supply chain or some limited part of it).
5. Identify risks to operations in the supply chain – both actual and potential.

6. Find the probability that risky events will actually occur.
7. Analyse the consequences of events and their expected values, establishing relationships between risks, events, responses and consequences.
8. Use the consequences to prioritize risks, identify the most significant and assign priorities for action and resources.
9. Design appropriate responses to the risk, listing alternatives and identifying the best.
10. Plan the implementation of responses, communicate findings, get support, assign responsibilities, train staff, define procedures and so on.
11. Monitor operations to check for events that actually occur or to look for critical events or operations that are out of control.
12. When necessary, implement the planned response, moving from theoretical ideas to positive actions, see if things work as planned and take necessary actions to manage the risk.
13. Control responses, adjusting procedures so that organizations maintain the best possible responses to risk, and update the risk register.
14. Return to the top of the list (or an appropriate point) to keep cycling through the SCRM process.

Although this is a daunting list, it is clearly a simplified view and is not meant to be a recipe for SCRM. Taken together, the steps outline a framework for moving SCRM from the initial ideas though to final implementation and control. The core steps of identification, analysis and response are covered in steps 5, 6–8 and 9 respectively.

Problems with this approach

This procedure gives an approach to SCRM, but nobody could suggest that this is easy. For instance, the whole process depends on step 5, which analyses activities in the supply chain and identifies the risks associated with them. This alone can be enormously difficult, and Stemmler (2006) says that simply identifying the risks 'poses an almost insurmountable challenge for line managers'. Step 6 puts a probability to the events, and again we hit problems, as these are often little more than subjective guesses (how else can you find the probability of an earthquake hitting an essential supplier?). Then step 7 looks at the consequences of events, and again it is difficult to give convincing figures, and managers have to rely on subjective estimates and accounting conventions.

Even an apparently straightforward part of the process – finding the expected values of outcomes – is extremely difficult in practice. Organizations can often make things easier by developing checklists for the most common threats and contingency plans to deal with them. For instance, if you want to open a new warehouse in Brazil, many specialized consultants (as well as firms that have already been through the process) will give you a standard checklist of risks you might face and ways of dealing with them.

Los Angeles Transport Infrastructure Board

The Los Angeles Transport Infrastructure Board has produced a guideline for managing risks in transport capital projects. Although each project is essentially different, these guidelines can be modified to allow for these differences. The following list of headings shows the main elements in the guidelines. You can also see that, despite minor differences from the list above, the overall approach is very similar:

1. *Preparation:*
   - Get commitment and resources from senior managers.
   - Identify key people and stakeholders in the project.
   - Identify relevant risk policies, aims, objectives and requirements.
   - Identify the general types of likely risks.
   - Review lessons learned from previous projects.
   - Prepare a schedule for risk management activities.
2. *Identify the risks:*
   - Form a risk management team for risk assessment.
   - Review their objectives, policies and methods.
   - Analyse the details of the activities involved.
   - Contact stakeholders and get their opinions.
   - Reassess risks already described in the database.
   - Draw up a definitive list of risks.
   - Analyse and categorize the risks using agreed procedures.
3. *Analyse and prioritize the risks:*
   - Get a consensus on the probability of each risk.
   - Get a consensus on the consequences of each risk.
   - Identify a time window when the risks could occur.
   - Prioritize risks according to their impact, likelihood and timing.
4. *Design responses to each risk:*
   - Design options for dealing with each risk.
   - Identify the risks that will be assumed (essentially low-level risks).
   - Identify the risks that will be avoided, transferred or mitigated.
   - Update the risk database with new decisions.
5. *Design the implementation:*
   - Design plans for implementing the designed responses.
   - Check the resources needed for the responses.
   - Check approvals, funding and procedures.
   - Plan all the remaining activities needed.
6. *Implement the plan:*
   - Make sure that all procedures are in place, especially those to monitor operations.

- – Check for triggers that activate the planned response.
- – Implement the response when necessary.
- – Manage the response for as long as necessary.
- – Report the progress and results from the response.
7. *Control risk management:*
  - – Periodically review risks, responses and plans.
  - – Proactively look for improvements and new procedures.
  - – Keep the risk database up to date.

Some principles of SCRM

We have now outlined the approach to SCRM, and develop this theme in the following chapters. There are so many different circumstances for SCRM that it is impossible to describe detailed procedures, but we can outline some general principles. For instance, we know that methods to improve operational efficiency seem to increase vulnerability to risk. The problem is that logistics managers usually base their decisions to improve efficiency on operating costs, with at best a token acknowledgement of some aspects of risk. SCRM takes a more detailed look at the risks and the details of their costs. When these costs are included the increased efficiency may come at surprisingly high cost.

The implication is that managers should look more carefully at the balance between vulnerability and efficiency, and they might find that there are benefits from introducing slack, thereby reducing operating efficiency but at the same time getting a significant reduction in vulnerability. This slack might appear as stock, spare capacity, backup systems, longer lead times or a variety of other mechanisms.

An extension to the first principle is summed up in the statement that 'Diversification reduces risk.' Then multiple sourcing is less risky than single sourcing, multiple locations are more secure than a single, centralized one, parallel transport links are less risky than single paths, and so on. A variation on this theme is the principle that agility reduces risk, and one way of increasing agility is to use modular processes and products. For instance, modular components use the same materials for a range of products – and this reduces risks from uncertain supplies, as materials can switch to the product in most need. Similarly, modular transport can be switched to the most urgent jobs when there is a threat of disruption.

Another principle we have developed is that SCRM must be proactive; waiting for risky events and then relying on good crisis management will not work. Risk management must prepare for events through the three core steps of identification, analysis and response. These steps explicitly include some quantifiable analyses – based on the old saying that 'What you can't measure you can't manage.' This quantification of risk is an essential part of SCRM, and without it there is no way of evaluating and comparing risks or deciding where resources should be focused (Rice *et al*, 2003).

In a different vein is the principle that SCRM is always cyclical rather than linear. In other words, it is never finished, but plans are continuously revised to take into account changing conditions. There are clear similarities here with TQM – which also relies on corporate culture, affects the whole organization, is continuous and never finished, and looks for continuous improvement to operations. So SCRM can use some of the methods and tools developed for TQM. For instance, a plan–do–check–act cycle gives one way of improving risk management, with a team of people using the cycle:

- ■ *plan* – looking at existing operations, collecting information, discussing alternatives and suggesting a way of improving risk management;
- ■ *do* – where the plan is implemented and data are collected on performance;
- ■ *check* – which analyses performance to see if the expected results actually appear;
- ■ *act* – if the plans work, they are made permanent, but, if there are problems, lessons are learned and the new plans are not adopted.

The team is continuously looking for new ways of managing risk, and at this point it returns to the beginning of the cycle and starts planning new ideas.

Risk management software

We could continue in this way, developing general ideas and themes for SCRM, but will take a more formal approach in the following chapters. One useful point, though, is that some of the analyses are so regimented that they can be automated. As risk management is increasingly recognized as a part of normal management, a range of software has been developed to help in different ways. Early work was done by oil companies, with both Norwegian Petroleum Consultants and BP developing programs for managing risks to projects in the North Sea. The 1980s saw a lot more software appearing, initially focusing on risk in projects and then moving to risk management in general. Now there are dozens of products around. As with any application, these range from the trivial (and free) that do basic calculations, through to the very sophisticated (and expensive) that give an integrated, tailored approach to risk management. Perhaps the best known is @RISK, which is an add-in for spreadsheets. Other programs are aimed at specific functions, such as Bancdirections (www.bancdirections.co.uk) to help financial institutions assess investment and market trading risks, KWI for the energy sector (www.kwi.com) and PSI2000 for health and safety risks (www.psi2000.com).

S-Crisk-Anal

S-Crisk-Anal is a risk management package developed by Szchewski Software and is currently being implemented by logistics companies in Eastern Europe. It is not widely available, but its users report very favourably on performance, claiming that its main benefit is the formal structure that forces them to understand and analyse the risks. The following description gives a brief feel for its capabilities:

- The program is based on the ownership of risks in the supply chain by specified managers. Then risks that are under the control of the focus firm need the risk owners to approve any decisions relating to them.
- The program develops a detailed map of the logistics activities within the focus organization (and if necessary tiers of customers and suppliers beyond). Associated with this are definitions of management responsibilities, reporting lines, internal communication and decision-making authority.
- Risk owners are the managers responsible for risks within specified operations, and they have to identify the risks.
- The software guides risk owners to assess:
  - the nature of the risk to the organization (supply problems, financial, accidental damage, natural disaster, etc);
  - the probability of it occurring (either on the normal scale of 0 to 1, or classified in some way);
  - the scale of the potential threat (short-term disruption, damage to reputation, closure of facilities, bankruptcy, etc).
- The software guides risk owners to develop alternative procedures for dealing with these risks and compare them using extensive 'what-if' analyses. This allows owners to select the most appropriate responses and design the implementation.
- Risk owners have to decide whether to endorse this decision. In effect they have to show how happy they are with the result and whether it meets their requirements. The options range from accepting the decision entirely, through adding comments about concerns and reservations, and on to rejecting the decision and recommending further work.
- The program models the interactions between activities, risks and responses, and maintains an appropriate risk register.

In summary

Risk management has a long history, originally developing through gambling, insurance and actuarial studies. But this role has developed into a core element of general management, and has spread into other business functions – including logistics.

The context for risk management is laid by the organization's broad strategies, particularly its risk strategy, which is passed on to the separate functions and forms the basis of their own risk management. The supply chain is particularly vulnerable to risk, and supply chain risk management is clearly growing in importance. The overall aim of SCRM is to ensure uninterrupted flows of materials, but there are many more immediate goals for good SCRM.

The context for SCRM and its long-term direction is generally given in a separate supply chain risk strategy, which is designed by a mixture of top-down design and bottom-up emerging. More details are added to this, with the core activities of risk identification, analysis and response. Around these three core steps is a series of other activities, starting with preparation for SCRM and ending with monitoring and control of risks. These steps do not give a recipe for SCRM, but they outline a continuing process that evolves over time. This brings numerous benefits, centred on better decisions about logistics and reduced supply chain vulnerability.

Because circumstances vary so widely, it is difficult to describe actual procedures for SCRM, but there are some general principles, such as the need to balance operational efficiency and risk, take a proactive approach to risk management, and so on. We develop these themes in later chapters.

The next chapter considers the identification of risk, with the following chapters discussing the analysis and design of responses.

6

Identifying risks

Types of risk

At the heart of risk management are the activities to identify, analyse and respond to risk. In this chapter we look at the identification of risk, while the following chapters consider the analysis and responses.

- Risk identification produces a list of the risks that are likely to affect the supply chain and hence the broader organization.

Supply chain risks

Risks to the supply chain consist of anything that might interrupt the smooth flow of materials. You can see an immediate problem here, as there are a huge number of possible risks that can appear in almost endless variety. Most things can appear as a risk to the supply chain, and managers comment that when you put 'risk' after any other business word you find something else to worry about.

You can imagine the risks of accidents to delivery vehicles, fire at a logistics centre, industrial action, theft, loss at sea, non-payment by customers, shortage of materials, poor-quality products, lack of trained people, faults in information systems, and so on. Hendricks and Singhal (2003) found that 34 per cent of supply chain disruptions originated from internal operations, meaning that the firm itself was responsible for the disruptions; suppliers were primarily responsible for 15 per cent of disruptions, customers for 13 per cent, nature and government for 4 per cent each and various combinations of parties for 6 per cent. They found that shortage of parts was the primary reason for supply chain disruptions (in 22 per cent of incidents), followed by sudden changes in demand (9 per cent), order changes by customers (9 per cent), various production problems (9 per cent), development problems (4 per cent) and quality (3 per cent). But how can you get anything like a complete list of risks?

Perhaps it helps to classify different types of risk, in the way that Chapter 1 described risks as either internal (that appear in normal operations) or external (that come from outside the supply chain). In practice, internal and external risks are not necessarily distinct. For instance, a financial problem might start outside the organization when a customer fails to pay a bill, but then it becomes an internal risk from the organization's subsequent cash flow problems. Or an external risk of rising prices for a raw material causes managers to increase stocks and hoard materials, thereby creating new internal risks of obsolescent stock, damage, loss, deterioration and all the other risks that come from excessive stocks. There is no clear border between internal and external risks, and we could argue that all internal risks are really triggered by some external event. Increasing production costs are triggered by variable customer demand, shortage of stock is triggered by late deliveries from suppliers, variable demand is triggered by customer preferences, and so on.

We can extend the classification of supply chain risks by seeing how they move along supply chains. Clearly diseases, such as foot-and-mouth disease in cattle and SARS, can move with the flow of materials and attack at any point of the chain. In the same way, computer viruses can be carried through connected IT systems. In reality, many other risks can also travel along supply chains, such as financial problems that are transferred between members, shortages of materials, uncertain demand for final products, and concerns for product quality. So a more detailed view of supply chain risk can describe risks as internal risks, which either are inherent or arise more directly from management decisions, risks within the supply chain, or risks in the external environment (Mason-Jones and Towill, 1998):

1. *Internal risks* arise from operations within an organization. They might be:
   - inherent risks in operations (such as accidents, the reliability of equipment, loss of an information technology system, human errors and quality issues);
   - risks that arise more directly from managers' decisions (such as the choice of batch sizes, safety stock levels, financial problems and delivery schedules).
2. *Supply chain risks* are external to the organizations, but within the supply chain. These occur from the interactions between members of the supply chain, and are principally:
   - risks from suppliers: reliability, availability of materials, lead times, delivery problems, industrial action, etc;

- risks from customers: variable demand, payments, problems with order processing, customized requirements, etc.

    The main causes of these risks are inadequate cooperation between members and lack of visibility.

3. *External risks* are external to the supply chain and arise from interactions with its environment – including accidents, extreme weather, legislation, pressure groups, crime, natural disasters, wars, etc.

Taken together, these types of risk define the vulnerability of a supply chain, allowing a more specific definition of supply chain vulnerability.

■ Supply chain vulnerability is the exposure of a supply chain to disruption arising from the risks to operations within each organization, to interactions within the supply chain, and from the external environment.

Other classifications

This classification of internal and external risks is only one option, and we can look at them in several different ways. An alternative is to consider risks to the three related flows of materials, money and information in a supply chain, and then add a fourth type of risk based on the ways that these flows are organized:

1. *Physical risks* are associated with the movement and storage of materials – and include risk to transport, storage, delivery, material movement, inventory systems, etc. These risks typically appear as late deliveries, interrupted transport, damage to goods, shortage of stock, missing products, accidents and so on.

2. *Financial risks* are associated with the flows of money – and include risks to payments, cash flows, debt, investments, accounting systems, etc. These risks appear as poor returns on investment, excessive costs, unpaid bills, shortage of cash, missing accounts and so on.

3. *Information risks* are associated with the systems and flows of information – and include data capture and transfer, integrity, information processing, market intelligence, system failure, etc. These risks appear as missing data, errors in information, breaches of data security, systems failure, incorrect transactions and so on.

4. *Organizational risks* arise from the links between members of the supply chain – and include relationships between suppliers and customers, alliances, shared benefits, etc. These risks appear as poor communications, lost customers, problems with supplies, disagreements over contracts, legal disputes, etc.

Other suggested categories of risks include environmental, demand and supply, process and control risks (Mason-Jones and Towill, 1998), and supply market, supplier, regulatory and supply strategy risks (Minahan, 2005). Merna and Smith (1999) give a somewhat longer list of risks to projects, and we will use this approach to give the following list of common risks to supply chains:

- ■ *strategic* – arising from strategic decisions made within organizations that directly increase the risk (as discussed in Chapter 4);
- ■ *natural* – arising from unforeseen natural events such as extreme weather, lightning, earthquakes, flood, landslides or outbreaks of diseases;
- ■ *political* – such as government instability, new legislation (such as the Sarbanes–Oxley Act), regulations, policies, permits, treaties, customs barriers, conflicts or wars;
- ■ *economic* – from the broad economic environment, including interest rates, inflation, currency exchange rates, taxes and growth;
- ■ *physical* – risks to buildings and facilities, such as traffic accidents, equipment failure, congestion or limited capacity;
- ■ *supply* – all issues with the movement of materials into an organization, including sources, supply market conditions, constraints, limited availability, supplier reliability, lead times, material costs, delays, etc;
- ■ *market* – all aspects of customer demand, such as level of demand, variability, alternative products, competition and patterns of change;
- ■ *transport* – for all movements of materials, including risks to the infrastructure, vehicles, facilities and loads;
- ■ *products* – risks arising from product features, including technology used, innovation, product mix, range, volumes, materials used and standardization;
- ■ *operations* – arising from the nature of activities in the organization, type of process, complexity, technology, special conditions, after-sales service, etc;
- ■ *financial* – all money transactions, including payments, prices, costs, sourcing of funds, profit and general financial performance;
- ■ *information* – including the availability of data, data transfer, accuracy, reliability, security of systems, etc;
- ■ *organization* – arising from the way the organization works, including its structure, disputes, types of interactions, subcontractors, communication flows, culture, etc;
- ■ *management* – and risks arising from their knowledge, skills, experience, decisions, real aims, etc;
- ■ *planning* – risks from the design and execution of plans for operations, including mismatch between supply and demand, inadequate detail, missed constraints, poor forecasting, lack of synchronization, etc;
- ■ *human* – from all the complex interactions between people, including working requirements, aims, culture, human errors and industrial action;

- *technical* – and new technology in processes, communications, new products, process designs and reliability;
- *criminal* – arising from all illegal activities, such as theft, fraud, bribery, vandalism and terrorism;
- *safety* – to people and facilities, including accidents, hazardous substances and fire;
- *environment* – eg pollution, use of resources, traffic and regulations;
- *local permits* – usually administered by local government and including planning permissions, land use, local policies, grants, etc.

This gives a daunting list – especially as it is by no means exhaustive and only suggests the main types of risk. A risk is any issue that might cause some concern. As supply chains span the world, these might be as diverse as a traffic jam in Prague that delays a delivery to Vancouver, a hurricane in Texas that causes fuel prices to rise in Spain, a rainstorm in Johannesburg that delays the start of a mining project in Quito, a missing payment from Nigeria that causes financial problems in Sri Lanka, and overcrowded trains in London that increase demand for cars from Japan. Even the most conscientious logistics managers cannot identify all the risks to a particular chain – in the way that you cannot list every possible risk when you go out shopping. The best they can do is list the most likely or most serious risks – or generally the most significant – and concentrate their efforts on these.

Risk register

The purpose of risk identification is to produce a list of the most significant risks to a supply chain, and this list is often described as a 'risk register' or 'risk portfolio'. This is a document – or more usually an entry in a risk database – that records the features of the risks. An initial format is illustrated in Figure 6.1. Beyond this, managers can add all sorts of details to give a fuller description of the risk.

Summary			Description		
Identification number	Date recognized	Owner	Description of risk	Description of impact	Probability
1					
2					
3					
4					
5					

Figure 6.1 Illustration of a basic risk register

The identification of risks is a difficult job, with Stemmler (2006) saying that identifying risks 'poses an almost insurmountable challenge for line managers'. But this is an essential step in risk management. For this reason it cannot be left to informal arrangements, but has to be properly organized using the best tools and methods. If this is not done, significant risks can be missed – or alternatively managers get carried away and list every risk that they think of, giving trivial risks too much weight. You can find examples of both of these effects – such as firms that do not notice that a major customer is going out of business, and conversely education authorities that ban all school trips because of the tiny chance that pupils might hurt themselves. In August 2006, the UK Health and Safety Executive became concerned that their advice was being used as an excuse for cancelling any public activity with even the slightest risk, and they started to give warnings against taking their advice to extremes (Hunt, 2006).

When we say that managers should identify the most significant risks to the supply chain, an obvious question is how many they should consider. Should they consider the main half-dozen risks, or are we talking about a few hundred? Unfortunately, each supply chain is unique and works in different circumstances, so we cannot really even give a guideline. Presumably a nuclear power station will consider far more risks than an accountant's office, but the decision about whether the risk register should contain two risks or two thousand must remain a matter of management judgement.

Identified risks

There is considerable variation – and disagreement – about the most significant risks facing supply chains. A survey for Accenture conducted by S Radoff Associates found that leading risks to supply chains are (Malone, 2006a):

■ raw material supply disruptions (50 per cent of respondents);
■ import operations and customs delays (36 per cent);
■ longer supply lines and lead times (36 per cent);
■ geopolitical instability (35 per cent);
■ shortage of skilled labour (35 per cent);
■ terrorist infiltration of cargo (30 per cent).

A similar survey by AMR Research found that the main risks are (Malone, 2006b):

■ supplier failure (28 per cent);
■ strategic risk (17 per cent);
■ natural disaster (15 per cent);

- geopolitical events (11 per cent);
- regulatory risk (11 per cent);
- logistics failure (10 per cent);
- intellectual property infringement (7 per cent).

A survey by Richmond and Associates (2007) found that the risks most commonly identified by European supply chain managers were:

- loss of the information system;
- loss of the site;
- government regulations;
- currency fluctuations;
- fire;
- extreme weather;
- floods and other natural disasters;
- industrial action;
- pressure group protest;
- product safety;
- health and safety issues;
- loss of suppliers;
- single sourcing;
- supplier reliability;
- poor forecasting;
- shortage of key materials;
- lean operations;
- long supply chains;
- delays at frontiers;
- lack of flexibility;
- capacity problems;
- traffic congestion;
- shortage of key employees;
- equipment failure;
- political unrest or warfare;
- terrorism.

Organizational and industry risk

We know that risks are not limited to individual members of a supply chain but are transmitted to all members, and the lesson is that organizations should not work in isolation but should coordinate their risk management to tackle their common problems. Another facet of shared risks is the difference between organization-specific and industry-wide risks. An organization-specific risk affects an individual business (or more accurately its supply chain), typically reducing its market share, income, profitability, competitiveness and performance in general. The point is that one organization is losing out to others in the same industry. These effects may be short-term, but with serious problems they can become very long-term or even permanent. On the other hand, an industry-wide risk affects all organizations in the same industry, leaving them all in the same boat – in the way that all transport companies suffer when fuel prices rise and all investment companies suffer when stock markets fall.

The importance of this difference appears with the type of response. An organization-specific risk encourages each firm to work in isolation, looking after its own interests and looking for a competitive advantage over competitors hit by problems. An industry-wide risk encourages cooperation, with competitors working together to overcome risks for their mutual benefit. This gives a clear message that the scope of the risk determines the best type of response – and particularly whether it is best to work in isolation or cooperate with other members of the chain or industry. With this in mind, Christopher *et al* (2002) describe risk as occurring at four levels:

- *Level 1: risk to underlying operations.* This views the supply chain as a simple pipeline, with risk affecting the smooth flow of materials, money and information. Risks come from problems with material flow, variability in demand and other market conditions. Then the best approach to risk management is to improve visibility, giving more efficient flows and better-controlled operations.
- *Level 2: risk to assets and infrastructure.* This considers the assets used to move the materials, money and information considered at level 1, with the supply chain defined in terms of its infrastructure. The nodes in the supply chain are the facilities that house assets (such as factories, logistics centres, retail outlets, etc) and these are linked through the infrastructure (roads, pipelines, communications, etc). Now the risks appear as potential damage to the links or nodes – and these are typically tackled by actuarial analyses based on historical data.
- *Level 3: risk to organizations and inter-organizational networks.* This steps back to consider supply chains as networks of trading relationships between organizations that own and manage the assets. Now risks appear as failed relationships between these organizations, arising through outsourcing, business failures, mergers, acquisitions, dominant organizations and all other potential problems with such networks. The best ways to manage such risks include closer, long-term relationships, partnerships, multiple sourcing and outsourcing.
- *Level 4: risk from the environment.* This includes all aspects of the industry, market, business and physical environment within which the supply chain works. The problem here is that risks are outside the control of

supply chain managers, but they can plan their response. For example, a new technological development might make demand for an existing product less certain; a company cannot avoid this risk, but it can make contingency plans, perhaps becoming more agile to respond quickly to changing markets.

Identifying risks

Risk identification reviews the uncertainties in a supply chain and lists the consequent risks. We already know that it is virtually impossible to list every conceivable risk, so it is fairer to say that identification gives a list of the most significant risks. This is a key activity, which forms the foundation for all other aspects of SCRM, so it must be done properly.

Personal knowledge

You might think that a reasonable way of identifying risks is to ask people who are familiar with the operations for their opinions. Provided they have an intimate knowledge of the organization, its operations and its environment, this can give reasonable results. Consultants and outside bodies can give some valuable insights, but it is generally much better to have internal people who are familiar with all conditions, communicating well, using trusted methods and creating in-house ownership.

However, this is only part of the story. People working on operations presumably have a detailed knowledge of how they work. But this does not necessarily mean that they can identify the risks, which needs a completely different set of skills. So a major failing of personal observation is that it is unreliable, recognizing the most obvious risks rather than the most significant, completely missing important risks and listing trivial ones. Another point is that some managers are reluctant to admit any risks, as this suggests some kind of failure or weakness. And they will inevitably focus on the risks they will be held responsible for, rather than the most significant – so they are more likely to plan for the minor risks from excess stocks (for which they are responsible) rather than for the major risks from terrorism (for which they will not be held responsible). This could be the reason why firms are apparently not concerned by major events (such as the Bhopal chemical plant explosion, Chernobyl nuclear power plant accident, Hurricane Andrew or the Kobe earthquake) before they actually happen.

The conclusion is that organizations really cannot rely on personal knowledge and informal procedures, but need some more formal arrangement for identifying risks. Then we can summarize the risk identification process (shown in Figure 6.2) as taking inputs (details of products, operations, the business environment, suppliers, finances and everything else needed to give a detailed description of the supply chain), using tools on these and giving the outputs (a list of risks, their sources, symptoms, triggers and consequences, as recorded in the risk register).

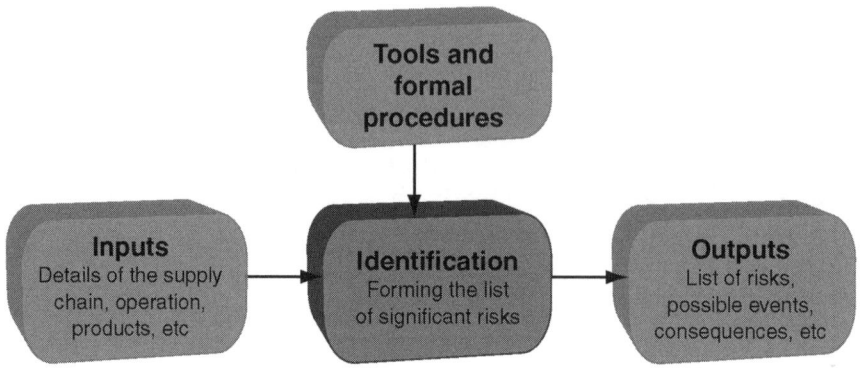

Figure 6.2 A summary of risk identification

Procedure for risk identification

In principle, there is a general procedure for identifying the risks in a supply chain. This divides the whole supply chain process into a series of distinct operations, studies the details of each and systematically assesses the risks in each.

> The general procedure for risk identification has the steps:
> 1. Define the overall supply chain process.
> 2. Divide this into a series of distinct, related operations.
> 3. Systematically consider the details of each operation.
> 4. Identify the risks in each operation and their main features.
> 5. Describe the most significant risks in a register.

It is never easy to identify risks, and a range of formal tools has been developed for the actual identification of risk in step 4. Some of these tools are general in that they can be used to identify any kind of risk (such as analyses of historical data, brainstorming, cause-and-effect analyses, fault trees, process mapping, likelihood–impact matrices and scenario planning); some are specifically aimed at the supply chain (such as supply chain mapping and audit, critical path identification, relative importance to the supplier and relative importance to the customer). Some tools work by analysing past events, some by collecting opinions and others by directly analysing operations. The choice of appropriate tools depends on circumstances, and particularly:

- the size and complexity of operations;
- the organizational experience with risk management;
- the type of information needed and already available;
- the availability of resources, particularly people and time;
- the levels of skills and knowledge.

First Western Bank of Canada

Operations in the supply chain need financing, and the subsequent borrowing, exchange and cash flows always involve risk. The First Western Bank of Canada has developed the following list of financial risks. Its advice for anyone who has to deal with financial risks is always to use specialized financial services with appropriate skills and expertise:

1. *Interest rates* – with risks from varying rates and conditions. These risks can be reduced by interest rate forward agreements that fix rates for periods in the future, or interest rate swaps between organizations.

2. *Liquidity* – and the risk of not generating enough cash to pay the bills. This is often caused by the need to invest money up front but wait for an extended period to generate income. The way to avoid such risks is through careful management of cash flows, short-term loans, selling assets or arranging a debt-for-equity swap.

3. *Operating costs* – the risk that expenses are higher than expected, perhaps suggesting that they are not efficient enough.

4. *Delays* – risks that operations are not done when planned, with consequent disruption, penalties and delays in generating revenues.

5. *Capital or equity* – the risk of not being able to raise enough capital to continue working. This is often caused by variations in the share price, which gives a rough measure of the perceived health of a company. Such risks can be managed through hedging, reinsurance, or some positive actions to adjust share price, such as issuing new shares or repurchase programmes.

6. *Counter-party* – inherent risks with any financial transaction involving two or more parties, where each party runs the risk that other parties will default on the agreement.

7. *Credit risk* – that a lender will not be repaid a loan as agreed (which has caused most bank failures over the years).

8. *Exchange rates* – risks caused by varying exchange rates and incurred whenever funds cross international borders. At a broad level, these risks are reduced by using hard currencies, such as the euro and US dollar. At a corporate level they can be mitigated by

forward exchange that fixes rates over specified future periods, or currency swaps between organizations.

9. *Taxation* – presumably organizations have the foresight to include taxes in their analyses, but there are always risks from changing rates and conditions. Conversely there may be various government incentives to encourage desirable operations.

10. *Country risk* – includes all the other risks of operating in foreign countries, which can only be managed through a complete country risk assessment.

11. *Fraud or criminal action* – risks that someone will steal or illegally drain money from an organization.

12. *Corporate bonds* – forms of IOU that are repayable at a fixed point in the future (with security below debts and above equity). Credit rating agencies, such as Standard and Poor's, and Moody's, assess the level of risk with bonds.

13. *Reinvestment risk* – occurs when managers get income from one investment, but they may not be able to reinvest it in a way that gives the same rate of return.

14. *Other contingencies* – the unknown risks from other unspecified events, often allowed for by contingency allowances in budgets.

Tools for analysing past events

'Five whys'

When some risky event has actually happened, the easiest way of identifying future risk is to repeatedly ask questions about the cause of the past event and find the likelihood that it will reoccur. A session of this kind might run as follows:

Question: What was the risky event?
Answer: A customer complained because we couldn't serve her.
Question: Why?
Answer: Because we had run out of stock.
Question: Why?
Answer: Because our suppliers were late in delivering.
Question: Why?
Answer: Because our order was sent in late.
Question: Why?

Answer: Because the purchasing department got behind with all its orders.
Question: Why?
Answer: Because it used new staff who were not properly trained.

By this point it is clear that something has gone wrong in the purchasing department, and particularly with the recruitment and training of staff. Now managers can assess the likelihood of this happening again and see if it presents a significant risk. For obvious reasons, this is called the 'five whys' method or – more formally – 'root cause analysis'. The strength of this method is that it investigates real risks that have occurred and clearly shows the relationships between symptoms and causes.

Cause-and-effect diagrams

We can show the relationship between risky events and their causes in a cause-and-effect-diagram – often described as a fish bone or Ishikawa diagram (Ishikawa *et al*, 1988). These can become quite complicated, but we can illustrate the principles by starting a diagram for the causes of a late delivery to customers. A reasoned analysis might suggest that the main reasons are a truck breakdown, traffic congestion, too many scheduled drops or late loading. Problems with a truck breakdown might be caused by its age, maintenance, distance travelled and so on. Figure 6.3 shows these relationships as a set of fish bones, and we could continue to give a fuller picture.

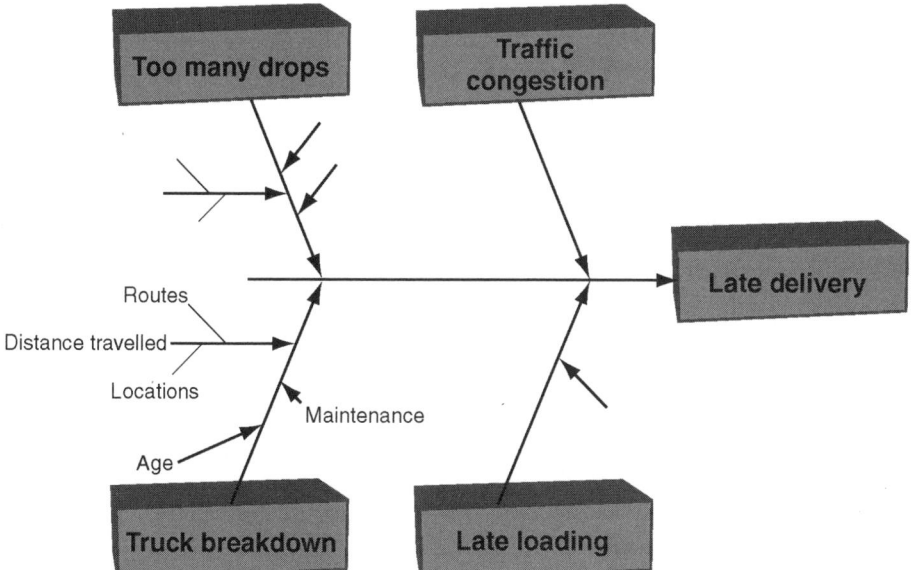

Figure 6.3 Fishbone diagram for a truck breakdown

Pareto analyses

A frequency diagram of risky events that actually occurred in the past can suggest those that are more likely to reoccur in the future. Pareto charts are based on the observation that 80 per cent of risks come from 20 per cent of causes – so that Tesco might find that 80 per cent of customer complaints come from 20 per cent of their products.

Waikiki Wholesalers

Waikiki Wholesalers is a well-established business distributing food items to supermarkets around Hawaii. Jose Samson is the owner of Waikiki and oversees all the administration, including records of the small number of customer complaints. Over the past three years he has collected the figures shown in Table 6.1.

Table 6.1 Waikiki customer complaints

Cause	Number of Complaints	Percentage of Complaints
Faults in the bill	39	49
Long lead time	16	20
Late delivery	9	11
Wrong goods delivered	6	8
Wrong amounts delivered	3	4
Range of products	2	3
Mixture of food and non-food items	2	3
Condition of fresh food	1	1
Condition of wine	1	1
Rudeness of staff	1	1

From these data, Jose drew the Pareto chart shown in Figure 6.4, which highlights the main areas for concern. There were almost no complaints about the materials delivered, so customers were clearly pleased with these. Half the complaints came from faults in the bill, and Jose reduced these by installing a new billing system. Sometimes deliveries were slow or delayed, and Jose worked out ways of reducing this problem with his transport managers. Tackling these problems dealt with almost all of the complaints, significantly reducing the risk of them reoccurring in the future.

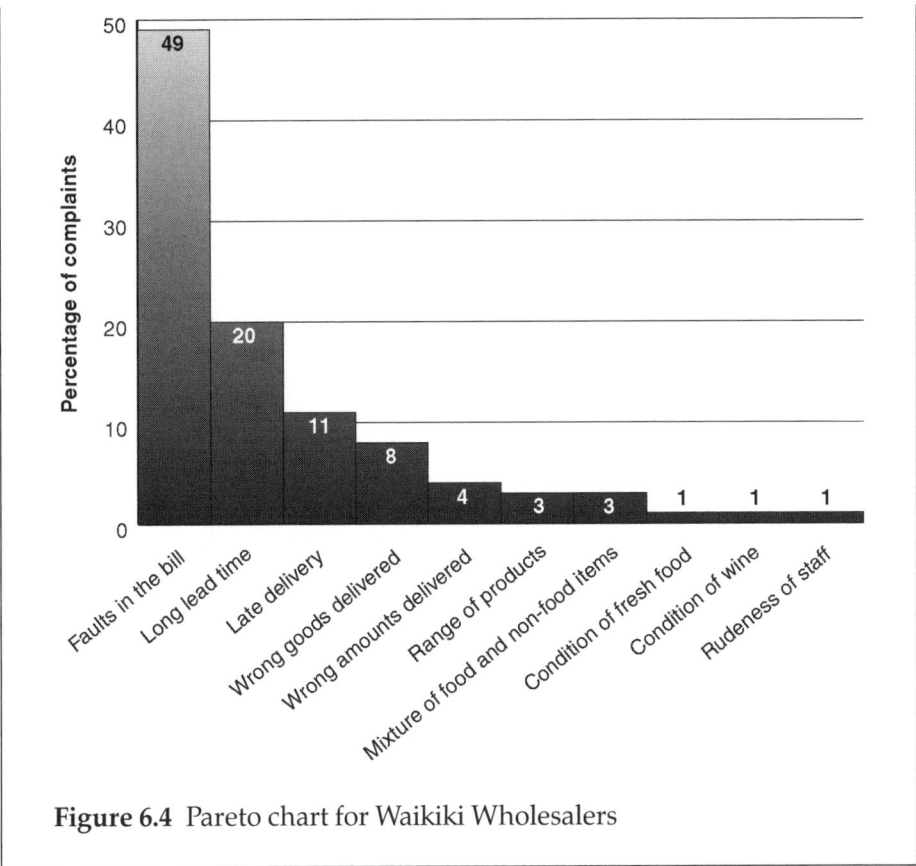

Figure 6.4 Pareto chart for Waikiki Wholesalers

Checklists

When there are common risks across a range of different operations an obvious way for managers to identify risks in their own supply chains is to see what risks have been identified in others. The usual way of presenting these is a checklist, derived from the risk register of other supply chains. This checklist can be transferred from another supply chain within the same organization, or it might come from another company, or it might be a standard list collected by industry forums, research institutions or consultants.

The benefits of checklists are that managers do not have to work from scratch but can build on previous experience and get results very quickly. On the other hand, they can be criticized for:

■ being too exhaustive and listing a huge numbers of potential risks, many of which are too trivial to warrant much attention;
■ alternatively, omitting risks that are really important to a particular firm;

- only considering routine risks, and omitting those that are essentially unknowable;
- listing too many possible responses, giving options but not enough guidance on their use;
- only giving routine responses, but missing innovative ones;
- relying too much on unsupported, subjective likelihoods of events;
- making assumptions about the true value of consequences, such as the loss of a key part of the supply chain;
- being preoccupied with risk as inherently harmful, and not analysing the trade-offs between the costs and benefits (Adams, 1999);
- often being based in separate risk management departments that are not integrated within other functions, have little knowledge of operations and have no power to implement findings;
- concentrating on risks to part of a single organization and ignoring broader effects on the supply chain.

A limited form of checklists is an 'assumptions analysis', which considers the assumptions made in any analysis. Then it sees if the assumptions are valid in a particular supply chain and considers the consequences if they are not. For example, the analysis for setting stock levels might assume a certain type of demand; assumption analysis asks if this assumption is valid and then finds the consequences if it is not.

Tools to collect opinions

Interviews

If analyses of past events do not give enough information about future risks, managers have to set about collecting new information. The most straightforward way of doing this is through interviews with knowledgeable individuals. This has the advantages of being easy to organize and fast, and of collecting detailed information about specific risks from the people who are most familiar with conditions. On the other hand we have already said that individual views have the disadvantage of being unreliable, relying on a few people's knowledge – as well as their ignorance, prejudice, lack of skills, inconsistency and general unpredictability.

Group meetings

If one person's views are unreliable, an alternative is to assemble a group of experts and ask them to discuss the operations and agree a list of significant risks. The structure of these meetings can range from rigid and very formal through to informal and unstructured.

A formal meeting might start with presentations, followed by a discussion, agreement and a summary of the conclusions. But this formality has problems, particularly for those who do not speak well at meetings or who feel stifled by the formality – and formal groups tend to reach conservative and unimaginative conclusions. This last observation might be surprising, as groups tend to make riskier decisions than individuals, because of the dispersed responsibility and the reality that more outspoken and influential members generally have more extreme views than moderate and silent members (Bowman and Ash, 1987).

A way of avoiding the problems with formal meetings is to reduce the formality, perhaps under the general title of brainstorming (for example, Chapman, 1998; Rawlinson, 1986). The principle of brainstorming is that all group members are encouraged to make innovative suggestions in a judgement-free environment, with the main features being:

- A group of around 10 knowledgeable people are collected to discuss risk in the supply chain.
- Before the meeting everyone is given a brief, which describes the background and clearly defines the purpose of the meeting.
- The meeting has a strict time limit, which might be anything from 15 minutes to a full day, but is typically two to three hours.
- The meeting starts with a brief review, and then everyone is encouraged to participate in a general discussion and share their ideas.
- The group is encouraged to generate large numbers of new and innovative ideas, with no initial judgement and using the principle that no idea is bad.
- A facilitator records ideas and makes sure that they are visible.
- The group develops initial ideas, with a more detailed evaluation after the meeting.
- Perhaps a follow-up meeting expands the most useful ideas.

Delphi method

Any group meeting has problems with people who do not perform well in groups – or alternatively dominate the group, work to their own agenda, always agree with the boss, speak for too long or introduce other problems. A way around this is to collect information through questionnaires.

The Delphi method gives an extension to basic questionnaires by allowing iterative adjustments to views. It selects a group of around 15 experts in the supply chain and sends each of these a questionnaire to get individual views about risks. These views are collected and analysed, with a summary sent back to members. Then each is asked if he or she would like to revise any opinions in light of the replies given by the rest of the group. All replies are anonymous, so there are no problems with face-to-face contacts, group pressure, conformity or the status of respondents. This process of asking questions, summarizing views and asking for adjustments is repeated a number of times, usually between three and six, and by this time the group should be closer to a consensus – or at least the range of opinion should be narrow enough for useful decisions (Waters, 2002; Wright and Goodwin, 1998).

Tools to analyse operations

Process charts

The final method of collecting information systematically studies the operations and identifies the risks at each stage. This needs a process chart to break down the supply chain operations into a series of distinct activities. For instance, one point of a supply chain might have goods moving from a delivery truck and into stores. The activities for this might be:

■ Use a forklift to take pallets out of the delivery truck.
■ Move the pallets to the receiving area.
■ Take the goods off the pallets and remove transport packing.
■ Check the goods and inspect them.
■ Move goods into bulk storage.
■ Keep them until needed in the picking stores.

After creating a full list for the whole supply chain, managers can study this list, critically analyse each activity and identify risks in each. Rather than start with a simple list, it is usually easier to describe a process in a diagram. There are several formats for this, with a basic one using a standard flow chart. A more formal process chart (illustrated in Figure 6.5) describes each activity as one of the following:

■ *operation* – where something is actually done;
■ *movement* – where products are moved;
■ *storage* – where products are put away until they are needed;
■ *delay* – where products wait for something to happen;
■ *inspection* – to test the quality.

Adding information to each activity can focus on the sources of risk. For instance, we can show the time spent on each activity in a Gantt chart, which has a horizontal timescale and all activities listed down a vertical scale, with the time activities are done blocked off in the body of the table (illustrated in Figure 6.6). A more complicated format has two time axes to differentiate between horizontal time when something is happening (such as materials being moved) and vertical time when nothing is happening (such as materials waiting in stock) (Christopher, 1998).

A survey by Jüttner (2005) shows that process mapping and brainstorming are the most common methods of identifying supply chain risks, with both always or usually used by around 60 per cent of firms.

Process chart – chain EP/42 Step AR/7

Step	Description	Op	Move	Insp	Delay	Store	Time (mins)	Distance (metres)
1	Arrive	x					2	150
2	Wait for unloading				x		10	
3	Check paperwork	x					2	
4	Move to unloading bay		x				2	40
5	Wait for forklift				x		4	
6	Check delivery details	x					1	
7	Take off truck	x					2	
8	Move to receiving area		x				3	20
9	Take off wrapping	x					10	
10	Check condition			x			10	
11	Check details			x			1	
12	Update goods received	x					3	
13	Move to main storage		x				5	50
14	Wait for crane				x		4	
15	Put on to shelf	x					2	
16	Keep in store					x		

Summary				
	Number	Time	Actions	16
Operations	7	22	Time	61
Movements	3	10	Distance	260
Inspections	2	11		
Delays	3	18		
Storage	1			

Figure 6.5 Illustration of a process chart

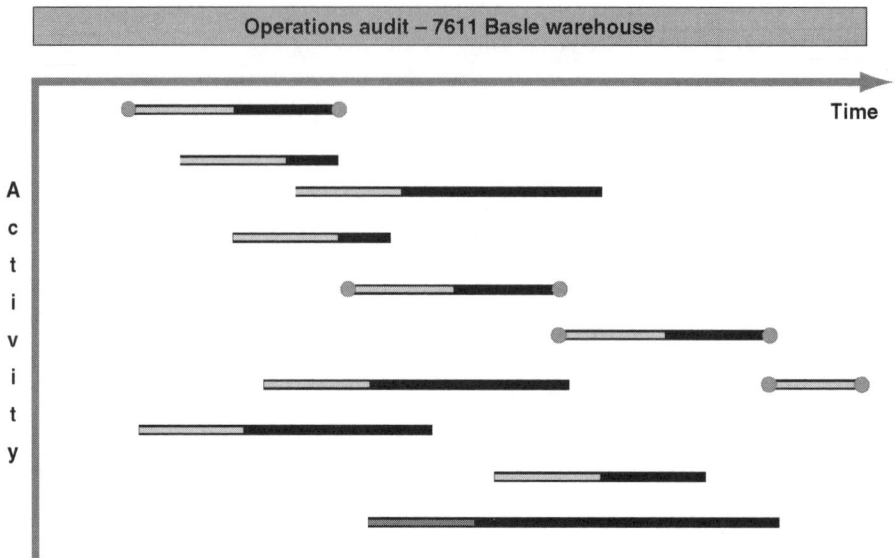

Figure 6.6 Example of a Gantt chart

Process control

No matter how good the operations, there is always some variation in supply chain performance. Differences in materials, traffic, weather, equipment, employees, moods, time, stress and a whole range of other things combine to give these, apparently random, variations. These variations may be small, but they are always present, which is why there is always some variation in, say, delivery lead time. One view says that risk appears from variation from plans for the supply chain, so to identify the main areas of risk we should monitor operations and find the areas with greatest variability.

The easiest way of monitoring the variations over time uses a 'process control chart'. This has a target performance and two acceptance limits, and provided the variation stays within the limits the process is under control and the risks are small. When there is a clear trend, or poor individual results, the risk is increasing.

James Bulwark & Sons

James Bulwark runs a UK warehouse for fruit and vegetables on the outskirts of Birmingham. Deliveries come from over 100 suppliers within the European Union. James Bulwark notices that suppliers usually quote performance in terms of lead time, but he finds that the greatest risk comes from those with most variability rather than the longest time. He monitors the lead time of each delivery and builds up a picture for each supplier. There is inevitably some variation about the mean, but provided the actual lead time is not too far from the target he assumes that operations are working normally and there is little risk. But if there is a sudden jump in the lead time, or a trend away from the mean, he assumes that the process is out of control, risk is increasing and some remedial action is needed. To see when this happens, he defines two limits – an upper control limit and a lower control limit, each about two standard deviations from the mean. When the lead time moves outside these control limits it is time for remedial action (as shown in Figure 6.7).

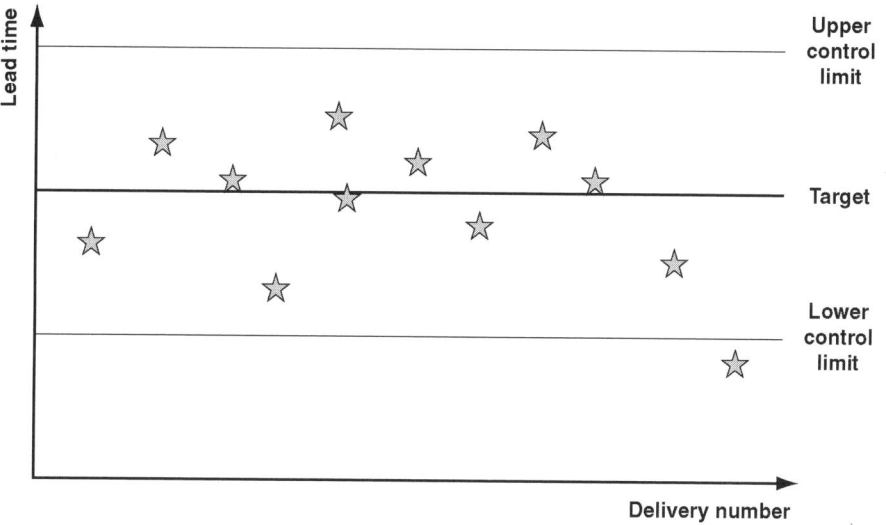

Figure 6.7 Process control chart for James Bulwark & Sons

Supply chain event management (SCEM)

SCEM is a rather broad term that describes different types of process control (Ansell and Wharton, 1995). The most common format uses structured brainstorming, where a group of experts systematically examine the operations of a supply chain to find deviations from planned performance. Then they investigate the deviations and find ways of eliminating their causes or take other actions to minimize the consequences. The principle here is that a systematic review will improve operations, reducing both variability and risk.

Techcons Inc

Techcons is a construction company that specializes in major capital projects. These are typically public works (such as rail links, road tunnels, bridges or airports) or major industrial works (such as oil pipelines, refineries, mine sites or chemical works). They have a well-established procedure for identifying risks. This starts with a checklist derived from many other projects and reinforced by specialized knowledge of a particular project. Many of their projects are in difficult environments, such as Alaska, Siberia and Saudi Arabia, so they are particularly aware of the risk from the physical environment. The following list is obviously not complete, but it suggests the type of risk they consider:

- *Management risk:*
  - risk strategies, aims and objectives;
  - management structure;
  - management systems;
  - industry and market stability;
  - product quality;
  - partner stability;
  - audits and inspections.
- *Financial risk:*
  - investment;
  - payments and cash flow;
  - profit;
  - capital turnover;
  - liability;
  - ownership.
- *Risks in the physical environment (natural):*
  - blizzard, snow, ice, avalanche, winter storms;
  - drought and extreme heat;
  - floods;

- forest or brush fires;
- high winds, hurricanes and tornadoes;
- lightning and thunderstorms;
- landslides and mud flows;
- earthquakes, tsunamis and volcano eruptions.

■ *Risks in the physical environment (artificial):*
- dams, canals and waterways;
- production processes;
- materials and other resources;
- buildings and facilities;
- environmental pollution;
- fire and explosions;
- transport infrastructure;
- transport incidents.

■ *Risk to operations:*
- property and site protection;
- fire and damage prevention;
- material sourcing;
- hazardous materials, processes and products;
- inward logistics;
- outward logistics;
- critical equipment and tools;
- service, maintenance and spares;
- capacity and bottlenecks;
- employees;
- information security.

Managers use such checklists to focus their discussions in a series of informal meetings. In these, they systematically look at the details of the process and see if the risks listed appear.

Problems with risk identification

In principle, when a firm sets about risk identification in a systematic way it should end up with a register of the most significant risks. But there are often difficulties that make this very difficult. We know that risk management starts with the recognition that risks exist and need proper management, but some firms do not even reach this stage. Someone within an organization has to recognize the importance of risk management and be senior enough to make the necessary arrangements. Then the assumption is that the benefits of risk management become so clear that the firm will quickly adopt its principles and it will eventually become a part of the corporate culture. But it may not be in everyone's interest to identify a risk. For instance, imagine a group of managers who are aware of some risk, but reporting it to senior managers might appear as a failure in their own abilities. The implication is that they have not understood their operations well enough to eliminate the risk, or their lack of skills means that they are facing problems that they cannot solve. When an admission that risks exist is seen as a sign of incomplete knowledge or inadequate skills, the managers will try to hide any risks by simply denying their existence. And another incentive to ignore some risks comes from the practical observation that the people who identify a risk are often given responsibility for dealing with it – even when they are not in the best position, they do not have the necessary knowledge and skills, and it is outside their control.

The same effect also appears at an organizational level. Each member of a supply chain wants the other members to present low risks. This leaves each member reluctant to admit their own risks, as they might lose business to competitors who are not so open. This returns to the discussion of integration, where working together has clear benefits – but there are also clear incentives for each partner to withhold information that might cause them commercial damage or embarrassment.

A variation on this theme has the significance of a risk depending on the perceptions of the person considering it. In other words, different people view the same risks in different ways. For example, an accountant might consider the risks from accounting anomalies as less serious – or possibly more serious – than equivalent risks to operations. It usually seems that the risks facing other people are inherently less severe than those we face ourselves, but, as they are less successful in dealing with them, our risks become considerably less worrying.

Even when there is the will to identify risks, the sheer size of the problem can give practical problems. There are always a huge number of risks to an organization, but these are amplified when managers begin to look for risks in the broader supply chain and consider the risks to their trading partners. But we have already suggested that ignoring risks to other members of the supply chain gives poor results, as it effectively hides them until the harmful events actually occur – at which point it is too late to react. And when every organization focuses on its own risks, there is an implicit transfer of risk from stronger members of a chain to weaker members that are less able to deal with it (Kendall, 1998).

Unknowable risks

Perhaps the greatest problem with identifying risks is the one we mentioned in Chapter 2, that it is simply impossible to identify every conceivable risk.

Even when managers put a lot of effort into forecasts and do every conceivable analysis, the future is essentially unpredictable and there will still be unforeseen events. For instance, a major earthquake in a stable region is essentially unforeseeable – as is a terrorist attack, the outbreak of SARS, industrial action, fuel shortages and many other external events that can disrupt supply chains. There are four reasons why events are unforeseeable:

1. *Inherently unknowable risks* are the true unknowns, where risks are completely hidden and only emerge when unexpected events suddenly hit a supply chain. As there are no signs of inherently unknowable risks before their events actually appear, we could argue that they are not really risks at all. Risk implies at least some minimal knowledge of future events, but with inherently unknowable risks we have complete ignorance until something actually happens. Business continuity management is the only way of dealing with such problems (as we shall see in Chapter 11).
2. *Time-dependent risks* only emerge with the passing of time. Risk identification can only work for some limited time in the future, and any risks beyond this time horizon remain hidden. These risks only appear when they move into the visible time horizon.
3. *Progress-dependent risks* depend on the way that operations move forward, and they only appear when a certain amount of progress has been made in a particular direction. So these depend on both the passage of time and the direction in which the organization moves. For instance, if managers decide to introduce leaner operations to their supply chain, some risks will emerge when they have moved some way in this direction. Another factor here is that managers' perspectives will also change when they move in one direction, so their perception of risks will also change.
4. *Response-dependent or secondary risks* only appear when action is taken to respond to an existing identified risk. So the sequence of events has an identified risk, followed by management response, which then creates a new risk. For instance, managers might identify a risk from material shortage, so they respond by increasing stocks, which increases the risks associated with excessive stock levels. Until managers take action these risks do not exist, so they cannot be seen before the response is implemented.

Apart from the inherently unknowable risks, all of these depend to some extent on time – as time moves on, the risks change. This simply reinforces our earlier warning that risk management is not a job that is ever completed, but it is a continuing process.

In reality, many risks do not suddenly appear but emerge over time – particularly socio-political risks (protests, strikes, new legislation, regulatory changes, etc), geopolitical shifts (such as the growth of the European Union, the collapse of the former Soviet Union, and the emergence of China as a major exporter) and changing economic conditions (currency fluctuations, business cycles, interest rates, etc). Routine scanning of the business environment to detect the early sign of such changes is an essential part of risk management.

Risk identification is a complex process – and it is by no means an exact science. There is always the huge number of possible risks, as well as unknowable ones, that we cannot recognize and that appear out of the blue. Using formal procedures for identification, along with regular reviews, should minimize the surprises. And remember that the alternative is to sit back and wait until you are hit by the inevitable unforeseen events that can cause irreparable damage to your operations.

Thermionic Sheve GmbH

Thermionic installs high-pressure reaction vessels in customers' facilities, which are generally large chemical works. Each installation is a distinct project, and the company has a standard format for identifying the risks. This is based on analyses of 30 different risk factors, and for each factor there are between 12 and 30 specific questions (the exact number varies from project to project). The following list shows the first 12 questions for the risk factor 'management', and then illustrates the type of questions for other risk factors:

■ *Management* – the ability to plan, resource, administer, monitor, control and generally run the project:
   - Do project managers have the necessary skills and experience?
   - Can project managers meet corporate executives when necessary?
   - Are there frequent changes in management?
   - Does the project have adequately documented procedures?
   - Do project managers know all stakeholders and understand their priorities?
   - Are the administrative arrangements reasonable?
   - Are the project budget, cost and schedule reasonable?
   - Are there enough resources to finish the project?
   - Are the stakeholders' contributions reasonable?
   - Would additional resources need additional funding?
   - Is the project given a high enough priority?
   - Are project managers committed to delivering a high-quality product?
■ *Purpose* – defining the overall aims of the project:
   - Have all the project requirements been identified?
   - Are these clearly stated and understood?

- – Have the requirements been successfully met in similar projects?
- ■ *Facilities* – the buildings, equipment and other assets:
  - – Does the project need dedicated facilities or capital equipment?
  - – Were these considered sufficiently during the project design?
  - – Is there enough infrastructure in terms of office space, facilities, supplies, etc?
- ■ *Systems engineering* – ensuring that technical solutions provided by the project meet operational requirements:
  - – Will the finished project satisfy end-users?
  - – Have the implications of the design been considered sufficiently?
  - – Does the design rely on new or untried technology?
- ■ *Testing* – procedures for giving information about performance:
  - – How is performance measured?
  - – What are acceptable standards for these measures?
  - – Were test procedures designed early enough in the project?
- ■ *Human resources* – the number of people available:
  - – Have human resource requirements been identified properly?
  - – Are there enough people available to meet these requirements?
  - – How do these requirements change during the project life cycle?
- ■ *Skills* – the capabilities needed to complete the project:
  - – Have the knowledge, skills and abilities required by the project been properly identified?
  - – Are these skills available?
  - – How can skill shortages be overcome?
- ■ *Training* – giving everyone the necessary skills, knowledge, values and attitudes:
  - – What training is needed for people working on the project?
  - – How is the training done?
  - – Who will do the training?
- ■ *Human factors* – the allowances for human abilities, characteristics, behaviour, motivation and performance requirements:
  - – Does the project make unusual requirements of its staff?
  - – Are there many manual operations to consider?
  - – Are there high levels of stress?
- ■ *Cost* – the funding available:
  - – Were realistic cost objectives established early?
  - – Have realistic costs been assigned to each activity?
  - – Is enough funding available for the project?
- ■ *Accounting* – monetary control:
  - – Is the funding under the control of the project manager?
  - – Are there adequate controls over cash flows?
  - – Is expenditure reviewed periodically to monitor progress?

■ *Schedule* – the timing of activities:
  – Have all activities been identified for the project?
  – Has each been scheduled properly into an assigned time slot?
  – Has enough time been allocated to complete the whole project?
■ *Tools* – supporting management tools, techniques, etc:
  – What management tools does the project need?
  – How are the tools chosen?
  – Are project staff familiar with these tools?
■ *Software* – computer programs, procedures, information processing and associated documentation:
  – Are the software requirements known and documented?
  – Is appropriate software already available?
  – What new software is needed and where will it come from?
■ *Procurement* – procedures for acquiring materials:
  – What materials are needed?
  – Who are the suppliers and how are they chosen?
  – Are the procurement procedures good enough?
■ *Contracting* – specific arrangements for contracting services:
  – What services have to be contracted?
  – Who are the contractors and how are they chosen?
  – Can the contractors meet the specific requirements?
■ *Logistics* – the inward and outward flows of materials:
  – How are materials moved into and out of the project?
  – Who provides and manages the transport?
  – What backup facilities are available?
■ *Environment* – the context in which the project works:
  – Do all aspects of the project comply with international, national and local laws?
  – Are there issues with intellectual property rights, copyrights, patents, trade secrets and confidentiality agreements?
  – How are policy changes transmitted?
■ *Health hazards* – potential risks to people employed:
  – Are there any health hazards specific to the project?
  – How can these hazards be removed or minimized?
  – What procedures are available to deal with hazards?
■ *Safety* – procedures in place to minimize the occurrence of accidents and injuries:
  – Are there specific sources of potential accidents?
  – How can these sources be eliminated or minimized?
  – Are there any particularly hazardous materials or operations?

In summary

The first of the three core activities of SCRM is to identify the risks. This is a notoriously difficult task, as there are a huge number of possible risks and forms in which they appear. It is best to focus on the most significant types of risk, and to help with this we can define different categories. A standard classification describes risks in the internal operations of supply chain members, risks within the supply chain itself and risks from the external environment.

Managers need some formal method of identifying risk. The usual approach breaks the overall supply chain process into a series of activities, systematically examines each activity in turn and identifies the risks in each. Many tools have been developed to help with this, and they work in three ways – by analysing past events, collecting opinions or directly analysing operations.

In principle, risk identification leads to a register of significant risks to the supply chain. But there are always problems. Apart from the inherent difficulty of identifying risk, managers can be reluctant to accept that risks exist and that they have to take appropriate action to deal with them. Other risks are simply unknowable in advance.

After compiling a list of the most significant risks, managers have to do something about them. The next step is to analyse each risk, which we discuss in the following chapter.

7

Analysing risks

Measuring risk

The last chapter described ways of identifying risk to the supply chain and forming a register. Now we can take this list, consider the features of the risks and analyse their possible impact, so that managers can give highest priority to risks with the highest potential impact.

There are two approaches to analysing risk. The first is purely qualitative, taking the risk register and describing the features of each entry, perhaps giving:

- nature of the risk – with a qualitative description of the risk;
- consequences – with a qualitative view of potential losses or gains;
- likelihood – giving a subjective view of whether the risk will materialize;
- scope – areas affected, such as supplies, deliveries, costs, service, etc;
- responsibility – ownership of the risk and responsibility for its control;
- stakeholders – people affected by the risk and their expectations;
- objectives – that risk management is trying to achieve;
- relationship to other risks;
- subsequent changes to operations – perhaps to mitigate the effects of the risk;
- current methods of risks management, and their levels of success;
- suggestions for improvement to risk management and new policies.

Such detailed views are useful for describing the nature of a risk and getting a better understanding of its effects and consequences. They give a very good basis for discussion, but – by definition – they are limited by not giving any numerical measures.

Some numerical measures could be added to the list, and this gives the second approach of quantitative analyses. These give a precise and objective description of the seriousness of a risk and its consequences.

Quantitative measures

There are many types of quantitative analyses for risk, but they are all based on two factors: 1) the likelihood of a risky event occurring; and 2) the consequences when the event does occur. The importance of these two factors is that we can calculate an expected value and use this to rank risks. We saw in Chapter 2 that the expected value of an event is calculated as follows:

expected value of an event = probability × consequence

When there is a 10 per cent chance that a delivery will be delayed, and any delay costs €20,000:

expected value of a delay = 0.1 × 20,000 = €2,000

But we have to give a warning here. When we discussed the expected value we emphasized that it gives the average result when a risk occurs a large number of times, but not the result each time you face a risk. Here there is a 90 per cent chance of no delay and, therefore, no cost. There is a smaller chance of actually having a delay with a cost of €20,000 – but the real cost will certainly not be €2,000. This illustrates an interesting point, that for many risks there is no actual impact at all unless the associated risky events actually occur. There may be a risk of fire in a warehouse, but this has no real impact unless there actually is a fire.

But even with this proviso, risk analysis is difficult. How can you find the probability of a fire in a warehouse? Or put a realistic value on the outcome of a fire? You might be able to say that a serious fire is quite unlikely and it would be very damaging – and you might even estimate the expected cost of physical damage. But all fires are different, and the probabilities and amounts of damage can range from virtually nothing to the destruction of the centre. And then there are the secondary costs of lost sales, confidence and reputation, and all the other intangible effects.

Perhaps a more reasonable approach accepts that the expected value is useful for ranking risks, but it does not suggest actual values that might occur. Then it becomes a tool for prioritizing risks, and allows us to put them into an ordered list or spectrum. At one end of the spectrum are risks that are so unlikely or their effects are so small that they have virtually no impact and we can often ignore them. Moving along the spectrum gives risks with greater impacts, such as the normal trading risks of varying customer demand, unreliable delivery, equipment failures, price rises and so on. The probability of risky events is higher and the consequences are more serious, so managers need to have reasonable safeguards to mitigate their effects. As we continue further along the spectrum we get to major crises – the disasters that can destroy supply chains and prevent firms from working at all. Managers should clearly consider these risks seriously and put most effort into avoiding them.

So the essence of risk analysis is to define a spectrum of possible impacts and place each risk on it, to give a prioritized list.

■ The aim of risk analysis is to give a prioritized list of risks.
■ This identifies the most significant risks that need positive attention, and the less significant ones that can be ignored.

In addition to the two key factors of probability and consequences, some people add other elements. Typically they suggest a third factor to take into account the imperfections of risk management. This might appear as a probability that managers can detect a risk and take remedial action before events occur, or probabilities of correctly identifying a risk, having it occur, being able to design a response, changing the consequences, increasing other risks, and so on. These models can get much more complicated, without necessarily improving the results.

Likelihood of a risky event occurring

The first problem for quantitative analyses is to find the probability of a risky event occurring. We know that this has a value between 0 and 1:

■ When values are close to 1, events are so common that they usually occur and can define normal operations. Managers should consider these events as part of normal work and make decisions on the basis that they will occur.
■ With probabilities in the middle – around 0.5 – events are equally likely to occur as not, so they are normal variations in operations. Managers should make some allowance for them, but not assume that they are inevitable.
■ Probabilities close to 0 mean that events are so rare that managers can assume they will not occur. These are unusual events and managers should not include them to any extent in their normal plans.

Although rare events are – by definition – unusual, this does not mean that they never occur and they can give major crises with disastrous consequences. For instance, it is very unusual for floods to hit New Orleans, and virtually all companies assumed that it would never happen; but when

Hurricane Katrina hit it in 2005 most of the city was flooded, with disastrous consequences. Deloitte (2005) found that many of the greatest losses in market capitalization were attributable to events that were considered extremely unlikely and for which companies had apparently failed to plan. Many affected companies lost more than 20 per cent of their market value in the month after an event, and it often took more than a year before their shares regained their original levels (see also Knight and Petty, 2001). Perhaps not surprisingly, risk managers are now putting more emphasis on this kind of rare event, moving away from their traditional view of 'It can't happen to us so there is no point in worrying about it' to the more useful view of 'It probably won't happen – but what can we do if it does?'

In Chapter 2 we described three approaches to finding the probabilities of events:

1. Use knowledge of a situation to calculate a theoretical or a priori probability. This is the most reliable method, and should be used whenever possible. Unfortunately, real circumstances are so complicated that we can rarely do calculations that cover all circumstances and give convincing results. For instance, it would be impossible to use any rational arguments to find an a priori probability that an IT system will break down.
2. Use historical data to see how often an event actually happened in the past, and use this to give an experimental or empirical probability. This usually gives good results and if, say, a daily delivery is late on average once a month a reasonable estimate for the probability it is late is $1/30 = 0.03$. However, this does make assumptions, especially that nothing has changed and past conditions are still relevant to the future.
3. Ask people for their subjective views about the likelihood of an event. This is the least reliable method, as it depends on people's judgement and opinions – as well as their ignorance, inexperience, lack of judgement, prejudice and so on. It is not usually recommended, but is often the only method available for complex circumstances. And even when the results are not as accurate as we would like, they can be reliable enough to help with decisions.

The first two of these methods seem to give objective measures of risk, and when the Royal Society discussed risk in 1983 it made a clear distinction between objective risk, with its precise, quantifiable measures, and perceived risk, which is less reliable and reflects people's perceptions of risk. However, this can be misleading, as when managers make decisions they always include some subjective perception of a risk. When the Royal Society returned to this question in 1992, a cross-section of social scientists moved to the view that objective and perceived risk were inseparable – and risk is not an objective phenomenon but is a consequence of human perception. This means that people modify their behaviour – and hence their exposure to risk

– in response to their subjective perceptions of that risk. The result is that risk can never be objectively measured. Unfortunately, this leaves us with the problem that subjective views are inherently unreliable and we always have to use them with caution. On the positive side, though, managers only want tools to help with their decisions – and probabilities do not have to be accurate to six places of decimals to achieve this.

Ranges of probability

The conclusion is that risks to the supply chain are much more complex and fuzzy than straightforward mathematical ideals, and their management always needs subjective input. Nonetheless, some probabilities are clearly more reliable than others. Perhaps we should recognize that probabilities are usually approximations, like risk impact itself, so we are not so concerned with the detailed calculation. Perhaps we can define a spectrum. At one end of this are rare events that are relatively scarce, at the other end are events that are relatively common, and the bulk of events come somewhere in between.

We can take three routes to this. The first is fairly complex and looks for a probability distribution for the events. Then instead of saying that there is a probability of 0.3 that a delivery will be late, we might say that there is a probability of 0.05 that it will be up to one day late, 0.15 that it will be one or two days late, and 0.1 that it will be more than two days late. Or we might use a standard distribution and say that the lead time is normally distributed. Such distributions have the advantage of giving a more precise picture of risks, but the disadvantage that a lot more effort is needed to collect reliable figures and use them in meaningful analyses. In practice, the benefit gained is rarely worth the extra effort of data collection and analysis.

A second route is to replace the point estimate for a probability by a range. Then instead of saying that there is a probability of 0.3 that a delivery will be late, we use the less precise view that the probability is somewhere in the range of 0.2 to 0.4. This gives the general impression of being fairly unlikely, which is accurate enough for most analyses.

The third route is even less precise and replaces the range by a description of the likelihood. Then we might describe the chance of a delay as 'fairly unlikely'. Again, these ranges are usually good enough for decisions, provided that managers agree the definitions and use a consistent approach. Table 7.1 shows one such classification for probabilities, along with the interpretation.

As events with a probability of 1 or 0 are certain to happen or certain not to happen respectively, they involve no risk. People generally use more categories, typically describing the probability of events as very low, low, medium, high or very high. Then the exact interpretation of these probabilities depends on the perception of people involved, circumstances and corporate culture. For instance, a risk-averse organization might consider a harmful

Table 7.1 A classification for probabilities

Description of Probability	Likely Value of Probability	Interpretation
Impossible	0	Will never occur
Low	>0 to 0.25	Unlikely to occur
Medium	0.25 to 0.75	About an even chance of occurring
High	0.75 to <1	Likely to occur
Certain	1	Will always occur

event with a probability around 0.25 as 'high risk', while a risk-taking organization will consider it as 'low risk'. You get a feel for this difference of perception by asking people of different ages what risks they are prepared to take with their pension fund.

A slightly less mechanical view of probabilities shows how often a person might expect to meet events with different probabilities, along the lines of:

■ *category 1*: very unlikely – an event that might happen, but so rarely that most people will never meet it;
■ *category 2*: rare – an occasional event that people might expect to meet once or twice in their working lives;
■ *category 3*: occasional – an event that occurs sometimes, with people meeting it sporadically throughout their working lives;
■ *category 4*: frequent – an event that occurs regularly, with people commonly meeting it;
■ *category 5*: very likely – an event that occurs often, with people meeting it continuously and accepting it as normal.

Lost containers

It is difficult to get exact figures, but somewhere between 2,000 and 10,000 containers are lost over the side of ships each year. At any particular time, there are probably around 6 million boxes in transit, so the probability that any one will be lost is very small. It is unclear whether this risk is increasing or not. On the one hand, there have been continuing improvements in the methods of securing containers to decks, and monitoring their positions and safety. On the other hand, international trade means that more containers are being moved. And changing designs of container ships are increasing some risks. For instance, deckhouses used to be at the front of the ship, protecting the containers from water and aiding navigation, but now they have moved backwards and been replaced by a breakwater (or nothing at all); stacks are six high (close to the limit for crushing those on the lowest level); three-quarters of containers are now lashed on deck; and the ship sides have been lowered to ease loading. The results of these changes include poor stability in rough seas, worse visibility from the bridge, worse manoeuvrability at low speeds, and more containers exposed to weather and seas.

The number of containers lost may be small – but the few that are lost can cause significant damage to their owners, and risks to the environment if they sink or their contents are washed ashore, and to other shipping if they float. Rough weather and waves break open the boxes, and there are many stories of lost containers spreading their contents around the world. In 1990 Nike lost 80,000 pairs of tennis shoes from a container ship in the Pacific, and there were still reports of them being washed ashore some 10 years later (10 years is about the maximum time that trainers will float in the ocean). In 1999 the container ship MV *P&O Nedlloyd Auckland* was hit by a hurricane in mid-Pacific and lost a dozen 40-foot containers overboard. Two of these again were filled with Nike trainers. In 1997 three containers with 5 million pieces of Lego fell overboard in the Atlantic when MV *Tokio Express* ran into a storm. These are expected to drift north into the Arctic Ocean and then through the Northeast Passage before turning south, where they are expected to come ashore on beaches in Alaska by 2012 and in Washington by 2020.

Less common are reports of ships being damaged by hitting partly submerged containers. An empty container weighs between 2 and 4 tonnes, and is generally weatherproof rather than watertight, so it soon fills with water and sinks. However, a full container might have trapped air or light contents, and float for some time. Roughly speaking, a sealed 20-foot container would have to weigh more than 16 tonnes before it began to sink, and weight restrictions should keep it below this, so sealed containers should float. In reality, containers usually fill with water and sink. If the seals are in poor condition this will happen quickly, but if the seals are good a light container might remain afloat for more than six months.

Consequences when a risk occurs

The second part of analysing a risk is to put a value on the consequence of a risky event occurring. Sometimes this seems fairly straightforward, particularly when there is some direct measure of the consequences. The most common measure is phrased in terms of a cost (or gain), and there are often actuarial calculations or historical data to give reasonable values. For instance, a lost load of goods might have a clear monetary value, such as a replacement cost of $20,000. Unfortunately, the monetary value is not usually this clear. For instance, a delivery may be running late, and this will incur some penalty cost; but there can be several ways of speeding up the delivery, each with different probabilities of success and costs.

A more pressing problem is that not all consequences can be viewed in financial terms. Some certainly have monetary values; some can be translated into monetary amounts; but others are so intangible or difficult to evaluate that they cannot be translated into any reliable financial terms. There may be alternative measures. For instance, the performance of a project might be judged by its completion by a specified date, or a fire service by the time it takes to put out a fire. Some aspect of timing is probably the second most common measure of consequences after cost.

Even when they exist, such absolute measures are not as straightforward as they seem. A delay in delivering a product will be viewed differently in different organizations. A company that has a mission of giving the highest possible customer service will say that any delay that reduces this service has a high cost; on the other hand, a company that has a mission of maximizing profit is likely to put a lower value on a delay and a greater value on lost revenue. So we should really relate the consequences of risks to the extent that they affect the organization's ability to achieve its aims. But suppose that the risks do not have consequences at the corporate level, but their main impact is lower down the organization. Then the people managing a risk are more likely to focus on the way that it affects their own activities. For example, warehouse managers are more likely to avoid risks from low stock levels, while finance departments are more likely to avoid the risks that come from high stock levels.

The message is that even quantifiable consequences are not straightforward. And most consequences are even more difficult to deal with, as they cannot be translated into quantifiable terms. So, as with probabilities, we have to accept that the values for consequences are generally approximations that depend on interpretation. So again we might use the same solution, and instead of using point estimates we can define ranges in which the consequences appear.

Ranges of consequences

As with probabilities, an option for dealing with consequences is to use ranges of values. Again we can simply specify a range, such as £20,000–£30,000. Or again we can describe a spectrum of possibilities, ranging from 'negligible' through to 'catastrophic'. Again, we are using this method to prioritize consequences, rather than look for actual values. Specifically, we might describe the impact of an event as:

- *category 1*: negligible – an insignificant effect on the working of the supply chain;
- *category 2*: minor – causing some inconvenience with minor disruptions, delays and increased costs to some parts of the chain, but with most functions unaffected;
- *category 3*: moderate – causing some disruption to parts of the supply chain, but with the main functions continuing to meet requirements;
- *category 4*: serious – major disruptions to the essential operations of the supply chain, causing serious delays and a high cost of recovery;
- *category 5*: critical – failure of the whole supply chain for an extended time, with major cost and effort needed for recovery;
- *category 6*: catastrophic – causing complete and irrecoverable failure of the supply chain and possibly whole organizations.

Boots plc

In October 1997 a single aerosol can being stored in a distribution centre owned by the high street chemist Boots exploded. This caused a fire, which destroyed the distribution centre. It is reported that insurance companies paid £15 million for the damage – but Boots lost £30 million in sales from disrupted supplies during the busy pre-Christmas period.

The consequences of unexpected events can often be far wider than expected. Insurance can compensate for actual damage to the supply chain, but it rarely covers all the subsequent disruption and intangible injury – in the way that fire insurance on your house will pay for the actual damage but not all of the inconvenience and emotional harm. When a delivery truck has an accident, insurance will cover damage to the vehicle and goods – but not the disruption to operations arising from the loss.

Evaluating consequences

When managers have estimates for the probability of an event and its consequences they can do some analysis – notably multiplying the two together to calculate an expected value. Then we can summarize the essence of risk analysis as looking at the register of risks, finding the expected value of each risk, using this to assign priorities to each, and identifying the ones that need most attention (as shown in Figure 7.1). The result of risk analysis is an ordered list of prioritized risks – at the top of the list are the most significant risks, and at the bottom are the least significant.

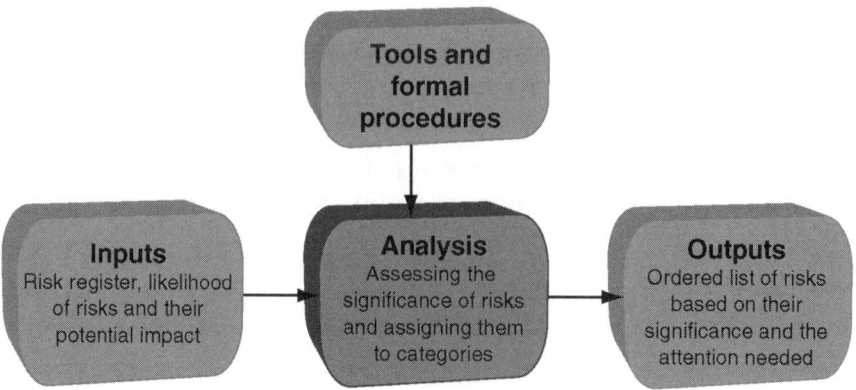

Figure 7.1 A summary of risk analysis

Managers should clearly give highest priority to the most significant risks – which means events at the top of the list with the highest probabilities and greatest consequences. Risks that have a low probability are unlikely to occur, so managers can pay less attention to them, even when the consequences are severe; risks that have minor consequences do not need much attention, even when they have a high probability. And the least important risks have low probabilities and minor consequences, so managers can virtually ignore them.

An ABC analysis – also called a Pareto analysis or rule of 80/20 – gives a way of describing different categories of risk, based on the observation that 20 per cent of the risks cause 80 per cent of concerns, while the remaining 80 per cent of risks only cause 20 per cent of concerns. In particular, we can identify three categories of risk:

■ *A risks*: the most severe that need special attention;
■ *B risks*: the medium ones that need normal attention;
■ *C risks*: the low ones that need little attention.

Then we might typically find the pattern shown in Table 7.2.

Table 7.2 Identifying categories of risk

Category	Percentage of Risks	Cumulative Percentage of Risks	Percentage of Concerns	Cumulative Percentage of Concerns
A	10	10	70	70
B	20	30	20	90
C	70	100	10	100

We can translate this table into a graph of the ABC analysis, with the cumulative percentage of risks along the horizontal axis, and the cumulative percentage of consequences up the vertical axis. Then the most significant, A, risks are near the origin on the horizontal axis, and the least significant, C, risks are further out (as shown in Figure 7.2).

Categories of risk

The expected value often seems convincing, but we have to remember that both the probability and the consequences are approximations. So we really should ask how reliable the results are. If an event has a probability of 0.05 and estimated consequences valued at $1 million, how accurate is the expected value of $50,000 – and what exactly does it mean? As Stemmler (2006) says, 'The quantification, estimating both probabilities of occurrence and the monetary level of impact, is limited through the lack of (reliable) data of past experiences of similar events.'

We can make three comments here. First, the values may be estimates, but they should be the best available and give the most accurate view of what is likely to happen. All managers' decisions rely on forecasts of future events, so this is a normal way for working. Second, the models are meant to give

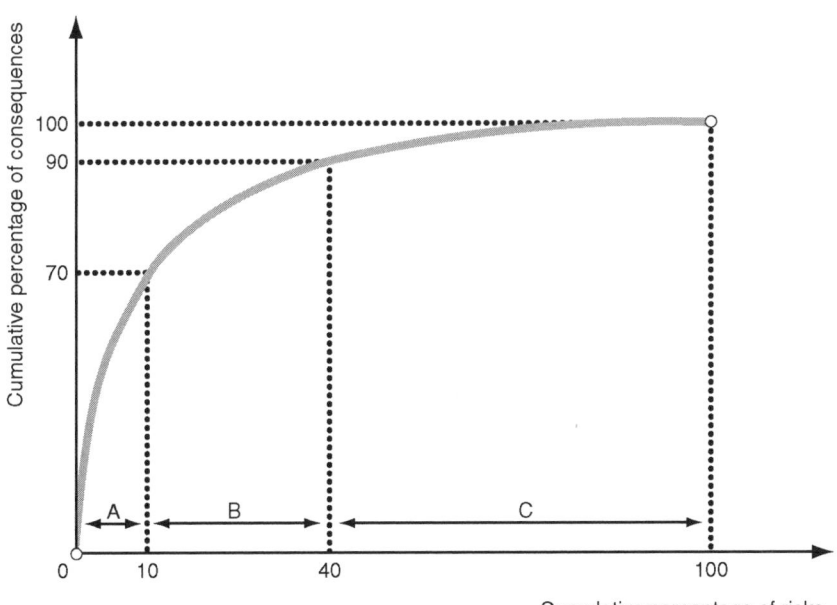

Figure 7.2 ABC analysis of risks

useful information to help managers make their decisions, but they are not meant to give definitive answers. No manager would ever make decisions based on a simple calculation, but they would consider this, along with all other factors, before making their informed decisions. Third, the results are not used to give definitive values for the effects of risks, but risk managers use them to compare different risks and identify those that need particular attention.

However, despite these comments, the figures are often so unconvincing that managers prefer to work with the categories for both probabilities and consequences rather than the figures. They feel that these give a more realistic view and 'feel' for the situation.

It is useful to describe the categories of risk in a diagram that shows the relative seriousness. The most common format for this is a risk map. This shows individual risks as points on a graph, with the vertical axis showing the probability of events and the horizontal axis showing the consequences (illustrated in Figure 7.3). Here managers should clearly pay most attention to risks that are furthest from the origin and less attention to those that are nearest to the origin.

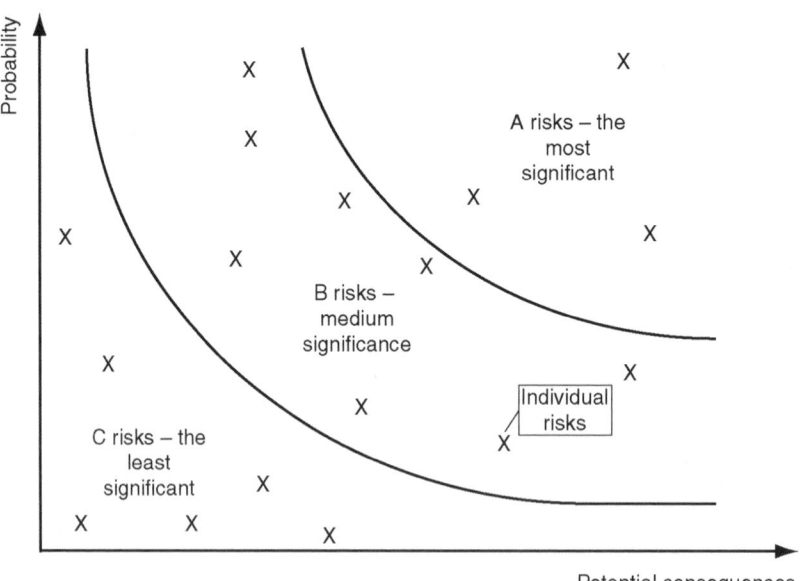

Figure 7.3 Structure of a risk map

Hewlett-Packard

Hewlett-Packard's procurement risk management programme is estimated to have saved the company $100 million over five years. Its main use is to assess the risks to supplies of its component, based on:

■ uncertainty in demand;
■ cost of components;
■ availability of components.

Each of these is analysed for uncertainty and risk, with forecasts made of future performance. Then managers assess the risk for each component and assign it a score, together with a review of the availability and costs of materials used to make the components. This information is used to prioritize risks and proactively manage the risk associated with each component.

Options for dealing with the risk range from agreements to share risks with suppliers through to switching to new, less risky suppliers.

Probability–impact matrices

A probability–impact matrix is another common diagram for describing classes of risk. It has essentially the same format as a risk map, but now we replace the actual values of probability and consequences by the more general categories. So the vertical axis shows probability categories and the horizontal axis shows categories of consequences. The result becomes a table rather than a graph, with descriptions of the risks put in the appropriate boxes in the body of the table. For instance, Table 7.3 shows a general format, and we can enter risks in the appropriate cells. We have also labelled the squares to show which risks deserve more attention, and have stuck to the three categories of risk – A, B and C – but could add more if needed.

Even when we use categories for both the probability and the potential consequences, we still get useful results for allocating resources. We can even calculate a surrogate expected value to reinforce this view. For this, each category of probability is given a notional numerical value, typically on a scale of 1 to about 5, as is each category of consequence. Then multiplying these two values together gives a score that reflects the impact of the risk.

Table 7.3 Format of a probability–impact matrix

		Potential consequences					
		Negligible	Minor	Moderate	Serious	Critical	Cata-strophic
Probability	Very high	B	B	A	A	A	A
	High	B	B	B	B	A	A
	Medium	C	B	B	B	A	A
	Low	C	C	B	B	A	A
	Very low	C	C	C	B	B	A

Lavalle-Pierceau

In 2006, managers at Lavalle-Pierceau, a transport company based in the south of France, introduced a new supply chain information system. They worked with a team of consultants from the system supplier, who described the risks from the installation using a probability–impact matrix. This had five categories of likelihood, with guidelines for the corresponding probabilities – 'very unlikely' meaning a probability of 0–10 per cent, 'unlikely' meaning 10–35 per cent, 'medium' meaning 35–65 per cent, 'likely' meaning 65–90 per cent and 'very likely' meaning more than 90 per cent. They assigned values of 1 to 5 respectively to each category. Similarly, they assessed the impact of risks as very low, low, medium, high and very high – so a delay of, say, 1 week in the project would have very low impact, a delay of 1 to 4 weeks would have low impact, a delay of 4 to 10 weeks would have medium impact, and so on. Then they assigned values of 1 to 5 respectively to these consequences (see Table 7.4).

By multiplying the two values together they got a notional value for the risk's severity. For instance, having a truck stolen during a journey was considered very unlikely (scoring 1) but the impact was high (scoring 4) – to give an overall score of 4.

The company assigned priorities based on these figures, with a very likely risk with a high impact (value 20) causing five times as much concern as an unlikely risk with a low impact (value 4). Risks giving values below 2 were not considered worth examining, risks from 3 to 8 were given some attention, 9 and 10 were given normal attention, 12 to 16 were given more attention, and most attention was focused on values above 20.

Table 7.4 Probability–impact matrix for Lavalle-Pierceau

			Impact				
			Very low	Low	Medium	High	Very high
			1	2	3	4	5
Likelihood	Very unlikely	1	1	2	3	4	5
	Unlikely	2	2	4	6	8	10
	Medium	3	3	6	9	12	15
	Likely	4	4	8	12	16	20
	Very likely	5	5	10	15	20	25

Tools for risk analysis

In reality, managers include many other factors in their decisions than probability and consequences. For instance, they could include the amount of change they can bring to a risk, where they might be tempted to put more effort into one risk that they can actually reduce, rather than another – perhaps bigger risk – that they have little chance of changing. They might also include a cost–benefit analysis to balance the cost of adjusting a risk with the potential benefits, and then concentrate on areas where the benefits are most significantly higher than the costs.

However, these need even more measures, and worsen the most obvious problem with risk analysis – which is the inability of managers to get reasonable measures for either the probability of an event or its consequences. Risk management needs some measure for both of these, but what happens when managers cannot provide them – either because of their own lack of skills, or because they are essentially unknowable? We partly get around this problem by not requiring precise figures, but using categories and subjective estimates. But this does not solve all the problems – such as the risks that are inherently unknowable. And a practical problem is dealing with the large number of risks that appear in a risk register. Then there is always the temptation to discard some risks as too trivial before doing any real analysis to confirm this belief.

So, as usual, the reality of risk analysis is more difficult than it at first appears. This is probably why a survey by the Aberdeen Group found that less than half 'have established metrics and procedures for assessing and managing supply risks' (Minahan, 2005). In practice, there are some tools that might help here, with the most common using systematic searches of operations such as 'failure modes and effects analysis'. Other useful tools include scenario analysis, simulation and network models.

Failure modes and effects analysis (FMEA)

FMEA systematically identifies possible modes of failure, and then establishes the impact of each type of failure. It starts by listing every activity in the supply chain and systematically identifying the ways in which each element can fail – effectively using a process analysis to produce a risk register. But the risks are usually considered in terms of hardware (from failures in vehicles, machines, equipment, etc) or activities (from problems arising when some activities cannot be done). Then for each potential failure it considers:

■ the probability of occurrence;
■ the severity of consequences;
■ the likelihood that remedial action can be taken before the failure becomes critical.

Each of these three factors is given a subjective score from 1 to 10, and multiplying the scores together gives a 'risk priority number' or measure out of 1,000 for the criticality. This number shows where managers should start looking for remedial action (Ansell and Wharton, 1995).

Scenario analysis

Scenario analysis analyses the possible effects of a series of decisions. So it assembles a small group of experts who construct a likely series of decisions, and then they construct a set of plausible future conditions that might follow from this series. By analysing the future conditions and adjusting the decisions, they can home in on a set of reasonable decisions that will probably give the desired results.

This is the same sort of approach as 'what-if' analyses, but it tends to focus on larger problems and the longer term. It is essentially qualitative, where designing the scenarios uses a mixture of expertise, judgement, brainstorming, analyses and guesswork – so it is unlikely that the experts could give convincing probabilities to their scenarios, but they can identify key features and get understanding and insights into the options and events that might lie ahead (Goodwin and Wright, 1998). If one logistics strategy allows a scenario of catastrophic failure, while a similar alternative expressly prohibits this, it makes sense for managers to prefer the second strategy.

Simulation

Simulation goes further than scenario analysis and gives a detailed quantitative analysis of events that might occur. It uses a dynamic representation of a situation, with a computer model imitating real operations over a typical period.

Suppose that you want some information about order picking in a warehouse. You could stand and watch the process for some time and record what actually happens. This would give a good idea of normal operations, but it would take a long time to get results and people would not work normally while you were watching. An alternative is to watch the process until you have a good idea of how it works and then simulate the process on a computer to generate some more typical – but artificial – results. Rather than collect a small number of actual timings, you get a computer to simulate a large number of typical results – and then analyse performance, find variations and compare results, giving a wide range of information.

The benefits of this approach are that it is easy to explore different options for operations without disrupting real operations (Evans and Olson, 2002). The problem, though, is designing and building a simulation model. Simulation languages can make this relatively straightforward, but it can still be a time-consuming process.

Jim's Drive Through Bottle Shop

Jim's Drive Through Bottle Shop sells alcoholic drinks in Brisbane, Australia. The prices are low and the shop is busy, with most customers apparently willing to accept some delays at checkouts to get cheap drinks. But at busy times the manager feels that he is losing customers.

The shop has a single line of cars driving past a service window. The obvious way of reducing delays is to have more service windows working in parallel, but the site is rather long and narrow, so this would be difficult.

The manager decided to try a number of improvements, such as dividing the service into a series of stages. He found the distributions of times for various operations, and then used a spreadsheet to simulate different options.

Figure 7.4 gives an idea of his approach. Here he put three servers in a series. The first server, A, took the customer's order, the second, B, looked after the bill and payment, and the third, C, delivered the goods. The spreadsheet follows 10 customers through the process. It generates times for each activity (randomly generated to follow actual distributions) and shows how the process performs during a typical short period. By following longer periods and more variations, the manager can look at different aspects of operations and see which configuration gives the best performance.

Simulation for Jim's Drive Through Bottle Shop

Customer	A			B			C		
	Join queue	Start service	Leave	Join queue	Start service	Leave	Join queue	Start service	Leave
1	8.45	8.47	8.51	8.52	8.55	9.00	9.01	9.02	9.04
2	8.45	8.51	8.53	8.53	9.00	9.01	9.01	9.04	9.07
3	8.58	8.58	9.01	9.02	9.07	9.09	9.10	9.10	9.13
4	9.00	9.01	9.04	9.05	9.09	9.10	9.11	9.13	9.16
5	9.05	9.05	9.06	9.06	9.10	9.13	9.13	9.16	9.18
6	9.20	9.20	9.21	9.21	9.21	9.23	9.23	9.23	9.25
7	9.20	9.21	9.24	9.25	9.25	9.28	9.29	9.29	9.33
8	9.22	9.24	9.26	9.27	9.28	9.30	9.30	9.33	9.35
9	9.25	9.26	9.29	9.30	9.30	9.34	9.35	9.35	9.38
10	9.25	9.29	9.32	9.33	9.35	9.38	9.39	9.39	9.44

Analysis

Number of customers	10.0		
Time in queue A	1.7	Service time A	2.5
Time in queue B	2.6	Service time B	2.6
Time in queue C	1.2	Service time C	2.9
Time in queues	5.5	Time being served	8.0
		Time in system	13.5

Figure 7.4 Simulation for Jim's Drive Through Bottle Shop

Network models

Supply chains are usually described in terms of networks of connected nodes, with risks occurring to the nodes or connections. A whole series of analyses is concerned with the flow through networks, often described in terms of 'graph theory' (Waters, 1998). For instance, a basic analysis considers the maximum amount of materials that can flow through a network. Managers can use this to find the maximum flow through a fully functioning supply chain and then repeat the analysis when various parts of the chain are deleted – with the difference showing the impact of losing parts of the chain. A related analysis finds the shortest path between two points in a network. Again managers can use this to find the shortest paths through a full network and then repeat the analysis to find the effects when some nodes or links are not available.

The key point in network models is that each node and link has a fixed capacity and takes a certain time to traverse. The capacity of the whole chain is set by the capacity of each link and the way that the links are configured. And one part of the chain always forms a bottleneck that limits overall capacity – with all other parts of the chain having spare capacity. It follows that the capacity of the whole chain can only be increased by increasing capacity at the bottleneck – and increasing the capacity of any other point has no effect except to give even more spare capacity. Conversely, reducing the capacity of the bottleneck will reduce the overall capacity of the chain, but reducing capacity elsewhere might have no effect (at least until all the slack is used). So these analyses identify the areas that are particularly vulnerable to risks. They show which parts of a supply chain are most important for maintaining the flows and where managers should put more effort into preventing problems.

Some specific types of network model find:

■ *maximum flow* – to give the maximum amount of materials that can move between two points in a network;
■ *the shortest path* – to find the shortest travel time or minimum distance between points in a network;
■ *transportation problems* – to assign customers to facilities, such as warehouses, to give the fastest or lowest-cost deliveries;
■ *set-covering* – to show the location of facilities needed to make sure that every customer is within a specified maximum distance of a facility;
■ *facilities locations* – to show the locations for facilities that give the lowest average distance to customers.

A slightly different approach to network analysis comes with critical path methods (CPM). These are most closely associated with planning activities in a project, but they also give a useful tool for planning material flow in supply chains. The characteristic approach divides the supply chain into separate activities and describes the relationships between them. Then by adding the times to complete each activity, managers can find the time at which each must occur. Some activities – the critical activities – have to be done at specified times or else there is a delay in final delivery (Waters, 2002).

Food scares

People are understandably concerned about the quality of the food they buy. We assume that it is perfectly safe, but occasionally something goes wrong and there is a small risk. As soon as a risk is discovered the product is immediately removed from shop shelves, but some people will already have bought it and they have to be warned. This needs a difficult balance between warning consumers about the risks and panicking them. You can often see examples of panic where, say, one person gets indigestion after eating a meat pie made by a local butcher, and sales of all meat products throughout the country plummet.

The media play an important role in telling people about risks. Many countries are very pragmatic in describing the risks, but in the UK everything becomes a major scare. For instance, in 2002 a possible risk from prawns led to 'Natural Prawn Killers'; in 2004 'Farmed salmon is full of cancer toxins' and 'Bird flu will be worse than SARS'; in 2006 illegal use of a food colourant led to 'The Red Killer'; and salmonella in imported chickens 'could end the Sunday roast'.

Many food scares are generic – such as Edwina Currie's statement in 1988 that British eggs contained salmonella, or the foot-and-mouth and BSE epidemics – and these affect all sales of a product. Other scares refer to a specific brand, which is then in danger of never recovering (Corbett, 2005).

In summary

The last chapter discussed the identification of risks, and here we looked at their potential impact. There are two approaches to this. The first is a qualitative description of risk features. The second has quantitative analyses giving more detailed, objective and useful information.

Quantitative analyses of risk are based on two key factors – the likelihood of a risky event occurring and the consequences when it does occur. Multiplying these together gives an expected value. Managers can use this to suggest a relative importance for risks, identifying the risks to which they should give highest priority and attention. Unfortunately, both factors – probability and consequences – can be difficult to evaluate, so managers often use broad estimates, subjective values or agreed categories.

The types of risk can be shown in different diagrams, such as an ABC analysis, risk map and, most commonly, a probability–impact matrix.

Several useful tools can help with these analyses, with the most common based on systematic searches of operations such as 'failure modes and effects analysis'. Other useful tools include scenario analysis, simulation and network models.

At the end of risk analysis, managers have an ordered list of risks and have identified the level of concern for each. The next step is to consider appropriate responses – and this is discussed in the next chapter.

Responding to risks

Responses to risk

After analysing the risks, we have a prioritized list that shows the amount of attention that each deserves. But now we have to see what kinds of response are available. So our aim is to select and implement the best response to identified risks.

In the same way that there is a huge variety of risks, there is a correspondingly huge number of possible responses. Again it is impossible to list every option, but we can develop some principles, starting with the basic view that the best response depends on the risk's significance, and this is usually defined in terms of its potential impact. For insignificant risks – defined in the last chapter as type C, with both low probability and minor consequences – managers may simply ignore them. Then risk management consists of carrying on as usual and reacting when an unexpected event occurs. For type B risks – with higher probabilities and more severe consequences – managers may make adjustments to operations, such as holding more stock, adding slack time or building spare capacity into operations. Then type A risks need more serious attention, and it is here that we need to consider the options and choices more carefully.

The key point is that different kinds of risk are best dealt with by different responses. You would not expect managers to treat insignificant risks in the same way as disasters that threaten the organization's survival, so their job is to design and implement the most appropriate responses.

- The aim of risk response is to define the most appropriate way of dealing with all risks to the supply chain.
- Then actions are needed to implement the responses.

As a minimum, any response should:

■ allow the supply chain to continue working normally, or with minimum disruption;
■ be effective in dealing with the risks;
■ allow appropriate and efficient use of resources;
■ comply with all laws and regulations.

We can illustrate some different types of response with the observation in Chapter 6 that some risks affect a single organization while others affect the whole industry in which it works. An organization-specific risk means that one may lose out to other firms in the same industry, and this encourages each to work in isolation, trying to maintain or recover its position relative to competitors. This needs rapid, positive action to overcome obvious problems. At the same time, competitors that are not affected may adopt a passive policy, carrying on as normal and learning lessons for the time when they might be hit by a similar problem. Alternatively, they may be opportunistic and try to gain an even greater advantage by focused marketing campaigns, cornering markets, stockpiling scarce materials, charging inflated prices for assistance, developing new sources and markets, introducing new products, changing operations, and so on.

An industry-wide risk affects all organizations in the same industry, in the way that all transport companies suffer when fuel prices rise. Here a whole industry might be concerned about its survival and the best responses are collaborative, with firms cooperating to solve mutual problems. Such efforts may be coordinated by trade bodies, such as the Freight Transport Association – and, when the survival of the industry has been ensured, firms can return to their normal competitive activities.

Of course, any positive response means that managers really want to deal with the risks – but we have already mentioned the occasions when they prefer to ignore them. So the initial requirements for a response are that managers want to deal with the risk, are responsible for operations in the supply chain, appreciate the significance of risks and their consequences – and have the necessary knowledge, skills, information and motivation. This combination seems surprisingly rare, and risks in most supply chains are not well managed – or not managed at all. A survey by the Aberdeen Group found that 'Most companies lack a strategic approach to supply risk management' and many firms 'lack sufficient market intelligence, skills, and information systems to effectively predict and mitigate supply risks' (Minahan, 2005).

Alternative responses

A simple view says that managers either respond to a risk or they do not. The choice not to respond suggests that they have analysed a risk and found that it is not worth worrying about – presumably because it has a low probability of occurring and very minor consequences. Then they decide that any response would be more costly or difficult than the expected consequences, so they accept the risk and do nothing about it.

If they decide to make a response, managers can choose from different types that range from the very easy to the enormously difficult. At one extreme, we have seen that the easiest response is to simply ignore a risk. At the other extreme are very severe responses that managers only use when a risk is so serious that it threatens the organization's survival. Within this range of responses we can identify several different types:

1. Ignore or accept the risk.
2. Reduce the probability of the risk.
3. Reduce or limit the consequences.
4. Transfer, share or deflect the risk.
5. Make contingency plans.
6. Adapt to it.
7. Oppose a change.
8. Move to another environment.

Each of these is best suited to different circumstances. In principle, prevention is better than cure, so the preferred options, in descending order of preference, are preventing a harmful event from happening, then reducing the consequences if it does happen, and finally seeking redress for damage after it has happened (Pauchant and Mitroff, 1992). As usual, the descriptions of these responses tend to be phrased in terms of harm to be avoided rather than benefits to be encouraged, but remember that this is just for convenience.

1. Ignore or accept the risk

Taking a basic view, managers have two options for risks: either they can ignore it and do nothing, or else they can respond and do something. As a general rule, it is easier and cheaper to sit back and do nothing, so it seems sensible to view this as the preferred option. But to justify it, managers have to identify a risk, analyse it and find that the expected impact is small – because both the probability of an event and the possible consequences are small. In particular, the expected value from a risk must be less than the cost of any remedial action. This means that even the most risk-averse organizations ignore some risk, which they describe in terms of risk acceptance, retention or internalization.

Retaining a risk means that an organization accepts the complete impact of all possible events, so this is usually limited to the smallest risks. It is certainly the option for many trivial risks, but remember that it can leave organizations unprepared for risky events that actually occur. Even when the impact is small, it can be annoying and time-consuming to have to start a response from scratch.

In different circumstances, managers can also decide to accept more significant risks, particularly when the cost of making a positive response is high or where mitigating actions could make the situation even worse. For example, imagine a shop working in a traditional town centre, where sales have declined as customers have been attracted to an out-of-town shopping mall. By staying in the old town centre the shop runs the risk of lower profits, which it could avoid by moving to new premises in the shopping mall. But this would be expensive, and it would introduce significant new risks.

Another point about risk retention is that it is not always a positive decision. When managers fail to identify a risk they effectively ignore it, not as a positive decision but by inadvertently not recognizing it. In the same way, they may underestimate possible consequences and mistakenly accept a risk that is too severe.

Perrier and Tylenol

In 1990 the French mineral water company Perrier received reports that several of its bottles in the United States were contaminated with traces of benzene. At the time, Perrier accounted for 80 per cent of imported water and was widely held up as a model of purity and good taste. The company's initial response was to say that this was an isolated incident and they recalled a limited number of bottles. But other contaminated bottles appeared in Europe, suggesting a much broader problem. And now the company's response was considered slow and unconvincing, to the point where some people suggested that it was unethical. It seemed that the company might have known for several months that customers could be drinking water containing a recognized carcinogen.

Eventually, Perrier realized the damage and recalled 160 million bottles with a value of $200 million. But harm had already been done, their market share fell dramatically, and share value dropped to the level where the company became vulnerable. It was soon taken over by Nestlé, which had to virtually relaunch the brand.

Perrier's response was compared unfavourably to Johnson & Johnson's a decade earlier when some samples of its painkiller Tylenol were laced with cyanide in the United States. The company instantly alerted consumers not to take any Tylenol product and recalled everything from the market. This showed Johnson & Johnson's concern for protecting its customers, even at the expense of sales and profits. It took Perrier years to recover from its problems, while the Tylenol brand recovered almost immediately.

In 2000 there was another scare when some bottles of Perrier in the United States were tampered with, and in 2005 more traces of benzene were found in some bottles. The new owners dealt with the issues immediately and effectively, and there were no significant adverse effects.

2. Reduce the probability of the risk

Here managers take actions to reduce the probability that a risky event will occur. For instance, being attacked by pirates is a surprisingly high risk for cargo ship operators in some parts of the world; a way of reducing the risk is to use other routes that avoid the most dangerous areas. A firm that is worried by environmental or political factor risks can move to a location where these cause less concern. At a more basic level, warehouses can reduce the risk of shortages by increasing their stocks; delivery firms can reduce their chance of late arrivals by allowing more time for journeys; a firm that is worried by uncertain demand can improve its forecasting, and so on.

These examples suggest that there are essentially two ways of reducing the probabilities: 1) take actions to reduce the probability that an event will occur – for example, increasing stocks of materials with widely varying demand; 2) avoid operations where the risk occurs – for example, finding substitute products that have less variable demand.

As an example, imagine the risk that a key supplier will hit financial troubles. Two ways of reducing the probability of this risk are to pay a reasonable amount for materials (making it less likely that the supplier will have financial problems) and switching to another supplier (avoiding the problem). Other ways of reducing the probability of disruption include careful choice of locations, having good relations with partners, partnerships, arrangements for arbitration and negotiation, using security systems, free flows of information, using quality management, adequate safety measures, learning from experiences, solving underlying problems, involving everyone in the organization, identifying problems early, and a host of other methods.

3. Reduce or limit the consequences

Often it is easier for managers to reduce the consequences of a risk rather than the likelihood that it will happen. For example, car seat belts do not necessarily reduce the probability of an accident, but they reduce the effects on the people involved. In the same way, reducing the lead time of deliveries from suppliers will reduce the consequences of material shortages.

This illustrates the obvious point that there are two ways of reducing the expected value of a risk – reducing the probability that it will occur and reducing the consequences if it does occur. For example, warehouse managers can reduce the harm from falling objects by either revising practices to reduce the number of objects that fall or by insisting that everyone wears hard hats and protective clothing to lessen harm. Ideally, of course, managers would reduce both the probability of harmful events and their consequences.

4. Transfer, share or deflect the risk

Risk transfer moves some or all of the risk from one organization in the supply chain to someone more able or willing to handle it. Managers do not generally like risk, so they are inclined to transfer any, especially those where the cost of transfer is significantly lower than the expected cost of internal management.

An important point is that transferring a risk neither eliminates nor reduces it. In practice, the overall risk to a supply chain might even increase when one organization transfers a risk to another organization that is less able to handle it. For instance, there may be a dominant manufacturer in a supply chain, like an automobile manufacturer, that routinely transfers risks to other members of the chain. Then a major company with considerable resources and knowledge may pass risks to smaller companies that are less able to handle them. Flanagan and Norman (1993) point out that, 'In some cases, transfer can significantly increase risk because the party to whom it is being transferred may not be aware of the risk they are being asked to absorb.'

Insurance is the most common way of formally transferring risk from one organization to another. This has an insurance company accepting the risk of, say, a fire in return for an agreed premium. The essence of insurance is that the potential loss from a risk is too high for one organization to accept, but an insurance company can pool the risks from a large number of organizations and share the costs. The potential loss from having your house burn down is so high that you probably cannot accept the risk yourself – but an insurance company can pool the risks from a large number of houses, find the average cost and set an acceptable premium:

Insurance premium = expected value of loss + operating costs + profit

Not surprisingly, the greater the risk the greater the premium. On average insurance raises the cost of a risk, as it has to cover additional operating costs and give a reasonable profit, but everyone insured shares this cost, rather than having some individuals critically affected.

Insurance gives some recompense for direct damage, but organizations themselves still suffer the disruptions to their own operations and intangible

harm. In other words, they do not really transfer the risks and their consequences, but are only given some compensation. Some people say that it is
misleading to talk about risk transfer, and we should really talk about
compensation, deflection or, at best, risk sharing.

Risk sharing is also common in finance, where there are many different
arrangements, such as the forward or futures market. When a company
knows that it will have to buy a large amount of some commodity, say oil, at
some point in the future, it can simply wait and buy the oil on the spot market.
But when there is uncertainty about the future price, the company can reduce
the risk by agreeing a price now with traders that will deliver the oil at the
future date. In effect, the traders are taking the chance that the spot price will
be lower than the agreed price, so they make a profit; the company is taking
the chance that the spot price will be higher than the agreed price, so it pays
less. (And, of course, the traders need not buy on the spot market but can also
buy on the futures market.) There are many variations on this hedging against
future conditions, which is the reason that financial markets are so big.
Southwest Airlines used hedging in 2005 to fix 85 per cent of its fuel purchases
when oil cost $26 a barrel. Shortly afterwards the price of oil soared to more
than $70 a barrel, and Southwest is estimated to have saved more than $200
million in fuel costs.

Another form of sharing risks comes with third-party logistics or subcontracting. When a firm agrees to deliver a load to a customer by a specified
date, it can subcontract a transport company to make the move and share
some of the risks. The responsibilities of each partner are specified in the
contract, including the allocation of risk. If the transport company accepts the
risk of, say, delays in delivery, it pays the penalties but would expect a higher
fee; if the original firm keeps the risk it pays the penalties, but pays the
transport company a lower fee. The partitioning of risk is largely done by
negotiation and agreement – and then other factors come into play, such as
relative power and attitudes towards risk. The actual division of risk depends
on a number of factors, including:

■ the relative power of organizations, with more powerful ones passing
  risks to less powerful ones;
■ the attitude to risk, with risk-averse organizations keen to pass on more
  risk and paying an appropriate price for this;
■ the control, where organizations that have most control over the risk
  should accept a larger responsibility;
■ the premiums or fees that organizations are willing to pay or receive for
  accepting a risk;
■ the expertise and experience, which allow some organizations to deal
  much more efficiently with a risk;
■ the views and analyses of the risk, which might differ in each organization.

Trans Balkan Trans

Trans Balkan Trans have a fleet of heavy, long-distance trucks that move goods from countries in the South-East of Europe to the main markets in the West. A rough estimate suggests a probability of 0.005 that a truck will have an accident next year that will cause it to be written off at a cost of $200,000. The expected value is $0.005 \times 200{,}000 = \$1{,}000$. But this is the average cost for each truck, and the real cost will either be nothing or $200,000. The possibility of losing $200,000 is so daunting to a relatively small company that it cannot take the risk and must take out insurance.

The insurance company spreads the risks over a large number of companies, where it expects to pay an average of $1,000 a truck. It charges a premium that is higher than this to cover administration, expenses and profit. A premium of $1,400 a truck would cover the company's expected accident cost and leave an excess of $400. For each thousand trucks on its books, it would generate $1{,}000 \times 1{,}400 =$ $1.4 million, and five of the trucks would be written off at a cost of $1 million.

---

5. Make contingency plans

Contingency plans come into effect after a risky event actually occurs, so this option has managers taking no immediate action, but preparing plans to deal with an event that might occur. Then if the event does not occur, they carry on as before – but if the event does occur, they activate the contingency plans. A contingency plan is often referred to as 'plan B', which is only activated when an event occurs and changes are needed to the usual 'plan A'. For example, a company's normal plans might include moving goods by low-cost road transport, but if there is a sudden emergency order it has a contingency plan of using higher-cost air freight.

6. Adapt to it

This is a somewhat passive response, where managers accept that an event is inevitable and they try to adapt operations to fit in to the new circumstances. For example, when there is a risk that demand for a product might suddenly fall, managers modify their operations so that they would still be profitable with the lower demand. For this to work, the organization must be agile and able to change operations quickly enough to respond to changing conditions.

The difference between this and contingency plans is that managers take steps immediately to activate the plans. This has the benefit of encouraging flexible operations that react quickly to changing conditions and, as changes in the environment affect all competitors, the most flexible can seize their opportunities and gain a competitive advantage. On the other hand, the weakness of this reactive approach is that the environment, and not the organization itself, controls the rate and direction of change.

7. Oppose a change

Sometimes managers get prior notice that an event is going to happen, such as a government announcing that new regulations will come into force at some point in the future. Then instead of accepting that the event is inevitable, an organization can resist and try to prevent it happening. Individual organizations might campaign against a proposed change, but usually several combine their efforts to form a joint pressure group. For example, the UK government might propose legislation to limit the working hours of truck drivers; transport operators generally oppose such changes as they increase costs, so the Freight Transport Association might lead a campaign against the change.

It is usually difficult to oppose a change that has been well prepared and where decisions have already been made, so this option is often seen as a last resort or sign of desperation when all other options have failed. Presumably, most resistance comes from organizations that are harmed by proposed changes, and their chance of success depends on their relative power. Realistically, managers must be careful not to spend an inordinate effort opposing changes when they have little chance of success. Unhappily, you often see people continuing to resist events that are inevitable, when they would be better spending time and resources adjusting to the new conditions.

8. Move to another environment

This is probably the most extreme option and admits that some events are so risky that an organization cannot work with them. If no other option seems to be feasible, an organization can reorganize and move to another market or industry that does not have the risk. For example, in the 1990s managers of ICI, one of the world's largest chemical companies, decided that the risks of remaining in the bulk chemical industry were too great, so it changed its strategic direction, moved out of bulk chemicals and became a much smaller provider of specialized products.

An acute version of this occurs when an organization finds it too risky to stay in its own business environment, but cannot identify another to move into – so it stops working and closes down. Essentially, the potential consequences are too severe, with continuing operations having a negative expected value. Occasionally, the risks are so severe that all organizations in a particular industry or market close down, and then the sector ceases to exist.

Types of responses

A well-known illustration of the alternative responses to risk appears when you want to walk across a busy road. You can identify the main risk, that you are hit by a car. Now you can analyse the risk and design appropriate responses. For instance, you can:

1. ignore the risk, by closing your eyes and walking across;
2. reduce the probability of being hit, by moving to a quieter part of the road or crossing at a quiet time;
3. reduce the consequences, by wearing protective clothing;
4. transfer the risk, by getting someone else to cross the road for you;
5. draw up contingency plans, by phoning an ambulance to be ready in case you are hit;
6. adapt to it, accepting that you would ordinarily be hit, so become more agile to avoid the cars;
7. oppose it, campaigning to prohibit traffic from using the road;
8. move to another environment, so that you do not need to cross the road.

Defining options

Now we have a list of the main types of response to a risk, and can begin translating these into actual operations, in other words adding the details that move from general principles to concrete methods for achieving the planned results. When managers identify a risk of fluctuating demand and decide to reduce the consequences, they now want to know how they can actually do this.

Some risks to supply chains are common to other business functions, such as risks to finances, information, staff, buildings, etc. These common concerns have had more attention – particularly those with finances and information security. Of more interest to logistics managers are the risks that occur uniquely – or at least predominantly – to supply chains, in other words risks directly to the movement and storage of materials. There are specific ways of dealing with such risks, involving both the design of supply chains and the way that the flow of materials is controlled. There are many of these available, and we can suggest some common principles.

Adjust the design of the supply chain

Supply chains with different designs have different levels of inherent risk. Then an obvious response to risk is to adjust the design of the chain so that it has less risk.

Probably the most important feature of a low-risk supply chain is that it has parallel paths. Imagine the road down the Keys in Southern Florida; there is only one road, and when there are problems on this no traffic can get through. But when there were parallel roads, traffic could bypass problems on one by switching to the other. So one response to risk is to add more parallel paths to the supply chain, creating parallel paths that give routes around potential problems. There are several variations on this theme, such as multiple sourcing, alternative transport routes and outsourcing.

Another response is to reduce the length of the chain. Despite the trend towards globalization, there are obvious benefits from having materials move through fewer organizations and travelling shorter distances. Specifically, there are fewer things to go wrong and less risk. Low-risk supply chains are clearly shorter and wider, and a number of other design features. We return to this theme of designing a resilient supply chain in Chapter 10.

Reduce variability

Some people argue that risk emerges from variability, so a valid response is to reduce the variability in operations. This has been a continuing theme of quality management, which says that organizations can benefit by making products with perfect quality, and this means reducing variability to a minimum.

There has been a marked change in attitudes towards variability in recent years. A traditional view specifies an acceptable range for specifications, and performance is considered acceptable if it stays within this range. For instance, deliveries might be considered on time if they arrive with a lead time between 43 and 53 hours – but anything outside this range is unsatisfactory. However, Taguchi (1986) pointed out the inherent weakness of this approach, which is that lead times of 43, 48 and 53 hours are all equally acceptable. But customers would probably not agree that taking 53 hours is as good as taking 43 hours. On the other hand, there might be little real difference between taking 53 hours (which is acceptable) and taking 54 hours (which is unacceptable). The reality, of course, is that there is no clear cut-off. If you are aiming for a target, the further you are away from the target the worse your performance. We can describe this effect in a 'loss function', which gives a notional cost of missing the target (Figure 8.1). Organizations should clearly aim at minimizing the cost in this loss function, and this means getting the actual performance as close to the target as possible. And this means reducing the variability – and hence the risk – in a process. In practice, most organizations actively do this as part of their quality management function, so risk becomes inextricably linked with product quality.

Keep more stock

Stocks are the traditional way of reducing risks, so a reasonable response is to increase stock levels. Stocks give a buffer between uncertain and variable supply and uncertain and variable demand. When there are risks with suppliers, an organization can hold stocks of raw materials; when there are risks of fluctuating demand, the organization can hold stocks of finished goods; when there are risks to operations, the organization can hold stocks of work in progress. And the greater the risk, the higher the stock levels needed to give an effective buffer.

But what is a reasonable amount of stock? The traditional answer looks for a balance between too much stock (with high holding costs) and too little (with high shortage costs). Then it defines two types of stock: 1) working stock, which is the essential amount that is needed when everything works normally; and 2) safety stock, which is an additional allowance to cover any uncertainty and risks (Waters, 2003a).

The safety stock is not usually used, but it becomes available when risky events actually occur. For instance, when a delivery is delayed, operations continue by using the safety stock of raw materials. An important point is that

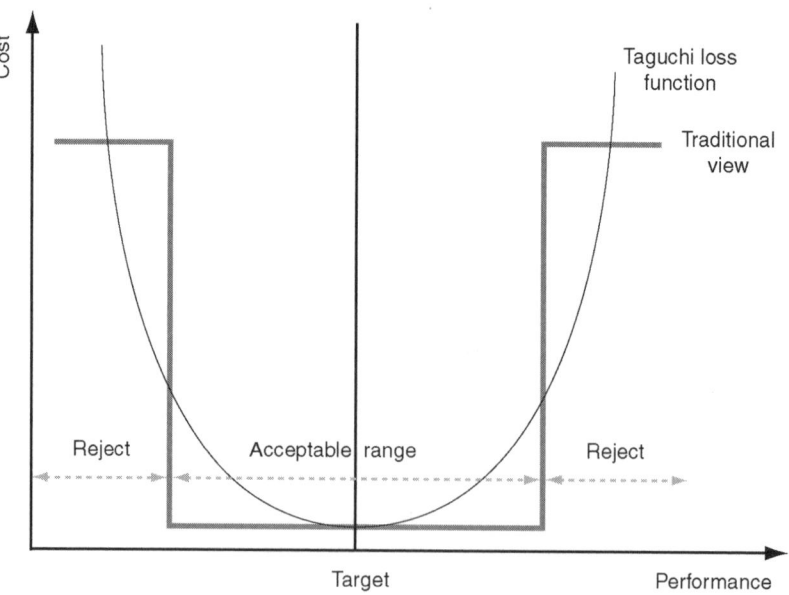

Figure 8.1 Taguchi loss function

safety stock is designed to cover risk, and the amount held should be related to the amount of risk. So when companies say 'We keep three days of demand for safety', they are making the mistake of relating safety stock to average demand rather than risk.

The main problem with safety stock is its cost, and we have already seen that there is a trend for organizations to move towards lean operations and lower stock levels (Waters, 2006). But this leaves them vulnerable to unforeseen events, and even something as minor as traffic congestion can disrupt operations.

Cisco Systems

At its peak, Cisco Systems had the highest market capitalization of US companies. It made network infrastructure products for the rapidly growing market, and during the 1990s often had difficulty keeping up with demands for its products. To give some security and slack in operations, the company would place big orders with its suppliers of key items like chips, optical lasers and circuit boards. But other companies in the supply chain were doing the same thing, holding large stocks, placing big orders, using multiple orders to ensure supply – and generally distorting the actual demand.

Then in 2001 the realities began to emerge, when 'the dot-com bubble burst'. Demand for Cisco's equipment fell and economic conditions in the industry quickly deteriorated. Cisco was suddenly left with huge amounts of excess stock. Most of this was specifically made for the company, so it could not be resold and had to be scrapped and recycled. The company lost $300 million on memory products alone, and had a total inventory charge of $2.25 billion.

Add spare capacity

This is the operational equivalent of holding safety stock, as it holds a reserve stock of spare capacity that can be used for unexpected events. A warehouse might calculate the amount of storage it needs for normal operations, and then add an extra amount of spare capacity to cover for unexpected events; a transport operator might calculate the number of vehicles it needs, and then add some spare to cover for accidents or unexpected demands.

Again, the main question is how much spare capacity to have – and again this should relate to the amount of risk. Greater uncertainty needs more spare capacity, so a company that simply 'adds 10 per cent of capacity to cover emergencies' is making a mistake. As with stock, the real answer is to balance the cost of providing and maintaining spare capacity with the expected cost of risky events.

Increase agility

Agility refers to the flexibility of an organization to adapt quickly to changing conditions. This suggests another response to risk, which is to increase the amount of agility in the supply chain so that it is flexible enough to cope with unexpected events. For instance, rather than holding stock to allow for unexpectedly high demand, a firm can use agile operations that make and deliver new products with very short lead times.

There are many ways of introducing agility (which we discuss in Chapter 10). The overwhelming theme is short lead times, so that organizations can respond quickly to risk events, but there are several other standard methods, such as postponement (which delays the finishing and final adjustment of products until the last possible moment), standardization (so that the same parts can be used in different products), concurrent operations (which do tasks in parallel rather than sequentially), cross-trained employees (so they can do the most pressing job at any time), alternative suppliers (to ensure reliable, rapid supplies) and so on.

Improve forecasts and planning

A common reason for problems in the supply chain stems from inaccurate forecasts. They mean that an organization plans on one level of expected demand, but unexpectedly has to perform for another level. Obviously the risks can be reduced by improving the forecasts. The usual way of achieving this is to move to more formal quantitative forecasting methods. Other considerations are that short-term forecasts are inherently more accurate than longer-term ones, and aggregate forecasts are more accurate than disaggregated ones.

The more accurate forecasts should include an idea of the likely variation, and this helps with subsequent planning. The plans can also be improved by improved procedures, and closer cooperation between the people who design the plans and those who have to execute them. There is often an artificial break between these two functions, but better coordination – with integrated planning and execution – can reduce many risks.

Increase collaboration

Risks often occur because trading partners do not work closely together. Then the actions of one partner come as a surprise to another partner, and this increases the general level of risk. An obvious response to this risk has trading partners working together and jointly looking for ways of reducing risk. In a straightforward case, one company might work with its suppliers and customers to reduce the uncertainty and potential disruptions. We have already seen that this collaboration can take many forms, ranging from informal discussion through to strategic alliances. The more formal arrangements need a lot of commitment, and in practice the most common methods of reducing risk are sharing information, joint forecasts, shared planning – and perhaps moving on to vendor-managed inventory (VMI), collaborative planning, forecasting and replenishment (CPFR) and synchronized material movement.

The key point about such collaboration is that it increases visibility within the supply chain. In other words, each member has a clear view of what is happening throughout the chain. This inevitably reduces the uncertainty and is a key factor in reducing risk.

Vendor rating

For most organizations, suppliers are a major source of risk. One way of reducing this risk is to use multiple sources, but this is contrary to current beliefs in the benefits of reducing the number of suppliers. An alternative is to use fewer suppliers, but be more careful in their selection. In other words, organizations should positively evaluate potential suppliers and choose the ones that give least risk.

Supplier or vendor rating is a general term for seeing how well a supplier matches the requirements of a customer. It can be organized in many ways, ranging from an informal, subjective review through to formal and sophisticated evaluation procedures. Usually a compromise gives a reasonable view, commonly based on a checklist of important factors. This checklist might ask whether the supplier is financially sound; how long its lead time is; whether it delivers on time; if material quality is high enough; if there is technical support; whether the price is competitive; where it is located, and so on. If a supplier does not meet any criterion, a customer has the options of looking for other suppliers or discussing improvements.

An extension to simple checklists uses a scoring model to evaluate different aspects of the supplier's performance. For example, a supplier might score 8 out of 10 for on-time delivery, 4 out of 10 for cost, and so on. If a score drifts down below some acceptable level, the customer can again look for another supplier, or discuss ways of improving performance in a process of 'supplier development'. The obvious difficulty with this kind of approach is the need to identify the critical factors of supplier performance, the relative importance of each, the actual performance and the lowest acceptable performance.

Philips Semiconductors, Stadskanaal

Philips' plant in Stadskanaal, the Netherlands, makes millions of diodes a year. These are made on an automated assembly line, using just-in-time operations, so materials (such as glass, wires and connectors) have to be delivered with perfect quality at exactly the right time. Over 65 per cent of the plant's cost is materials, and Philips puts exacting demands on its suppliers. It tolerates only a few defects per million parts, and typically demands decreases in price each year.

To make sure that supplier performance is satisfactory, Philips uses a supplier rating system that focuses on five aspects of performance:

Criteria	Performance required
Delivery performance	99.5 per cent delivered on time, with average deliveries twice a week
Quality	Fewer than 3–5 parts per million defective
Price	Expected to fall by up to 7 per cent a year
Responsiveness	Supplier feedback within two hours for critical problems
Audit score	Compiled from scores achieved in different aspects of performance measured by Philips' audit system

Make to order

There are four basic types of operation, with varying types of risk. An organization can respond to risks by moving to a more appropriate type of operation – which are, in increasing order of customization:

■ *Make to stock*, which keeps stocks of finished goods, so that customer demand can be met immediately. This is the most responsive, but there can be risks of unused stock. These risks can be reduced by using efficient operations with common components, short lead times, small batches, narrow product ranges, accurate forecasts and efficient inventory management.
■ *Finish to order*, which is the basis of postponement, but it can go further and keep stocks of common modules, sub-assemblies or semi-finished goods. This increases flexibility, as a wide range of products can be supplied from a limited stock of materials. But customer response is not immediate, so there are the risks from worse service. These risks are reduced by flexible operations that reduce finishing times, narrower product ranges and lines, more standardization and so on.

■ *Make to order*, which only makes products to meet specific customer orders. This can meet more varied demands with low stocks, but it has the risks of slow delivery. Ways of reducing risk are to use common components to reduce stocks of materials, flexible automation to reduce lead times, short lead times for materials from suppliers, etc.

■ *Design to order*, which is the most flexible, but with the longest lead times. Also it tends to be limited to small quantities of unique products, with the corresponding risks of variable demand and high costs. These risks can be reduced by shorter lead times, offering variations on a range of generic products, using common designs, collaboration with customers to get early warning of demands, high-technology designing, and flexible automation.

Consider the make-or-buy decision

When organizations want any component for a product, they have the option of making the component internally or buying it from a supplier. Economies of scale, specialization, expertise, outsourcing and other factors are increasingly moving this balance away from internal sourcing and towards outsourcing. But this makes organizations increasingly reliant on suppliers, particularly those supplying critical materials, and the loss of control inevitably raises the level of risk.

Organizations should look at this make-or-buy question carefully, to see how the increased cost of risks from outsourcing offsets the lower acquisition costs. Ways of reducing the risk of buying components are to keep some in-house capacity, use several suppliers, specify service levels and performance guarantees, and insist on reserved capacity at suppliers when there are constraints on capacity.

Rationalize the product range

This might seem like a minor adjustment to operations, but a company can significantly adjust its exposure to risk by its choice of products. The obvious response here is to avoid products with higher risks – typically with a retailer deciding not to stock an item with high risks, wherever these risks originate.

Binding contracts

An apparently straightforward way of reducing risk has organizations tied to trading partners by legally binding contracts that specify the obligations of each. Then if anything goes wrong, the contracts say who is responsible.

However, even this apparently foolproof approach still has problems. For a start, it is very difficult to draw up such definite contracts, and it is probably even more difficult to get trading partners to agree to them. And integrated supply chains blur the boundaries between organizations at an operational level, so that it becomes difficult to separate responsibility and risk. For instance, who is really responsible when agency staff pack goods delivered from a manufacturer, on to vehicles owned by a rental company, organized by a third-party transport provider, at the premises of a third-party warehouse operator, before delivering them to different customers?

Perhaps a more pressing problem is the considerable evidence to show that in times of trouble even the most rigid contractual arrangements break down. For instance, when a supplier is short of materials it will inevitably divert these to its largest, regular or most profitable customers – even though it has binding agreements with other less significant customers. This procedure is so automatic that business systems are usually programmed to automatically divert supplies to the most valuable accounts.

Using insurance

We have already mentioned insurance as a way of mitigating risks, but it is worth mentioning again as it is somewhat different from other responses to risk. In particular, it does not try to maintain a supply chain, but offers compensation when things go wrong. In essence, most ways of dealing with risk try to avoid its effects – using methods that we can combine under the heading of 'continuity planning', which tries to maintain normal operations through unexpected circumstances.

There is even an argument that insurance discourages other responses to risk as, arguably, a firm that will be recompensed for any disruptions is likely to put less effort into avoiding them. And when one member of a supply chain is less worried about maintaining smooth operations, risks to the whole supply chain increase.

A common concern with insurance arises from disagreements about the responsibility for risks. In an integrated supply chain the operating boundaries become blurred and ownership of risks becomes less distinct. Then when something goes wrong it can be difficult to say who exactly is responsible and who should be compensated. And the size of compensation is also debatable, as it becomes difficult to draw a boundary around the consequences. Do these include the loss of goodwill, image or future business – and if they do, how much is this worth? Insurance may cover the direct loss of materials and physical damage to a facility, but it is more difficult to include less tangible effects – and with most claims it seems that the insurer is in a stronger position than the people insured.

Mitigating the risks of crime

The UK's Security Service (MI5) lists the following ways of dealing with the threats of crime. The first three give general principles, and the remaining seven give specific advice:

1. Do a risk assessment to identify the risks, their likelihood and their consequences.
2. If you are building or acquiring new premises, consider security at the planning stage (it is cheaper and more effective than adding measures later).
3. Make senior managers responsible for risk management, and instil an awareness of risk in the corporate culture.
4. Use good housekeeping to keep public areas well lit, tidy and without unnecessary furniture.
5. Keep a minimum number of access points, issue passes to staff and visitors, and where possible do not allow visiting vehicles too close to buildings.
6. Install appropriate equipment, including locks, alarms, CCTV surveillance and lighting.
7. Examine mail-handling procedures and consider establishing a mail room at a distance from the main premises.
8. When recruiting staff or hiring contractors, check identities and follow up references.
9. Use the best ways to protect information and keep IT systems secure.
10. Plan and test business continuity plans.

Choosing the best response

We have now listed some of the most common responses to risk in a supply chain, but there are clearly many other options that depend on specific circumstances. Some of the responses change the actual design of the supply chain (its length, number of paths, capacities, relationships, etc) while other responses change the way that materials move (keeping stocks, binding contracts, taking out insurance, etc). The best response is presumably the one that keeps materials moving efficiently through the chain with the lowest cost – or perhaps achieves some equivalent objectives. But it is by no means clear which response does this, and it also depends on prevailing conditions. Sometimes it is best for a company to do nothing about a risk, at other times it is best to make minor adjustments to the flow of materials, and at other times it is better to make major changes to the chain or even close down.

The usual route to choosing the best response has two stages. In the first stage a long list of responses is considered, and from this a reasonable shortlist of leading options is identified. In the second stage the shortlist of options is considered and the best is chosen. This means that risk managers should have some formal procedures for choosing the best. This procedure should contain some quantitative analyses, but in practice it is likely to put more emphasis on management judgement and opinion.

There is a broad range of tools to help with such decisions, which we can illustrate with two methods: systematic analysis and decision trees.

Systematic analysis

We said that, when identifying risks, a general procedure divides the whole supply chain process into a series of distinct operations, studies the details of each and systematically assesses the risks. Then during the analysis we took this register of risks and considered the likely impact of each so that we could form a prioritized list. Now we can do the next step and systematically consider the list of risks and decide the best response to each.

Because of the practical difficulties, this kind of systematic analysis usually concentrates on qualitative views. So a reasonable procedure systematically breaks a supply chain into distinct parts, and then a brainstorming session takes each part in turn and asks the related questions 'What can go wrong?', 'How significant are the risks?' and 'How can we best deal with these risks?' From these sessions a list of viable solutions will emerge, and managers can analyse these in more detail to identify the most effective. This procedure is repeated for each part of the chain, giving an ordered list of preferred options for dealing with risks. Adding these details to the risk register in Figure 6.1 gives the basic structure shown in Figure 8.2.

This approach obviously needs a lot of effort, but it is fairly straightforward and can give a lot of related information. For instance, by giving a detailed analysis of the risk at every point in the supply chain and the actions needed to deal with it, managers can see where more resources or new operations are needed, where unnecessary operations can be eliminated, the paths that minimize total risk, the best alternative paths when there are problems, and so on.

Decision trees

These give a more quantitative view, with the problem of choosing the best response represented as a tree. The branches of the tree represent alternatives or events, and they emerge from nodes that are either: decision nodes, where

Summary			Description		
Identification number	Date recognized	Owner	Description of risk	Description of impact	Probability
1					
2					
3					
4					
5					

	Analysis			Response		
Identification number	Likelihood rating	Impact rating	Priority rating	Risk reduction	Impact reduction	Mitigation
1						
2						
3						
4						
5						

Figure 8.2 More details added to the risk register

we choose the best alternative – or branch – leaving the node; or random nodes, where we calculate the expected value of events following the node.

The analysis of a decision tree is in two parts, with the first drawing the tree to represent the problem and to show all the alternatives, events, probabilities and consequences. Then the second analyses the tree, working backwards from the final consequences until we identify the best path through the tree.

Decision tree

Consider the artificially simple example of a company choosing between three responses to a given risk:

■ Do nothing and accept the probability of 0.4 that an event will occur and do damage of £30,000.
■ Spend £5,000 reducing the risk of the event occurring to 0.2.
■ Spend £6,000 reducing the consequences of the risk to £20,000.

Figure 8.3 shows a decision tree of this problem. As you can see, the expected values of the decisions are:

Node 1, reduce the probability	0.2×35,000 + 0.8×5,000	= £11,000
Node 2, do nothing	0.4×30,000 + 0.6×0	= £12,000
Node 3, reduce consequences	0.4×26,000 + 0.6×6,000	= £14,000

Clearly, the best option here is to spend £6,000 reducing the probability of the risk, and giving it an expected value of £11,000.

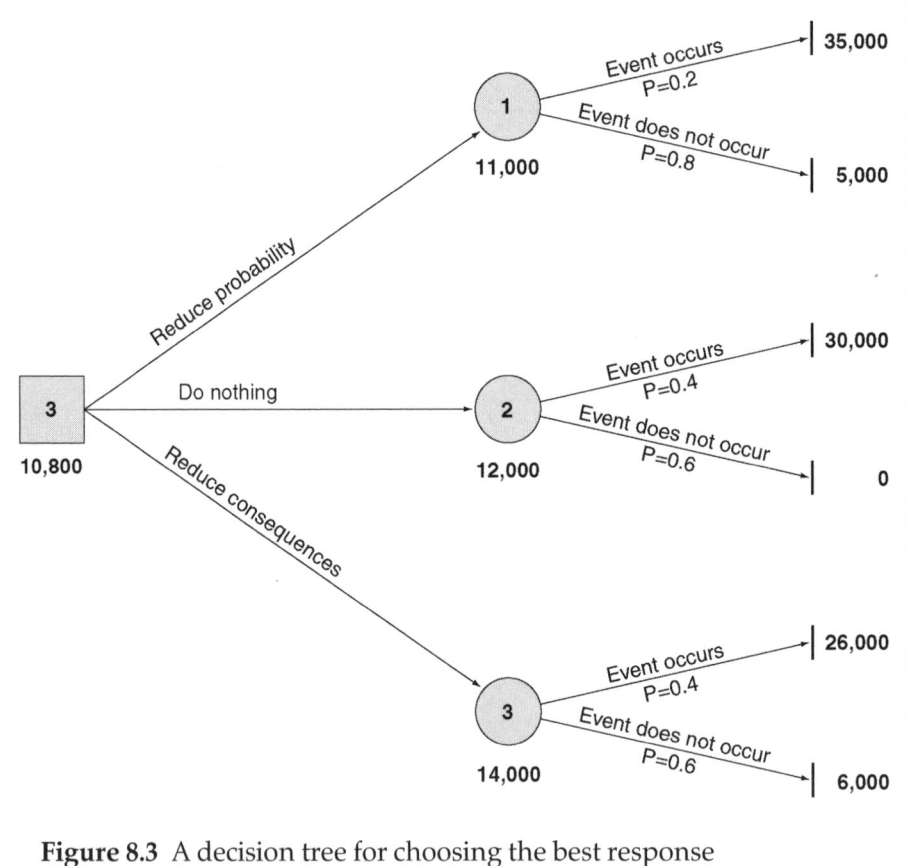

Figure 8.3 A decision tree for choosing the best response

Inappropriate responses

Even when carefully designing a response, managers can make a mistake, and it is fairly easy to find examples of risk management that has gone wrong. For instance, schools have responded to the risk of accidents during swimming lessons by stopping teaching children to swim – an inappropriate response that has considerably increased the risk of children drowning outside the lesson (Hunt, 2006). There are many examples of managers apparently putting inappropriate effort into avoiding risks, with many examples quoted for the US government following the terrorist attack on the World Trade Center. To take a small illustration, the government immediately tightened security at its borders and shut down US airspace – so all the companies that had set up low-cost operations in Mexico were now hit by delays at the border, and just-in-time operations that included international movements were interrupted. As a result, Chrysler had intermittent plant closures during the following weeks, and Ford reduced production by 13 per cent in the fourth quarter of 2001. These disruptions were not a consequence of any terrorist attacks, but were caused by the government's reaction.

Of course, at times of crisis governments have to restore public confidence by acting quickly and decisively. When the UK government announced that it had warnings of a significant risk to flights in August 2006, it immediately introduced new security measures at airports. These caused considerable difficulty – often amounting to chaos – and by November no harmful event had occurred so the restrictions were slightly reduced. People were divided between those who were grateful that the government had taken positive action to avoid threats and those who felt that the government had panicked in the face of unspecified threats that had never really existed.

It is never really easy to decide how much effort should be put into managing a risk. And this is most evident with risks that have potentially disastrous consequences, but very little chance of occurring – as illustrated by terrorist attacks. Ignoring these would leave the organization open to possible crippling consequences, but when the probability and expected value are small it is difficult to justify a lot of effort. In practice, there are two responses when managers put a lot of effort into a risk that does not actually occur. The first is to praise managers for putting in the effort needed to make sure the consequences never materialized; the second is to criticize them for wasting resources on a risk that never really existed. This alone is an incentive for using risk management – as the worst that can happen with risk management is some criticism for wasting resources, while the worst that can happen without it is the disastrous consequences and closure of the organization.

Foot-and-mouth disease

In 2001 the UK had a major outbreak of foot-and-mouth disease in cattle. This was the first outbreak for many years and, as its likelihood was considered low, little effort had been put into updating earlier plans or designing new ones. As a result, the country was largely unprepared for the latest outbreak. To overcome its lack of planning and demonstrate to a sceptical population that it was in control of the situation, the government introduced emergency measures to cull millions of animals, close off large areas of the countryside and pay farmers billions of pounds in compensation.

However, later analyses were critical, suggesting that:

1. the government was ill prepared for a major outbreak of disease and did not have adequate plans to deal with it;
2. the emergency actions taken were often hurried and inappropriate;
3. millions of animals that were neither infected nor in danger of infection were needlessly slaughtered;
4. closing the countryside to tourists had a greater economic impact than the disease itself (in a country with a relatively small agricultural industry, but major tourist industry);
5. the cost was excessive;
6. the disruption caused by the disease was far less than the disruption caused by the government's response.

Implementation and activation

Having designed an appropriate response to a risk, the next stage is to implement it. There are two stages to this: 1) implementation, which introduces the measures, policies, procedures, etc needed to deal with risky events should they arise, and includes everything needed to get an organization ready to deal with a risky event; and 2) activation, which monitors operations to see whether a risky event actually materializes, and if appropriate responses should be triggered.

You can imagine this with a company that delivers goods by rail. It recognizes that there is a risk of disruption to the rail service, and decides that the best response is to use more expensive air transport. Implementing this response means getting everything prepared for the air transport should it be needed; activation means using air transport when the rail service is actually disrupted.

Critical events

In principle it seems easy to identify when a risky event has occurred – a building burns down, a delivery does not appear, there is an earthquake, a supplier goes out of business, and so on. These clearly have critical events that mark the start of the risky event and show that it is time to activate the planned response. Then operations work normally until the critical event, at which point the planned response moves into action.

The problem is that the signs of a risk appearing are often more subtle than this. For instance, when a supplier runs into financial difficulties, there may be a long period during which its performance declines. Then there is no critical event, but at some point managers have to take action to safeguard operations from a further decline. In a similar vein, industrial disputes may have a strike as a critical event, but problems may have been growing for some time before this, and managers should monitor events and take actions before the strike actually starts.

It is important for risk managers to monitor performance, not just to keep the risk register up to date, but also to look for critical activities that trigger a response. Suppose that a supplier quotes a lead time of 72 hours. There is inevitably some variation, but if a delivery takes 76 hours is this a normal variation or is it time to activate a response? The odd late delivery is probably a random variation, but if the lead time consistently drifts towards 76 hours at some point customers will have to decide to activate a response. And the initial one is probably to discuss performance with the supplier. Control charts, which we mentioned in Chapter 6, give a useful tool to help monitor performance and give a warning when it is time to activate a response.

Even when there is a critical event it can be easy to miss. Virtually all organizations limit their view of risk to their immediate suppliers and customers. They become aware of risks at more remote points of the chain from information passed through their immediate partners – or possibly through informal relationships or general publicity. But it is easy to miss this, particularly when a small remote member of the chain hits problems.

Risk management in transport

Road transport is such a broad topic that it is clearly impossible to give a general list of all possible risks. When Scarborough (2007) reviewed the risks in transport companies he included the following points.

Risk identification

Risks appear in many different forms and with many variations. Three universal concerns are late deliveries, damage in transit and loss in transit:

■ *Late deliveries*. This is the most common problem with transport, which is often judged by its ability to deliver within a stated period.

Historically, organizations were fairly lax in their requirements, specifying delivery within a period of days or even weeks, but changing operations have tightened requirements. Now organizations ranging from JIT manufacturers through to supermarkets specify a delivery time slot that might be a couple of hours long, but is often as short as half an hour.

■ *Damage in transit.* Organizations put a lot of effort into product quality, so it is particularly disappointing when products are damaged in transit. Often it is worse to have goods damaged than to have them not delivered at all, as customers then have to organize the return of damaged goods as well as their replacement.

■ *Loss in transit.* For a variety of reasons goods are not delivered as expected, and they apparently disappear. The two main causes are mismanagement and theft. There might be some overlap between loss and damage when, say, a tank of liquid is lost as the result of an accident.

Risk analysis

Because of different circumstances, we cannot give figures for probabilities or potential consequences, but can mention some guidelines:

■ *Late deliveries.* Delays in transport are usually small compared with total lead time, but most organizations are less concerned with the total delay than the reliability with which a delivery comes at an expected time (Murphy and Hall,1995). The probability of this can usually be found from records of supplier performance. There is clearly wide variation in performance, but a 1997 survey of the UK food industry (DETR, 1998) found that 11 per cent of deliveries were at least half an hour later than scheduled. In 1998 a follow-up survey suggested that about a quarter of journey legs in food supply chains had significant delays (McKinnon, 1999).

An interesting point is that transport operators usually blame delays on traffic congestion, speed restrictions, industrial action, border delays, traffic bans and so on. But McKinnon found that most delays actually occur at the operator's premises rather than during transport, with the most common causes of delay being:
- problem at a delivery point (31 per cent);
- traffic congestion (23 per cent);
- company internal actions (13 per cent);
- problem at a collection point (10 per cent);
- equipment failure (2 per cent);
- lack of driver (2 per cent).

■ *Damage in transit.* Here it is even more difficult to give general figures, but each company can find them from transport records. Most damage occurs during loading and unloading of vehicles, or from deterioration during actual moves (typically caused by accidents, movement within vehicles, contamination or lack of temperature control).

■ *Loss in transit.* A survey by the Road Transport Association (2004) suggested that one in five UK companies had suffered some vehicle-related theft in the preceding year, with the value of stolen loads at around £210 million. Over 40 per cent of these losses occurred in the operator's own depot, compared with 25 per cent during transport.

Responding to risks

■ *Delays.* These can occur at five points in transport: at the point of collection from a supplier; during actual transport; at transshipment or intermodal depots; during security or customs checks; and at the point of delivery to a customer. Organizations can use many methods to reduce the risk of these delays. For instance, increasing the scheduled transport time to give more slack reduces the chance of missing a quoted delivery time. Other responses are to increase the length of delivery time slots, change delivery times to avoid congested periods and increase night-time deliveries. Delays can also be reduced by more efficient operations at depots, such as the numerous methods for rapid loading and unloading of vehicles, reducing paperwork, redesigning vehicle bays, and any improvements to goods reception procedures.

■ *Damage in transit.* The risk of damage is clearly related to the amount of handling, and improved methods can significantly cut risks. The other key factor is the quality of packaging used, but environmental pressures to reduce this might increase risks to products.

■ *Loss in transit.* Ways of improving the security of goods in transit include improved staff vetting and training, depot security, secure parking, anti-theft devices, and vehicle location devices. Tracking systems started with global positioning systems (GPS), which in addition to their routeing and planning functions continuously monitor locations and increase the chances of stolen vehicles being returned. Similar tracking systems follow loads and packages, initiated by parcel delivery services such as FedEx, UPS and DHL.

In summary

The last two chapters showed how to identify risks and analyse them. Now managers have to design the most appropriate responses. These depend on circumstances, and particularly the significance of the consequences. The usual choices for type of response are to ignore the risk, reduce its likelihood, reduce its consequences, transfer the risk, make contingency plans, adapt to it, oppose it or move to another environment.

This list shows the main options for dealing with risk, and the next stage is to translate these general methods into specific actions. For example, when managers decide to reduce the likely consequences of a risk, how can they actually do this? There are several practical ways of responding to risks, including keeping more stock, adding spare capacity, increasing agility, improving forecasts and planning, increasing collaboration, vendor rating, making to order, considering the make-or-buy decision, rationalizing the product range, using binding contracts and using insurance.

Having got a list of possible responses to a risk, managers have to choose the most appropriate. Many models can help with this decision, and we illustrated them by systematic analysis and decision trees. However, it can still be difficult to choose an appropriate response to a risk, especially when there can be severe consequences.

After designing the response, the next task is to implement it. This is in two parts, implementation (to prepare for a risky event) and activation (which actually does the required activities). Often a critical event causes activation, but it can be difficult to identify a specific trigger.

So far our view of risk management has largely focused on the risks within a particular organization. But we know that a risk to one organization can present a risk to the whole supply chain. Then the most appropriate response to a risk comes from the whole chain and not isolated members. We consider this problem in the next chapter.

9

A network view of risk

Shared risks

Each member of a supply chain is vulnerable to its own risk, risks to other members of the supply chain, and risks from outside the chain. In Chapter 6 we classified these risks as:

- *Internal or organizational* – the normal risks within the operations of an organization arising either from inherent risk or from management decisions.
- *Supply chain risks* – the risks that are external to an organization, but within the supply chain. These occur from lack of visibility or inadequate cooperation between members of the supply chain, and are principally risks from suppliers or customers. Chapman *et al* (2002) refer to these as endogenous risks, which typically arise from either:
    - integration risks from the cooperation itself, and include information flows, payments, liability, joint forecasting and planning, etc; or
    - coordination risks arising from the alignment of operations in different organizations, including quality issues, lead times, delivery reliability, stocks, cycle time, etc.
- *External risks* – the risks that are external to the supply chain and arise from interactions with its environment. Chapman *et al* (2002) refer to these as exogenous risks, which include the risks of natural disasters, legislation, cultural differences and so on.

Transmitted risks

Risks are transmitted through the chain, so a risk to any single member has, at least to some extent, consequences for the whole chain. For instance, if one company faces risks to its finances (which are essentially internal) it may not be able to pay its suppliers (creating broader supply chain risks). Similarly, a hurricane (an external risk to the chain) might disrupt supplies and encourage firms to give preferential treatment to bigger customers (a supply chain risk), causing other members to stockpile materials (with consequent internal risks).

The clear message is that even a minor incident in one part of a chain can escalate and have disastrous effects in other parts – or even destroy the chain's ability to deliver products to final customers. Svensson (2000) develops this idea of risks in one firm being linked to risks in others and distinguishes: direct or atomistic risks, which are the immediate risks that occur from interactions between an organization and its first-tier suppliers and customers; and indirect or holistic risks, which originate anywhere in the supply chain and are transmitted through the chain to an organization.

There can be hundreds or even thousands of members of an extended supply chain, but each organization deals only with a limited number of these. Therefore, it seems reasonable to suggest that events affecting more distant members will be more common than those affecting first-tier suppliers and customers. But these risks can only be identified with a broader, or holistic, view. Most organizations limit their risk management to their own operations and possibly their immediate suppliers and customers. Presumably this is the reason that, when managers were asked to identify risks to their supply chains, the overwhelming majority identified atomistic risks, but virtually none of the more remote holistic risks.

The amalgam of risks facing all parts of a supply chain describes its overall vulnerability. Peck (2003) describes vulnerability as 'an exposure to serious disturbance, arising from risks within the supply chain as well as risks external to the supply chain'. To be even broader, vulnerability describes the amalgam of risks that arises from the internal risks to individual members, risks from interactions within the supply chain, and risks from interactions with the external environment. The related idea of resilience shows how quickly a supply chain can return to normal working after it is hit by a risky event. In practice, resilience is more proactive than this, as it recognizes that the chain might not have been working in the best possible way before the event.

■ Resilience means that a supply chain can quickly return to a previous state or move to an alternative, more desirable one.

The obvious problem is that there are so many members of a complete supply chain that, even when the risks to each are small, the cumulative effect becomes significant. If only one firm in 10,000 has financial problems in a year, a supply chain with several thousand members can expect problems at some point. And as the risks are transferred to all members of the chain, it seems reasonable to suggest that they all should work together to mitigate the effects. If a key supplier faces closure, the other members of the chain can sit back and do nothing – in which case the whole supply chain faces closure – or they can cooperate to mitigate the effects of the threat.

Coordinated supply chain risk management

When all members of a supply chain work on their risk management in isolation (or realistically those members of the supply chain that do any risk management) the results are rarely good or even satisfactory. Lee (2004) and Christopher and Lee (2004) illustrate this with a description of managers who fear that they might have difficulties getting supplies. Their inevitable reaction is to hoard whatever becomes available, giving stocks that are unrelated to either supply or demand. Effectively they return to inefficient policies that increase investment in stock, risk of deterioration, obsolescence, warehouse facilities and finance required – as well as changing suppliers, using lower-quality substitute materials, distorting demand patterns, and a host of related problems.

Of course, all managers want to protect the operations under their direct control. And managers would presumably argue that they are in no position to identify risks in more remote areas of the supply chain – and, even if they did, they could do nothing about the risks. They might even argue that the best overall result comes from each firm looking after its own interests and even taking advantage of problems in competitors. But rather than reduce the level of risk, an independent approach tends to increase it and amplify the consequences. When one company reduces its exposure by holding less stock, this can increase the risk of shortages and disruptions throughout the whole chain – with greater supply chain risk more than offsetting the reduced internal risk in one company. In 2005 a tropical storm threatened oil facilities in the Gulf of Mexico; each oil company acted independently to protect its own supplies, buying extra stocks and creating a temporary shortage, which suddenly increased prices by $10 a barrel.

By acting independently, managers reduce their own exposure to risks, perhaps transferring risks to other members of their supply chains. With a narrow perspective this seems reasonable. But not everyone can gain by this manoeuvring, and moving risk from one member to another does not decrease overall risk – and it might even increase it, making the whole chain more vulnerable. When there are broad risks to the whole supply chain they can only really be tackled through a cooperative effort by all members, with each managing its own internal risks and accepting a broader responsibility for reducing the vulnerability of the whole chain.

Christopher *et al* (2002) support this view by defining supply chain risk management as 'the integration and management of risks within the supply chain and risks external to it through a co-ordinated approach amongst supply chain members to reduce supply chain vulnerability as a whole'. Similarly, Kajüter (2003) takes a holistic view of SCRM as 'a collaborative and structured approach to risk management, embedded in the planning and control processes of the supply chain, to handle risks that might adversely affect the achievement of the supply chain goals'.

■ The best approach to supply chain risk management does not have each member of a chain working in isolation, but has them working together in a coordinated effort to reduce the overall vulnerability of the whole supply chain.

To avoid confusion, we will refer to this broad, coordinated view that spans different organizations as 'integrated SCRM' – to differentiate it from ordinary SCRM that might exist within each organization. Of course, this is really a tautology, as SCRM should always involve an integrated view. Unfortunately, the reality is that most managers view SCRM as contained within their own organization, and the surveys by Christopher *et al* (2002) concluded that 'None of the managers interviewed... believed that their organisations had addressed the issue of supply chain vulnerability in a direct and comprehensive way from a general risk management perspective.'

Achieving an integrated approach

Stemmler (2006) suggests that the basic requirements for integration are that managers:

■ consider risks to all three flows of material, information and finance;
■ expand their interests beyond their own organization and on to cover all of the supply chain;
■ consider not only the broad principles of strategic risk, but also the details of operational risk;
■ expand risk management from a statutory reporting function into a planning function.

This implies that managers can recognize the benefits of an integrated approach and want to share them. But we know that there are real reasons why an organization might not want to cooperate. The first is the amount of effort needed. A principle of risk management is that it should give a net benefit rather than be a burden, but some managers still feel that it gives additional responsibilities – and these are multiplied when they also have to consider risks to other members of their supply chains. The second is the reluctance of some managers to admit risks to their own organization, as this might put them at a disadvantage compared with competitors that do not admit these risks. A third is a natural inclination to withhold some information about risks, particularly any that is commercially sensitive. This might encourage members of the chain to ask about the reliability of inputs from their partners, and this raises a fourth point of the necessary mutual trust, which may be absent.

The combination of these – and many other – factors suggests that complete integration is a theoretical concept that is unlikely to be achievable. Realistically, the best we can hope for is integration along parts of the chain, with cooperation between some tiers of partners.

To achieve even this basic level of integration needs three key requirements – identifying the need for integrated SCRM, having an incentive to actually introduce it, and creating the systems that make it possible.

1. Identifying the need for cooperation – the knowledge that integrated SCRM can bring benefits

We can make a case for the principle of cooperation in a supply chain, but managers really do have to acknowledge that risk management is essential for continuing operations in the chain, and the best approach is to use cooperation. Surprisingly, most organizations have not yet recognized this, and even those with procedures for mitigating internal risks have generally failed to recognize the broader need for coordinated action with other parts of the chain. Presumably managers do not recognize the extent to which risks in other parts of a supply chain can affect them – or else they recognize the risk but assume that other firms are in a better position to tackle it and will do whatever is necessary to reduce its effects. For instance, a manufacturer that uses small amounts of palladium will buy this from traders; it might not know that there are currently risks of world shortages, or it might recognize the possibility of a shortage but assume that other companies will sort out the problems and give continuing supplies.

The concept of joint risk management is still at an early stage of development, and most organizations work in isolation. In 1995, White noted that risk management rarely takes into account broader interactions, and in 2006 Peck could still say that 'risk management models have failed to keep pace with the realities of our networked world. They have failed to account for operational interdependencies between firms.' A symptom of this lack of recognition comes with a survey in 2004 (Computer Sciences Corporation), which found that only 35 per cent of firms agreed or strongly agreed with the statement 'My organization pays sufficient attention to supply chain vulnerability measures and risk mitigation action.'

2. Having an incentive to cooperate – the reason for undertaking integrated SCRM

There must be incentives for managers in the chain to cooperate and work together, and this means positive benefits to each organization rather than a nebulous feeling of communal good. Firms have to commit resources to any programme for integrated SCRM, and they have to be convinced that their direct benefits will outweigh their costs. A particularly sensitive problem occurs when one organization has to accept more risk to reduce the exposure to risk of the whole chain. Then it has to be confident that it will get proportionally greater benefits and will not be harmed by its new arrangements.

We have already mentioned similarities between integrated SCRM and TQM, and another is the way that requirements are passed back through a supply chain. Here, when one organization manages its own risks it has to insist that its suppliers have adequate methods in place to deal with their own risk. The suppliers, in turn, pass on the requirements to their own suppliers, and so the motivation for increasing risk management expands through a chain.

3. Creating the systems that allow cooperation – the means by which integration is achieved

Cooperation can only be achieved in a visible supply chain, where all members exchange relevant information and work together to solve mutual problems. But this needs appropriate systems for sharing information – and organizations are nervous about this. Perhaps they believe the benefits are not worth the effort of building the systems, or they may feel that information is commercially sensitive, or they may not want to reveal their own vulnerabilities. We return to this question of building systems for integrating SCRM in the next chapter.

Information recovery

Banks and financial institutions started to install huge computer systems in the 1960s, and the financial sector has continued to develop increasingly complex systems for moving and storing information. From the start, the industry was concerned about the reliability of such integrated networks, recognizing that disastrous consequences could appear from damage to even a small part. A fire in one building could close down the whole financial system.

Finance companies, also encouraged by considerable pressure from regulators, looked for ways of protecting their operations and their clients' money. Part of this response came with plans for disaster recovery, with companies working together to develop common crisis plans. At the heart of these plans are duplicate systems at a secure location that is remote from the original systems and safe from shared risks.

For the computer industry, disaster recovery has become an important new service to complement its equipment sales. In practice, it is rarely necessary to duplicate complete systems, and alternative formats allow backups for parts of the system, or simply copies of essential data. Data protection is particularly common, and anyone can subscribe to a disaster recovery service and use the internet to download the contents of a PC to a secure site. And the scope of disaster recovery has expanded beyond computer systems to include any other facilities that might be lost – including buildings, equipment, staff, systems, materials and so on.

Steps in supply chain risk management

In previous chapters we have described a general approach to SCRM, and although this is predominantly used for organizational risks we can extend it along the supply chain for integrated SCRM. So it starts with senior management support and appointing a risk champion and risk management team, and goes through the central activities of risk identification, analysis and response, implementing the findings and then monitoring and control.

In principle the same reasoning applies to the chain as to the individual organization, but we soon hit major problems. Appointing a risk champion and management team is difficult in a single organization, as the team will have different views and organizational responsibilities. But at least they are all working towards the same aims. With integrated SCRM there is now a large group of supply chain partners that want to achieve some common aims but also have a range of different objectives, constraints and agendas. It might be difficult to find an individual champion with enough status and dynamism for the cause of integrated SCRM; it might be difficult to identify a group of reasonable size to move the initiative forward; it might be difficult to agree common goals, beyond the broadest principles; it might be difficult to agree common responsibilities, plans and procedures for achieving these goals; it might be difficult to translate these broad ideas into practical operations.

The reality is that even preparing for integrated SCRM can be extremely complicated, and the next steps are equally difficult, as organizations struggle to agree joint policies and procedures. And only after this preparation can organizations move on to the core activities of risk identification, analysis and response.

Aberdeen Group

The Aberdeen Group surveyed 180 global enterprises and found that more than 80 per cent had been affected by disruptions to the supply chain within the preceding two years (Minahan, 2005). But despite this, less than half had any procedures for supply chain risk management.

It seems that five strategies are important for successful SCRM:

1. Define and enforce performance standards for risk management.
2. Make risk management a core business function.
3. Adopt sourcing methods that balance cost, performance and risk.
4. Use innovative technologies and information systems to improve risk management.
5. Work together with trading partners to identify and mitigate risks.

Businesses using these methods have demonstrably performed better than their competitors in terms of supply chain disruption, reliable deliveries, cycle times and quality.

Identifying risks

Assuming that the problems of initiating integrated SCRM can be overcome, the next stage is to move on to the core activities, with the team of managers from related organizations discussing the workings of their supply chain, identifying common risks and forming an agreed list of significant risks. In principle, the risks affecting the whole chain are the same as those affecting each member, including the usual diverse mixture of physical, financial, information, organizational and other risks – but the scope of these risks is now made more complex by interactions within the chain.

So the managers set about identifying risks using the methods that we described in Chapter 6, to analyse past events, collect opinions or analyse operations. But managers from each organization rarely have more than a passing knowledge of operations in other organizations. At best they might have some idea of operations in their first-tier suppliers and customers, be very hazy about second-tier suppliers and customers, and know almost nothing about operations further upstream and downstream. So they are rarely in a position to identify and analyse risks – or even take part in informed discussions about them. Then the primary route for risk identification is clearly through managers in their own organizations. They have to identify all risks and classify them according to whether they are largely internal or whether they have a broader impact on the supply chain. For instance, managers might identify constraints on capacity as a risk in their own company – and then they have to consider the risk constraints bring to other parts of the chain. If the risk is largely limited to the managers' own company, they can deal with it internally; if other companies could be seriously affected, they should deal with it jointly.

Risk identification depends on the ability of managers in each organization to identify relevant risks, assess their consequences, decide whether the risks are best dealt with internally, determine the amount of information that they are willing to share, and so on. This process can be particularly sensitive and can break down for reasons ranging from ignorance to commercial sensitivity. With integrated SCRM it becomes particularly difficult for some members to publicly acknowledge their vulnerability to risk, as other members may exert pressure to replace them by a competitor that is perceived as being less risky (or probably less open in disclosing risks). And when there is a dominant member of the chain, such as a manufacturer in the automobile industry, there is inevitably a tendency for the dominant member to transfer any risk identified from itself to other members of the chain (Kendall, 1998).

As getting managers in each organization to agree a list of joint risks is clearly difficult, an alternative is to replace the 'top-down' approach with a 'bottom-up' one. Here, people at lower levels in the organization notice risks in their normal work, and they transmit them upwards to the risk management team. This needs completely different flows of information, which are generally even more difficult to organize. And all managers insist that there are filters on these flows, to limit the type of information that is passed outside their own organization. Nonetheless, where possible this approach can give much better results, as they come from a broader range of people, who have a more intimate knowledge of the operations.

Another way of reducing the organizational effort is to piggyback risk management on to, say, quality management. This is likely to have well-established procedures in place for collecting broad opinions and transmitting them up to quality management teams. Even simple mechanisms like suggestion boxes and quality circles (or risk circles) can give surprisingly useful results.

Analysing and responding to risks

Now assuming that a list of significant risks can be identified, the next stage of integrated SCRM is to analyse these and prioritize them. Again we can use methods that we have already described, using probabilities and possible consequences to give a prioritized list of risks. But this again becomes more difficult when more firms are involved. Now there can be basic disagreements about the likelihood of events, and particularly their consequences. These disagreements might come from genuine differences of opinion, but are just as likely to stem from differing perspectives. One firm might view a risk as insignificant (when the risk is unlikely to affect the firm directly) while another firm views the same risk as serious (when it will be affected). So the contents of the risk register depend on negotiation and agreement, as well as more formal analysis.

By the end of the analysis, managers should have an agreed risk register that contains a prioritized list of risks. A significant difference between this and the register for an individual organization is the likely number of entries. In an organization, managers will list all risks that have a significant impact and that they can manage. It is impossible to suggest a reasonable number here, but it might be 20 or it might be 200. But with a supply chain, difficulty of getting agreement generally forces managers to focus on the handful of most serious risks. They can only really look at mitigating the most pressing risks that are accepted by the majority of the risk management team. Of course, it is possible to list many more than four or five risks, but as the list gets longer they tend to become less well supported, with less agreement about the details.

Alternatives for dealing with risks

The next step in integrated SCRM is to take the most urgent risks and agree ways of dealing with them. The options available were discussed in Chapter 8 – with the main alternatives of accepting, reducing the probability, reducing the consequences, transferring, contingency plans, adapting to it, opposing a change or moving to another environment.

Again, these methods need some adjusting before they can be used for integrated SCRM. For example, risk transfer is comparatively easy in a single firm, simply by agreeing a transfer of risk to another partner. But this now becomes more difficult, as we want to transfer risks somewhere that will reduce the level of risk for all members and not just shuffle the risk around trading partners.

A practical problem for integrated SCRM is the division of responsibility. There may be a risk management team with nominal responsibility for risk in the supply chain, but when they identify ways of mitigating risks they have no real power to implement the solutions within individual organizations. So one group of managers may identify the best way of reducing a risk, and find that this needs action by managers in another part of the chain, who are unable or unwilling to take any actions.

Some people suggest that the practical problems of integrated SCRM make it a theoretical ideal rather than a practical proposition. Others say that the problems can be overcome, but they need a more radical approach. Rather than introduce integrated SCRM to an existing supply chain, it is more successful to start from scratch and design a new resilient supply chain. Rather than look for iterative improvements to an existing supply chain, simply replace it by one with a better design and lower risks. This radical approach is more aligned with the ideas of re-engineering (Hammer and Champy, 1993), while organizational SCRM is more aligned with continuous improvement or kaizen (Imai, 1986).

Problems with integrating SCRM

We have perhaps laboured the point that integrated SCRM is very difficult in practice, but these difficulties can be overcome, and then there can be considerable benefits. The following list suggests some other specific problems that need attention:

■ *Knowledge.* Managers rarely look for risks beyond their own customers and suppliers, so the first hurdle is getting them to recognize the need for integrated risk management. In one sense, integrated SCRM is a natural progression of an integrated logistics function. As SCM is becoming ever more integrated, risk management is simply the next function to add. Unfortunately, many organizations have not really progressed far with cooperation in the supply chain, so cooperative risk management is an entirely new concept.

■ *Unclear responsibility.* Even when members of a supply chain can independently identify a risk, it may not be clear who is responsible for it or who is in the best position to deal with it. In a simple case, a delivery arrives late – but is this because the customer ordered it too late, the supplier was too slow in responding, the transport was inefficient, or someone else was at fault? The problems of assigning responsibility increase with outsourcing and more complicated operations that blur the operational boundaries between organizations.

■ *Incentives.* Even when the responsibility for a risk seems clear, as does the organization best able to deal with it, this does not automatically mean that anything will happen. An organization only does the things that give it a positive benefit – so it will not do things for the general good if its own benefits are less than the costs. In practice, most organizations believe that their own risk management is satisfactory, and their main risks stem from their partners. This discourages them from tackling their own risks, as they imagine greater problems continuing in other members.

■ *Unequal benefits.* Ideally joint mitigation reduces the risks to all members of a supply chain, but sometimes difficult compromises are needed – especially when one organization is asked to increase its own exposure in order to reduce risk to the whole chain. You can imagine this when one firm is hoarding materials that might be in short supply and the other members ask it to distribute the materials to other firms so that they can continue operations. Generally, such sharing of risks is reflected in the prices charged, so the company asked to distribute hoarded materials will presumably charge a higher price to cover its own increased exposure.

■ *Trust.* Most organizations do not have implicit trust in their trading partners – often for good reasons. Often a sense of commercial sensitivity is understandable and sensible, but at other times it seems ridiculous. Imagine a customer refusing to release its outline production plans to a key supplier – meaning that the supplier has to use its own forecasts of demand, which are inevitably less reliable and give less efficient operations. The result is more risk from uncertain demand and higher costs.

■ *Resources.* Developing integrated SCRM is a major exercise that needs considerable resources, particularly management time. It may be difficult to justify the costs involved when the results are, by definition, uncertain. Managers may find it difficult to build a convincing case for diverting money into risk avoidance, when they effectively measure success by the fact that nothing happens. This is a particular problem with small and medium-sized companies. But if these cannot find the resources, risk management becomes the preserve of large organizations, which are the ones more able to deal with any risky events. Arguably, this makes small businesses more vulnerable and helps the concentration of ownership in fewer, large firms.

■ *Communication.* In most supply chains there is fairly limited contact between members, typically limited to brief contacts between purchasing and sales departments. Integrated SCRM needs much more communication at different levels – with senior managers having to reconcile different aims and cultures at organizational level, and people at operational levels exchanging information to reduce the risks in specific activities. And it can still be difficult to get seamless and secure connections between the various systems.

■ *Sharing information.* Making sure that relevant information is available at all points in the supply chain – giving visibility – is at the heart of risk management. But we have already said that organizations are nervous about sharing information. One result is that only 40 per cent of firms allow even key customers and suppliers to view order status online (Computer Sciences Corporation, 2004). On the other hand, many organizations have gained considerable benefits by moving towards greater visibility, perhaps by simply passing on relevant information or through collaborative planning, forecasting and replenishment (CPFR) or enterprise resource planning (ERP).

■ *Terminology.* An apparently trivial – but surprisingly common – problem is that organizations use different terms for the same aspect of logistics, or use the same term to mean different things. This makes it difficult to exchange basic ideas and correspondingly more difficult to discuss common approaches to complex problems.

■ *Different working conditions.* Each organization in a supply chain has its own aims, constraints, values, culture, operations, systems, etc. These present practical barriers to cooperation, when each firm has different views of risks and the best ways of dealing with them. Of course, this is a basic weakness of all integration – that organizations can perform better if they work together, but they still have to work for their own self-interest.

■ *Operational incompatibility.* Each organization runs its operations in the way that best suits its own purposes. But this gives problems at the boundaries when different types of operation meet and have to cooperate. You can imagine this when, say, a traditional batch process passes materials to the just-in-time operations of its customer. However, over the long term such risks should decline as trading partners merge their operations, homing in on methods that reduce incompatibilities.

■ *Complex decisions.* Supply chains are long and complex, and it is unrealistic to expect every manager throughout the chain to always make the right decisions. So it is likely that something unexpected will happen some-where – perhaps by a manager making a mistake – and the consequences ripple through the chain.

■ *Risk expansion.* Forrester (1961) described the 'bullwhip effect', where risk is amplified as it moves through a supply chain. Imagine a retailer that notices that demand for a product rises by five units in a week. When it is time to place the next order, the retailer assumes that demand is rising and orders 10 extra units to make sure it has enough. The local wholesaler sees demand rise by 10 units, so it orders an extra 15 units to meet the growth. The regional wholesaler sees demand rise by 15 units, so it orders another 20 units. As this movement travels through the supply chain, a relatively small change in final demand is amplified into a major variation for upstream suppliers. Christopher *et al* (2002) say that these effects are a result of 'over-reactions, unnecessary interventions, second guessing, mistrust, and distorted information throughout a supply chain'.

■ *Inertia.* In complete contrast to agility is the concept of inertia in a supply chain, which is the reluctance to make any changes or adapt to any kind of new conditions. This might seem impossible in such a rapidly changing area, but imagine a complex network of firms that has taken years to develop relationships and is working well together. Any change would introduce new ideas, operations, procedures – and risks, so there is an understandable tendency to keep the chain as it is.

■ *Training.* Few organizations give their staff training in risk management, so they may not see potential problems or know how to deal with them. A widely reported illustration of this lack of training occurred with radio frequency identification (RFID) in the 2003 invasion of Iraq. Some RFIDs were used to track and monitor materials, but the army did not train logistics staff or soldiers in their use. As a result, no one knew what the tags were for and they simply threw them away.

Levels of SCRM integration

If a supply chain consists of thousands of members – or even a few dozen – it is clearly impossible to get them all to work together on risk management. So this combination of practical problems probably makes integrated SCRM a theoretical concept rather than a practicality. However, we can imagine it as an ideal that organizations should work towards. This is what they should be aiming for, even when they are making slow progress. A more realistic, intermediate target would have a small set of close partners working together. Perhaps a lead organization could start working with its key suppliers and customers to reduce localized risks. Over time this could be repeated in other parts of the chain so that most members are eventually involved in coordinated risk management.

Then we can describe the progress towards integrated SCRM as a spectrum. One end of this spectrum has organizations taking no interest in risk management at all. Initial progress away from this extreme has individual organizations identifying internal risks and taking steps to overcome them. The benefits from such individual actions are probably most obvious when an entire industry faces a risk, and then each firm uses risk management as a way of gaining a competitive advantage. For instance, when there is a risk of rising prices for raw materials, one company might sign long-term contracts as a way of getting a price advantage.

Further progress towards integration has an organization building on relationships with its immediate suppliers and customers. These can form a small group to consider immediate concerns, do a limited audit of the risks that are under their control, and decide on joint actions. This extends the normal cooperation that exists between trading partners into a new area, and is likely to be the easiest type of integration to implement. If this approach is used widely along a chain, different initiatives overlap, giving a more coherent view of risks. Of course, there can still be problems with missing links when a member is unwilling to work in this way.

An even more integrated approach extends cooperation along the supply chain, including further tiers of suppliers and customers in joint decisions. The more levels that are involved, the more complex and difficult become the practical difficulties. And the ideal of fully integrated SCRM with all members working together remains a theoretical concept rather than a practical proposition.

This view suggests five levels of SCRM:

1. no risk management at all;
2. risk management by individual companies working in isolation;
3. joint risk management with immediate trading partners;
4. integrated risk management along more of the supply chain;
5. integration along the whole chain.

In reality, most supply chain managers work in the first two of these stages, and largely see good risk management as a means of gaining a competitive advantage, rather than contributing to the overall good of the supply chain. Level 5 remains a theoretical target, and it is fair to say that almost no organizations really work at level 4.

Of course, this view assumes that there is an inevitable progression towards more integration, with organizations sorting out their own organizational risks and then moving on to the more complex areas of cooperation. This is the usual approach with all broadly based ideas, which start in isolated spots and grow over time. And there are certainly analogies with TQM, which started in isolated firms and then expanded down supply chains when it became clear that each firm could only achieve its aims by a coordinated approach. Now TQM is routinely adopted throughout supply chains, with all members working together to solve mutual problems. The same approach could certainly be used for integrated SCRM – and there are early signs that it is happening, with firms increasingly insisting that their trading partners have SCRM procedures in place.

Reawla Engineering

Reawla Engineering was founded in Chicago, United States, in 1947, and by 2003 its main products were pumps for the oil and gas industry. The company was exporting more to the growing markets in South-East Asia, and wanted to make deliveries to these markets as efficient as possible. To collect ideas, it organized a meeting of interested bodies in Singapore. This meeting discussed all aspects of supply chain management, including risks.

When different companies presented their profiles, one transport company said that there was a possibility of some political insecurity in its home country. The following year Reawla was reviewing its distribution in the region and decided to use a single transport company. Despite its history of good performance, the company that had admitted the possibility of political insecurity was not shortlisted. Opinion seemed divided over whether Reawla was making progressive moves towards integrated SCRM – or whether it was sending the wrong message that risks should be hidden rather than identified and openly discussed.

Principles for integrated SCRM

The general principles of integrated SCRM are essentially the same as those for organizational risk management, so we can summarize these as follows:

■ The main aim of integrated SCRM is to avoid disruption to the supply chain and maintain a free flow of material.

■ Integrated SCRM manages all the risks facing the entire supply chain. It aims at reducing the overall effects of harmful risks, rather than moving them around the chain.

■ A reasonable approach to integrated SCRM starts in isolated spots and expands along the supply chain. This follows the TQM model, with an organization insisting that its suppliers adopt reasonable methods for controlling their own risks. Realistically, there seems to be a limit to the amount of integration that is achievable.

■ Integrated SCRM needs visibility, as well as active understanding, cooperation, communication and supporting systems among members of the chain.

■ To work properly, there should be a culture of risk management throughout the supply chain.

■ The approach of integrated SCRM again has the core activities of risk identification, analysis and response. However, these become much more difficult than with organizational SCRM.

■ The result of integrated SCRM is a supply chain that is not inherently vulnerable to risks, and is resilient and agile enough to recover quickly from unexpected events.

In summary

There are several types of risk to a supply chain, which we described as internal, supply chain and external. In reality, these are not isolated, but are linked. As each member of a supply chain occupies a unique position, risks to any single member can be transmitted and expanded to give risk to the whole chain. The best way of dealing with these mutual risks is not to work in isolation but to have all members cooperating and working together to reduce the level of risk to the whole chain.

Although this seems a sensible idea, it is new to most organizations, and little real progress has been made. There are many practical reasons for this, ranging from unclear responsibilities through to communication problems. So most organizations tackle their own risks in isolation (assuming that they have an organizational policy for risk), and very few have made any progress towards integrated SCRM.

In principle, integrated SCRM is similar to organizational risk management. Then the core activities are risk identification, analysis and response – with preparation needed before this and monitoring and control afterwards. But now the process is much more complicated, as it needs cooperation between organizations with widely different operations, aims and views. Although the main tools are the ones we described in earlier chapters, they are much more difficult to apply to integrated SCRM.

The need for visibility, lack of commitment, different aims, and a whole range of practical difficulties mean that integrated SCRM is much more complex than organizational SCRM. Realistically this limits the amount of progress that can be made. But overcoming these difficulties can bring significant benefits.

We can describe some general principles for integrated SCRM, such as visibility and cooperation – but the most important point is to design a resilient supply chain in the first place. We discuss ways of doing this in the next chapter.

10

Creating resilient supply chains

Design of a resilient chain

In the last chapter we discussed the concept of integrated SCRM, where all members of a supply chain worked together to manage mutual risks. In practice, this is difficult to achieve and progress has been limited – but the result should be a resilient supply chain that is not vulnerable to risks. In this chapter we bring some more threads together and describe the design features that help to make a supply chain resilient. The important point about these features is that they are not revolutionary or needing dramatic new methods, but they generally reflect good SCM practice.

> ■ The design of a resilient supply chain – one that is not vulnerable to risks – is generally achieved by the normal practices of good logistics management.

Earlier on we said that current trends in SCM tend to increase the level of risk, such as lean operations removing the slack that can absorb minor variations. Now we are saying that good logistics management leads to resilient chains. So how can we reconcile these two views? One answer is that the trends do not necessarily reflect good management. Of course, lean operations give considerable benefits – but there comes a point where slack in the chain is removed solely for the sake of removing it, even when overall performance declines. Many firms blindly continue to eliminate stock, but their calculations do not include the increasing potential for disruptions. The result is more vulnerable supply chains. Good logistics management would not go so far down this path, but would include both efficiency and resilience in its analyses.

Importance of design

Chapter 8 discussed some principles for reducing risk, but these focused within an organization. Now we are looking more broadly and extending the principles to the design of the whole chain.

Perhaps the first thing to emphasize is that the supply chain design really does affect the level of risk. For instance, a long, narrow chain is inherently more risky than a short, wide one; when organizations work in isolation the overall level of risk is higher than when members cooperate to jointly solve problems; a chain without visibility is more risky than one with free information flows. We could develop these arguments, but it seems obvious that the basic design of a supply chain is a primary factor in determining its vulnerability and resilience. The clear implication is that managers should design chains with vulnerability in mind.

Few organizations really appreciate the concept of supply chain integration, let alone the need for an integrated approach to risk management. Unfortunately, this means that even major incidents are not analysed from a broad perspective. If materials are in short supply, customers blame the immediate supplier rather than searching for the root cause, and then underlying weaknesses in the supply chain design are missed. In the same way, when demand for a product varies, managers look for ways of levelling demand from their immediate customers, rather than looking for the underlying causes of the variation.

Jacques Chagal

Jacques Chagal uses organically grown, stoneground flour in his handmade breads. In 2006 the price of this flour was 40 per cent higher than it had been in the previous year. The miller explained that there had been a poor harvest and wheat prices had risen sharply, so he was just passing on the higher prices charged by the local farmers' cooperative. This seemed a reasonable explanation, so Jacques Chagal had no choice but to pass on the costs and raise his own prices.

There are three interesting points here. First, the miller was paying 40 per cent more for wheat, but his other costs had remained virtually constant. Wheat accounted for only 30 per cent of his total expenditure, so he could have covered the increased cost by raising his prices by 40 per cent × 30 per cent = 12 per cent. The second point is that there was no shortage of wheat. If the local farmers' cooperative had limited supplies, the miller could have looked for alternative sources from further afield – even in the next town.

The third, more interesting point is the background of a growing interest in various kinds of specialized and healthy breads. Jacques Chagal's breads were in this category, and this allowed him to charge higher prices. And in general, people were willing to pay a premium price for what they perceived as high-quality products. Supermarkets had obviously noticed this effect – and this identifies the real source of the problem. A supermarket chain had signed an agreement with the local farmers' cooperative, offering higher prices for wheat in return for guaranteed supplies. The cooperative had simply diverted their supplies away from the miller and Jacques Chagal, and towards the larger customer. If the farmers' cooperative, the miller and Jacques Chagal had maintained closer working relationships, they could have negotiated a much better deal.

Principles of designing a resilient supply chain

In the last chapter we described a progression of integration for SCRM starting with no risk management at all and moving through to a fully integrated approach (Kleindorfer and Saad, 2005). There are a number of basic principles involved with this move, such as the need for careful design, agile operations, visibility, relationships with customers and suppliers, culture, etc. We have already met most of these principles before, but can consolidate them here:

1. *Start within the organization.* The first principle is to get SCRM installed and working properly in your own organization before starting the ambitious move into collaboration. This step makes sure that senior management are committed, they have defined broad policies for risk, a risk management team has been appointed, necessary systems have been installed and tested, there are smooth information flows, an internal risk register has been designed, procedures have been tested, and so on. Only when everything is working internally can managers really expand their scope to consider other members of the chain. An opposing view says that managers can learn valuable lessons from working with others on their joint problems, so they should not approach trading partners with well-defined and inflexible ideas, but should go in a spirit of exploration. The best ideas will emerge from a cooperative approach, combining ideas and

experiences so that each can learn new ideas and methods that they can use within their own organizations. Perhaps the best answer is somewhere between these two, where managers make some progress on their own risk management, and then look to improve and consolidate their methods using inputs from other organizations.

2. *Take a strategic view.* In common with all major initiatives, SCRM needs commitment from senior managers who are aware of the issues and can allocate the resources. SCRM is a strategic initiative that can have profound effects on an organization and the way that it is run. To put it simply, with poor risk management there is less chance that an organization will survive into the long term. But this need for senior support becomes more obvious when it explicitly includes relationships with other organizations, as these inevitably need new strategies and policies.

3. *Understand the concept of supply chain risk.* Before they can successfully plan for risk along a supply chain, managers must clearly understand what they are studying. In other words, they must understand the concept of risk – and the members, roles, links, interactions, objectives, forces, dynamics, power and all the other elements that form the complex web of a supply chain. Then they can combine these two concepts in the integrated function of SCRM.

4. *Consider risk in the design.* This principle is the one that we have been stressing all along, that managers should explicitly include the effects of risk in their decisions. If they ignore risk, they will focus on leanness, efficiency or some other goals that inadvertently increase vulnerability. The best design needs a balance between resilience and normal measures of efficiency. For instance, a single path through any point in a supply chain creates a vulnerable point, and if anything happens at this point the whole chain is at risk. The way to avoid such risks is to design a chain with parallel paths, so that flows can be diverted away from a disrupted path to one that is working normally.

5. *The chain is only as strong as its weakest link.* Disruption at any point in a supply chain causes problems for the whole chain, so managers have to identify risks throughout the chain to find the weakest parts. We already know that this is difficult, but there is little point in managers building a resilient chain in the areas they control if adjacent areas are still vulnerable. There are always weak spots in a network, and these might include single paths, links with long lead times, members facing specific organizational risks, those that are unwilling to share information, members that do not manage risks properly, and so on. Sometimes parallel paths can be created around risky areas, but this may be difficult – for example, when there is only one container depot or a single port that can handle a cargo. Managers must be especially careful of the risks in vulnerable areas, particularly when these areas are outside their control. Then they might take steps to reduce the consequences of the risk, or try to influence the managers who are responsible by including them in the risk management

process. Or they can redesign the chain to bypass the area of weakness (Handfield and Nichols, 2002; Kunreuther and Heal, 2004).

6. *Look for collaboration.* The sharing of ideas, methods and information is a core part of supply chain management. This is the only way that members of the chain can identify mutual risks and design effective ways of dealing with them, gaining synergies from the collaboration.

7. *Prevention is better than cure.* The principle here is that it is always better to avoid harm rather than look for compensation after it has occurred (Michaels, 1996). To be more specific, we can characterize the best options for mitigation (in descending order of preference) as trying to prevent a harmful event from happening, then reducing the consequences if it does happen, and finally seeking redress for damage after it has happened.

8. *Create agility.* Risk is based on uncertainty, which exists in all operations. So despite our best plans we are always susceptible to unforeseeable events, and must have the flexibility to deal with them. There are many ways of increasing agility, such as spare capacity, backup systems, stocks of finished goods, holding cash reserves, postponement, short lead times, modular processes and so on.

9. *Have emergency procedures.* When a risky event occurs, flexible operations can avoid its worst effects and continue to work normally. But sometimes the effects are too severe for even the most flexible operations to deal with. For instance, if a delivery of materials is delayed, flexible operations will allow normal working, but if the supply of materials is completely eliminated, even the most flexible operations cannot find a solution. The alternative is to build contingency plans for emergencies. These are used as a last resort when all other aspects of risk management have failed, and they work on the basis that, if you do not know what will happen, the best plan is to be prepared for anything. The next chapter describes the features of such emergency plans.

United Technologies Corporation

United Technologies has a turnover of $40 billion from its range of high-technology products, largely for the aerospace and defence industries. In 2003 it introduced new systems for SCRM that combine lean operations and risk management across its 23,000 suppliers. This focused on four elements:

1. *Operations transformation leaders* – to train, improve and lead cooperation with suppliers. Their aim is to apply lean principles and risk management with first-tier suppliers, encouraging them to extend the same principles to second-tier suppliers.

2. *Supplier performance measurement system* – to establish standard measures for the quality and delivery performance of its 3,000 most critical suppliers.
3. *Supplier alert service* – United Technologies examines financial, market, regulatory and performance information from hundreds of sources to assess potential risks to its suppliers. It uses this to monitor the financial and operational health of more than 80 per cent of its suppliers.
4. *Lean assessments* – when the supplier alert service detects a risk, it informs the operations transformation leaders. These analyse the supplier's operations and identify opportunities for improvement.

The company estimates that this approach has improved stock turnover by 28 per cent and reduced the cost of poor quality by 32 per cent. And it routinely identifies supplier risk and takes mitigating action before events can affect the business.

Physical features of a resilient supply chain

Now we have described some principles for designing resilient supply chains, we can ask what the resulting chains look like. Although the details will vary, there are some common features. For convenience, we have divided these into physical features (length, breadth, capacity, etc) and relationships (collaboration, visibility, process integration, etc).

Design is matched to demand

The basic principle of supply chain design is to match the chain to its requirements. For instance, there is no point in having capacity to move 1 million tonnes a year when the demand is only 1,000 tonnes; or a supply chain shipping goods from around the world will not work when the demanded lead time is a few hours.

This match between design and requirements does not just happen, and there are many analyses that can help. Models that examine the flow of materials through networks of connected facilities are usually described in terms of 'graph theory' (Waters, 1998). These work on the principle that each node and link in a network has a fixed capacity and takes a certain time to traverse, and these can be used to analyse the features of the entire network. In particular, the overall capacity and lead times are defined by the features of each link and the way that these are configured.

A basic analysis of graph theory considers the maximum amount of materials that can flow through a network, and managers can use this to get the essential structure needed in a chain. A related analysis finds the shortest path between any two points in a network, so this can be used to analyse expected lead times. Similarly, managers can identify the bottleneck that limits overall capacity, remembering that the capacity of the whole chain can only be increased by increasing the capacity at the bottleneck, and increasing the capacity of any other point has no effect except to give even more spare capacity.

Parallel paths

We introduced this idea in Chapter 8, with the example of the road down the Keys in Southern Florida. When there is only one road, there is no way of avoiding any problem; but with parallel roads, traffic can bypass problems on one by switching to the other. This principle applies to whole supply chains, where problems can be bypassed by creating parallel paths. In practice, there are several variations on this theme, including:

1. Multiple sourcing, where a firm uses parallel suppliers, perhaps with rules of thumb like 'never let a manufacturer account for more than 20% of total revenue; never let a customer absorb more than 50% of total resources' (R Perry, quoted in Lawless, 1998).
2. More logistics channels to customers, including direct sales and e-trading, that remove layers of the supply chain. When these work together with traditional routes, such as Tesco's home delivery service, they give extra paths.
3. Outsourcing operations such as transport to several outside parties, or having them work in parallel with internal operations.

Shorter supply chains

Despite the trend towards globalization, there are obvious benefits from shorter supply chains. This means both fewer partners in the chain and shorter distances moved. The most obvious benefits are lower costs from less transport, and reduced lead times from closer suppliers. But these bring associated benefits of more flexibility, fewer delays, less loss and damage to goods, and so on. Just-in-time (JIT) operations recognize the benefits of local sourcing, insisting that suppliers are physically close to operations, so you often see clusters of suppliers around a main manufacturing plant. In practice, there is some debate about whether JIT or similar operations really encourage local sourcing, or whether their principles have got lost in the rush towards globalization.

Shape of the supply chain

It stands to reason that a complex supply chain has a higher chance of disruption than a simple one. More complex chains have more members and more links – and simply more things to go wrong. But this is only part of the story, and the vulnerability of a supply chain does not depend just on the number of members but also on the way that they are arranged.

Suppose we describe the reliability of one element of a supply chain as the probability that it continues to work throughout an entire period. A lorry might have a reliability of 0.98 of working properly for a delivery, a logistics centre might have a reliability of 0.97 of work without major disruptions for a year, and so on. We can use the reliability of each individual element to calculate the reliability of the supply chain as a whole.

If you take one element of a chain – say a transport link – then putting two identical elements in parallel increases the overall reliability. This assumes that the second element can still work when the first one fails, and that the chain can work normally with only one element. For instance, suppose a company finds that a transport operator delivers 90 per cent of items properly (for simplicity rather than accuracy), then its reliability is 0.9 and its probability of failure is $1 - 0.9 = 0.1$. If the company uses two similar transport operators, it opens two parallel paths, each with a reliability of 0.9. Then assuming that it can use the second operator when there are problems with the first, the supply chain only fails when both operators fail, and the probability of this is $0.1 \times 0.1 = 0.01$. So the chance of having at least one operator working is 0.99, clearly illustrating that parallel paths in a supply chain increase reliability and reduce risk. If the company wants to be even safer if can use more transport operators in parallel. Then with N operators, there are N parallel paths and the probability that they all fail is 0.1^N (as shown in Figure 10.1).

Now imagine what happens when a supply chain is made longer, with new elements added in a series. The whole chain only works when all the separate elements are working. When a factory distributes goods through a logistics centre, transport company and retailer, its goods are only delivered when all three elements are working properly.

Suppose that the reliability of one element in a chain is 0.9 (again for convenience rather than reality), then the probability that two elements in the series both remain working is $0.9 \times 0.9 = 0.81$. So elements in a series reduce the reliability of a chain and increase the risk. In general, when there are N elements in a series the probability that they all remain working falls to 0.9^N (as shown in Figure 10.2).

As long chains are inherently less reliable, and wide chains are inherently more reliable, the most reliable supply chains are clearly short and wide.

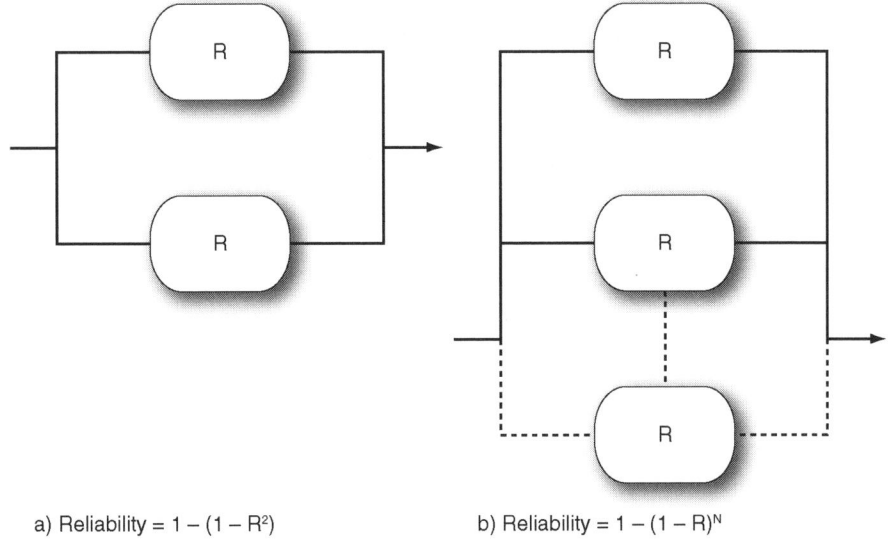

a) Reliability = $1 - (1 - R^2)$ b) Reliability = $1 - (1 - R)^N$

Figure 10.1 Elements in parallel increase reliability and reduce risk

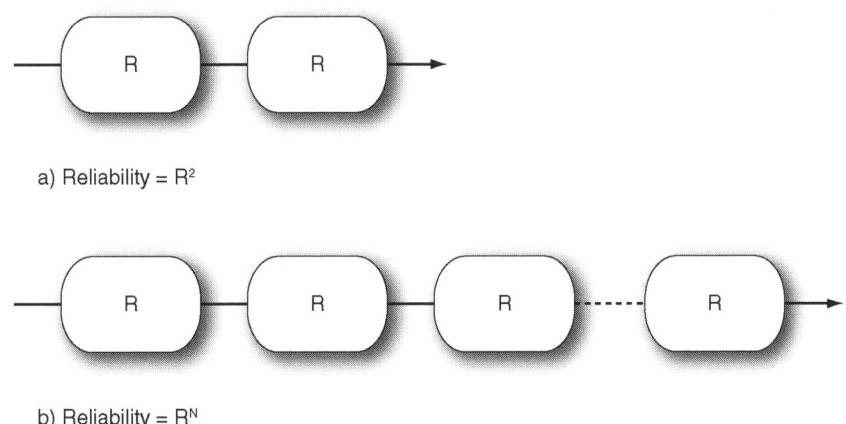

a) Reliability = R^2

b) Reliability = R^N

Figure 10.2 Elements in a series reduce reliability and increase risk

---

Calculating reliability

A very small part of a supply chain is shown in Figure 10.3. We can use the following logic to find the reliability of this section of the chain:

1. Take the top two elements, a and b, which are in a series and have a combined reliability of $0.95 \times 0.95 = 0.9025$. This is equivalent to

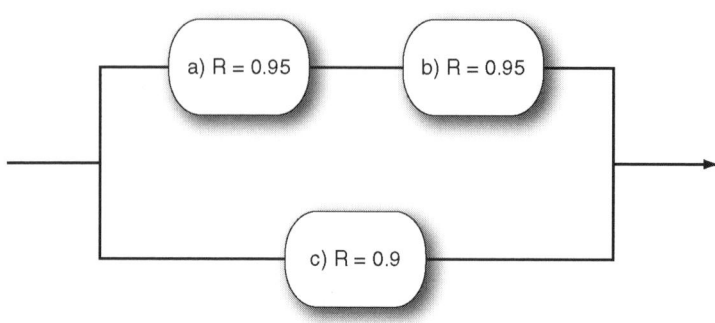

Figure 10.3 Part of a supply chain with a reliability of 0.99025

a single element, say d, with a reliability of 0.9025 (and probability of failure = 1 – 0.9025 = 0.0975) in parallel with element c.
2. The probability of both c and d failing is 0.1 × 0.0975 = 0.00975. So the combined reliability of these two is 1 – 0.00975 = 0.99025.

If we had more elements in the chain we could continue in this way, simplifying the elements to given an overall result for the whole chain.

The key point about parallel paths is that each should be isolated from risks in the other, rather than just giving that impression. This is sometimes not as obvious as it seems. For instance, Zbigniew Forwarders used two shipping lines to carry materials across the Atlantic. In 2005 Hurricane Katrina flooded large areas of New Orleans – and this was when Zbigniew realized that both shippers relied on the port of New Orleans for access to the Mississippi River. You can imagine a similar situation with multiple sourcing. Perhaps an electronics company uses a preferred supplier and an alternative for commodity chips, both of which have facilities in Taiwan. Then any unforeseen event in Taiwan could simultaneously remove both the main supplier and the alternative. On a more limited scale, apparently parallel paths might really share the same electricity supply, use the same transport system, buy raw materials from the same source, arrange finance through the same bank, and so on.

Higher stocks

We have already said that stocks give slack in a supply chain and reduce levels of risk. Then higher stocks of raw materials reduce the risks from suppliers; stocks of work in progress reduce the risks to operations; stocks of finished goods reduce the risks to demand. A firm always needs some basic working stocks for its normal operations – and to allow for risks it needs additional safety stock. This safety stock is above the company's perceived needs, but it holds it to allow for any unforeseen events. Such stocks do not give a long-term solution, but they overcome immediate problems and allow a firm to plan its recovery after any disruption. Unfortunately, they also bring their own risks of tied-up investment, damage, obsolescence and so on – and they have the major disadvantage of hiding underlying problems in operations. For instance, a supplier's unreliability can be hidden by safety stocks, so managers might not notice and have little incentive to improve things.

Spare capacity

It is clear that a process working at full capacity cannot suddenly change and start moving work around. Braithwaite and Hall (1999a, 1999b) say that 'flexibility and agility is simply not possible when the available resources are stretched to the limit'. The alternative is to build spare capacity into a process, typically in its facilities, operations, transport, staffing levels, etc. This gives the operational equivalent of holding safety stock, as it gives slack that can be used for unexpected events – in the way that a warehouse might calculate the amount of storage it needs for normal operations and then add some extra capacity to cover unexpected events.

Remember that spare capacity is not earmarked for other purposes, such as planned growth, but it is set aside for unexpected events. This means that companies sometimes refer to base capacity as their normal needs, and reactive capacity is needed for unexpected events. Then spare capacity is more flexible than stock, as it can be used for any purpose – while stock is already committed to its final form. Spare capacity can create more stock, but stock cannot be transformed into spare capacity.

There are many ways of providing extra capacity, such as building bigger facilities, renting or leasing facilities at short notice, subcontracting operations, moving to build-to-order operations or adjusting work patterns (perhaps by changing shifts or product mixes). All of these can increase operating costs and reduce efficiency, but they may be the best way of avoiding disruptions. As usual, managers have to find a balance between the cost of providing the extra capacity and the expected costs of associated risks.

Agility

Methods of increasing the flexibility of an organization to deal with unexpected events are generally clustered under the heading of agility. Then agility means that operations are flexible enough to deal efficiently with rapidly changing conditions. For instance, rather than hold stock to allow for unexpectedly high demand, a firm can use flexible operations to increase production and deliver products with short lead times.

In practice, it is often difficult to predict the details of events that might follow risks, so agility is often the best response. This can be achieved in many different ways, such as:

- Short lead times, so that all changes are done quickly, making it possible to recover quickly from disruptions.
- Postponement, which delays finishing products until the last possible moment. For instance, a manufacturer of electrical equipment does not add the packaging, plugs, transformers and instructions to its products until it receives actual orders, and then it can customize products to specific market requirements.
- Standardized materials, so the same parts are used in different products, cutting down on stocks of materials, delivery problems, work in progress, number of suppliers, and so on. The important point for agility is that operations can switch from one product to another without waiting for deliveries of new materials.
- Standardized operations for different products so that they can switch seamlessly between products, with cross-trained employees moving to areas of shortage.
- Rapid rescheduling of operations, diverting work and materials away from areas of surplus and towards areas with shortages.
- Moving operations between different locations when the risks to one location increase, perhaps moving storage from one warehouse to another.
- Concurrent development to speed up new methods and products.
- Flexible suppliers, using multiple sources with different features to meet differing needs, different kinds of contract, and spot markets.
- Building to order rather than building for stock.

Downstream decoupling point

The downstream parts of a supply chain are generally controlled by direct customer demand. Retailers obviously experience final customer demand, and then pass this back to their suppliers, and so on through the tiers of the supply chain. But the upstream parts of the supply chain are insulated from final customer demand by the intervening tiers of members. A decoupling point is the most upstream point where final customer demand actually penetrates. Downstream of the decoupling point, all operations are controlled by final customer demand; upstream of the decoupling point all operations are controlled by forecasts and plans.

The decoupling point is also the point at which postponement can most easily be arranged, so generic stocks are held upstream and customized stocks downstream. The best policy is to move the decoupling point as far down-stream as possible. This reduces the total amount of stock, makes the response time faster – and reduces vulnerability.

IKEA

The Swedish furniture manufacturer and retailer IKEA has doubled sales every five years since its founding in 1949. But by 2002 its rapid expansion into 32 countries had left its supply chain looking somewhat dated and inefficient. The company started a programme to both improve supply chain efficiency and reduce the risks from its 2,000 suppliers in 56 countries. Its programme included:

■ Improve planning and forecasting – to reduce stock levels in distribution centres by 10 per cent.
■ Improve order management and increase cooperation with suppliers.
■ Adopt a balanced sourcing approach – standardizing sourcing procedures, increasing automation and using low-cost countries.
■ Balance cost cutting with business objectives – maintaining both supplies and environmentally responsible policies (for example, sourcing the bulk of its wood products from low-cost areas in Eastern Europe, while protecting itself against unpredictable lead times and deliveries by maintaining other sources closer to home).

Relationships within a resilient supply chain

In addition to the physical shape of a supply chain, resilience depends on the way that it is managed, and particularly the relationships between the different members of a chain.

Collaboration

Arguably the most important way to ensure a resilient supply chain is through integration, with members working together to solve mutual problems. Without a basic level of cooperation it is simply impossible to make any progress towards an integrated SCRM. As we have seen, this collaboration can take many forms, and can range from informal discussion to strategic alliances. But the most common forms share information to increase visibility – with more formal arrangements of vendor-managed inventory

(VMI), collaborative planning, forecasting and replenishment (CPFR), and synchronized material movement. We know that there are various reasons why collaboration is difficult to achieve, but mechanisms do exist and managers have to be persuaded to use them.

Whatever the details of the arrangements, cooperation takes collective action to deal with problems. This might mean very close collaboration with a small number of firms working so closely together that failure of a single member would have disastrous consequences for the rest. Or it might mean more distant, arm's-length relations with a broader set of suppliers, where the failure of one member can be alleviated by using a parallel path through the others. Neither of these approaches is inherently right or wrong, and the most appropriate depends on circumstances. A particularly successful approach is illustrated by Dell, which includes strong single-supplier relationships with Intel for its processors and Microsoft for its operating systems, and more distant relations with several vendors for other components.

Confidence in partners

Cooperation in risk management is only possible when there is some level of trust between partners. You might imagine that there must be some trust already, or else they would not be partners – and certainly there must also be some level of confidence in product quality, ability to deliver, quoted lead times, suppliers' capability to deliver, financial security, capacity and so on. But a basic trading relationship does not really imply much confidence in partners, and collaborative risk management must go some way beyond this (Christopher and Lee, 2004). Specifically, there must be confidence that each member of the chain can give continuing performance, managing its own risks and reducing the risks for others. There must also be confidence in each partner's ability to identify and share information about the risks it faces. As we have seen, this is a bold step, as suppliers are often chosen on the basis of their reliability – or detachment from risk.

Conversely, with little trust between members there is, by definition, more risk in the supply chain. And this encourages managers to use all the usual buffering and mitigating procedures for dealing with risky trading partners, including high safety stocks, over-ordering, long lead times, slow movements, decoupling of operations, demand inflation, and so on.

Confidence is the sort of thing that grows slowly during an extended trading relationship. It also relies on reputation, and a firm that has a good reputation is likely to be trusted quickly in preference to an organization that for some reason has a poor reputation. One positive way of generating confidence, at least on some level, is to monitor performance over some period to check that performance really does reach an acceptable level over the period. This is routinely done during trials and comparison studies. On a more formal basis it moves to vendor rating, which collects information about new or potential suppliers.

FKML Synergies

FKML advises firms on procurement methods, and it recommends that a fairly large amount of data be collected to allow vendor rating. This usually has the following elements:

- *Market intelligence* – describing the environment in which suppliers work, such as availability of materials, growth, prices, suppliers, locations, competition, special conditions, etc.
- *Supplier intelligence* – to show the underlying stability of a supplier and review its overall operations. Relevant details typically include the corporate functions (business units, mission, industries, markets, aims, etc), financial performance (sales, profit, credit rating, financing, bankruptcies, etc), business performance (strategies, policies, ethics, etc) and operations performance (products, locations, technology, markets, etc).
- *Supplier performance* – measuring performance achieved, such as lead times, service level, prices, quality, reliability, satisfaction levels and responsiveness.
- *Spending analysis* – giving details of the firm's expenditure at a supplier, along with patterns, trends and contractual arrangements – and generally reviewing the importance of the supplier to operations.
- *Forecasts* – to show how much the supplier might be used in the future, considering ordering policies, price, stocks, etc.
- *Supplier comparisons* – including analytical tools to compare bids from different suppliers and relate them to sourcing objectives, risks and constraints.

Visibility

Sharing information throughout the supply chain is the basis of visibility, which means the extent to which one member of the supply chain can see what is happening at all points in the chain. This information typically includes stock levels, demands, seasonality, promotions, new product introductions, industry and market conditions, operations and purchasing schedules, performance, risks, unexpected events, lost sales and any other relevant information.

When this information is passed freely between organizations there is high visibility, and managers in, say, a retailer can follow the movement of products from early suppliers, through manufacturers and on to their shops. But, if there is distrust and poor information flows, routine information is not transmitted by organizations, and the retailer now only talks to a wholesaler, doing little more than arranging delivery size and time. This inevitably increases risks, but it can have more severe consequences when, say, one member identifies a major risk but does not pass this information on. Then no one else may be aware of the risk or able to take the actions needed to manage it.

Visibility encourages an underlying aim of logistics managers, which is replacing inventory by information. Then it has the two key benefits of: 1) allowing managers to make informed and efficient joint plans for dealing with risks; and 2) reducing risks that come from poor communications, such as demand amplification. It also means that information can be transferred quickly when a risky event actually happens. For instance, a disruption at any point of the chain is signalled to all members, which can immediately take mitigating actions. At a simple level, a company might take immediate action to overcome a problem with supplier delivery, rather than wait until the next order is overdue to hear of the problem.

Sharing information has been a developing area for some time, and we can identify some key steps in this:

1. The first step occurred some time ago, when companies realized that they could benefit by sharing information with other members of the supply chain, breaking away from the 'silo mentality', mistrust and confrontation, and moving towards cooperation. This laid the principle that cooperation is better than conflict.
2. The second step was to overcome mistrust and fears about security and commercial secrecy – and recognize that a firm's viability is rarely compromised by passing some basic information to its trading partners. This made the exchange of information a possibility.
3. The third step was to overcome technological problems and the difficulty of connecting information systems. But now immediate communications are taken for granted in even the most dispersed supply chains, so the exchange of information becomes easy.

Now an exchange of information is a routine part of many operations. This allows companies like Benetton, the Italian clothing company, to build an extensive EDI network that links design centres, outsourced manufacturers, sales agents, transportation firms, logistics centres and retail shops. The highly visible chain lets all supply chain partners continuously monitor operations and immediately notice any problems. When this visibility is combined with flexible manufacturing, postponement, and high-technology logistics centres, the result is a very agile supply chain.

A 2004 survey into the visibility of supply chains found that a surprisingly high 44 per cent of firms are often or always taking actions to improve the visibility of their supply chains, while only 27 per cent of firms never or hardly ever did this (Jüttner, 2005). On the downside, this puts an even greater stress on the reliability of support systems, and it seems inevitable that new operations will push visibility even further and put even more pressure on the supply chain to deliver.

Process convergence

Visibility brings benefits to risk management, but it can also lead to other benefits, including the convergence of operations. You can see this with JIT, which is initiated in one organization, but its specific demands encourage other members of the supply chain to move towards JIT themselves. In other words, operations tend to converge to common standards and are eventually accepted as the normal way of working. Other initiatives have the same effect, particularly TQM – and increasingly risk management.

High velocity

The velocity of a supply chain is simply the speed at which materials move through from original suppliers to final customers. With a low velocity, materials spend a lot of time in stock, waiting for operations, moving between operations, and so on. This suggests that a lot of time is simply wasted. Time compression – and leanness in general – tries to eliminate this wasted time and increase velocity, to remove stock, delays and other operations that add no value.

Obvious benefits of high velocity are shorter lead times, greater agility, lower stocks, more responsive operations, and so on. Of course, the question is how to achieve this – and there are basically two options: 1) make existing operations faster and more efficient, by simplifying work and using more efficient equipment, more skilled people, parallel operations, standard tasks, synchronized schedules, and all the other techniques that are part of process improvement; and 2) remove unnecessary operations from the process, analysing current processes and removing any that do not add value from a customer's perspective.

Sudan red 1

In 1953 there was a salmonella epidemic in Sweden – thought to have originated in a slaughterhouse – that killed almost 100 people. This sort of incident makes people very wary of risks in their food, and public reactions to food scares are arguably getting more severe.

New technologies and methods are improving food safety, and there is a general feeling of lower risks. However, others methods are noticeably increasing the risk to food, such as sourcing in regions with uncertain attitudes towards food safety, longer supply chains that move food around the world, and untried technology.

Sudan red 1 is an industrial dye that has been banned as a food colourant throughout the EU since 2003. In 2005 it was found in a batch of chilli powder used by Premier Foods in the UK to manufacture Worcester sauce. There was an immediate scare over Premier Foods' products – and any other product that contained red dye – so 500 products were taken off store shelves. In effect, one contaminated batch of one ingredient immediately stopped all production and sales of 500 products, and many other intermediate products used by food processors. This was unavoidable, as no food can be sold with the possibility of containing an illegal substance. But the reality is that no products were actually contaminated, and no one bought any product containing Sudan red 1.

On the positive side, an average supermarket stocks 50,000 food items, so even 500 is a relatively small number. And risk management procedures moved very quickly to prevent any harm. The UK government alerted food agencies in European countries, and the European Commission's rapid alert system, and within minutes retailers' information systems were updated, blacklisting affected products and immediately preventing further sales. It also issued automatic press releases, along with television and radio warnings.

Within the food industry integrated systems distributed information, alerting firms by e-mail, direct electronic links and phone calls. Links back through the supply chains immediately stopped further movement of suspect material.

Lea & Perrins is the major supplier of Worcestershire sauce, and although it was not involved in the scare its website quickly received 18,000 hits. Probably because of the prompt action all round, Lea & Perrins' initial concerns that its brand would be affected proved untrue and its sales were not affected (Corbett, 2005).

Supplier relationship management

Many aspects of collaboration in the supply chain are summarized in 'supplier relationship management'. This is an umbrella term for procedures that allow an organization to cultivate new supply chain partners, maintain existing partners, reduce interruptions by spreading business among suppliers and locations, and managing risk with sole sources. Some specific methods associated with supplier relationship management include:

- detailed and shared understanding of the supply markets and industries;
- clear statements of expectations from suppliers;
- defined measures of supplier performance;
- performance-based contracts that include risk management;
- continuous monitoring to ensure that suppliers are meeting expectations;
- supplier development programmes to ensure the performance of suppliers that are critical to the success of the supply chain and that cannot be easily replaced;
- collaboration to find ways of improving SCM and tackle problems of mutual concern;
- monitoring the supply market to identify alternative sources of supply and to track the competitiveness of existing suppliers;
- exploring substitution to expand the potential supply base.

Risk compensation and business continuity

The features of every supply chain are different, so we cannot describe the details you would see in every resilient chain. We have mentioned some broad principles, but there are two other effects that we should mention. The first is risk compensation, which tends to counteract the efforts of risk managers.

Risk compensation is a rather difficult idea for risk managers, as it suggests that people are happy working with a particular level of risk. Some people are risk takers and seem to be happy to work with very high levels of risk; others are risk-averse and are unhappy when any significant risk appears. But the point is that, if the risks are reduced, people are likely to adjust their habits – generally being more reckless – until risks return to the original level. The usual illustration for this effect is seat belts in cars. Wearing seat belts reduces the risks of driving, but it appears that people then drive more dangerously to return the risk to its original level. In a supply chain context, this means that using integrated SCRM to reduce the overall risk encourages members to behave more recklessly in their organizational decisions until the risk returns to its original level. Imagine a wholesaler that keeps a safety stock to give cover for an unreliable supplier. The wholesaler can replace the supplier by a more reliable one, thereby reducing its risk. But it will then reduce the safety stock to the level that raises risk to the same risk as before.

The consequences of risk compensation for SCRM are obvious, as they suggest that any attempts to reduce risk will be met by changing practices, carelessness or complacency that return the risks to their previous level. So measures designed to increase supply chain resilience are less effective than expected.

This is a very difficult type of problem to solve, and there is no immediate experience that can suggest a solution. The whole idea of risk compensation is open to some discussion, and its effects are not universally recognized. Nonetheless, there is evidence to support it from the insurance industry, where simply taking out insurance affects the events that might occur.

The second effect to mention is business continuity planning. We have discussed ways of dealing with risk in the supply chain, but we cannot identify, let alone mitigate the effects of, every possible risk. Some events will still come as complete surprises. The way of dealing with these is to design a general response that can be used for any severe disruption to the supply chain. This emergency plan can be used to deal with any kind of unexpected crisis – using the reasoning that, if you do not know exactly what will happen, you should be agile enough to cope with anything. This is the basis of emergency planning – or more generally business continuity planning – which we discuss in the following chapter.

In summary

In the last chapter we considered the idea of integrated SCRM. This chapter shows what this actually involves. And a key principle is that the design of a supply chain has a fundamental effect on the inherent risk, so managers should work together to design resilient chains. A number of standard principles apply to the design of resilient supply chains, such as starting within individual organizations, taking a strategic view, really understanding the concept of supply chain risk, designing chains with risk in mind, always looking for collaborative solutions, and so on.

All supply chains vary in detail, but there are some common features of resilient chains. Some of these are essentially physical features, with a resilient supply chain being short, wide and agile, with spare capacity, and so on. Other features refer to relationships, with a resilient chain having collaboration, confidence in partners, visibility, process integration, etc, to allow a joint solution of mutual problems.

Even the best risk management has unexpected events, and when these are severe they are generally described as crises or disasters. The way of dealing with these is to design emergency plans that can be used to deal with any crisis. We discuss these in the next chapter.

11

Business continuity management

Emergencies and crises

In the last few chapters we have developed a view of supply chain risk management that is based on the core activities of identifying, analysing and responding to risks. But we also know that some risks are inherently unknowable and cannot be identified in advance. These give events that managers cannot predict and they always come as complete surprises. So how can organizations deal with these? The answer comes from a different type of approach that is not based on an analysis of identified risks – but instead looks for ways of dealing with actual disruptions to a supply chain, regardless of how these disruptions occurred. For instance, an organization may consider the failure in a key transport link and see what it can do to get operations working again, regardless of how the damage was done to the transport link.

Here the aim is not to analyse a risk and see how to mitigate its effects, but to consider the elements of a supply chain, see what happens when the element is unavailable, and make plans to restore the flows of materials when the element is unavailable. This kind of planning is often associated with severe consequences – such as the catastrophic failure of some part of a supply chain – often causing crises or emergencies. So the approach has become known by different names, notably 'emergency planning', 'disaster recovery' and the more positive 'business continuity management' (BCM). Logistics managers are most likely to discuss 'crisis management' – a term they might use to describe anything from a late payment to the destruction of a substantial part of a supply chain.

- Crisis management designs procedures to deal with severe, unexpected disruption to a supply, however the disruptions were caused.
- The general term 'business continuity management' describes the methods that ensure the essential business functions continue to work through an emergency.

The Department of Trade and Industry (2006) gives a broad definition of business continuity management as 'a process developed to counteract systems failure'. In its website the Business Continuity Institute gives a more specific view of 'anticipating incidents which will affect mission critical functions and processes for the organisation and ensuring that it responds to any incident in a planned and rehearsed manner whilst the business recovers'. But this definition does not make it clear how BCM differs from standard approaches to risk management and their process of identification, analysis and response. Similarly, the British Standards Institute (2006) describes 'an holistic management process that identifies potential impacts that threaten an organisation and provides a framework for building resilience with the capability for an effective response that safeguards the interests of its key stakeholders, reputation, brand and value creating activities'.

Although views differ, the consensus is that risk management responds to specific identified risks, while BCM develops ways of responding to unidentified or unidentifiable risks. A company that considers the risk of storm damage to a warehouse is doing risk management; when it decides what to do if the warehouse becomes unavailable it is doing BCM. An organization that analyses the risks of a key supplier going bankrupt is doing risk analysis; one that plans its actions if supplies are unavailable is doing BCM. Depending on circumstances, the difference might be minor and subtle, or it might suggest fundamentally different approaches. For instance, you can take out insurance against storm damage, but BCM might make wider recommendations, such as having backup facilities that can be used in an emergency.

Risk management and BCM are clearly very closely related, and many people view the two as indistinguishable or at best different aspects of the same function. Some people say that risk management is really a part of broader BCM; others argue that BCM is really a part of broader risk management. Other people say that the two are distinct functions, and you can certainly find them run by different departments within a company. As usual, there are clearly differences in the terms, but these are often semantic rather than conceptual.

Perhaps the fairest view is that risk management is expanding in two directions. The first direction extends the traditional methods of risk management into new areas, which is increasingly known as 'operational risk management'. Our concern is how this expansion has led to SCRM. The second direction is towards a strategic view. Senior managers are looking at survival and viability during severe disruptions, which is increasingly described as 'enterprise risk management'.

Whatever we call the two directions, managing the risk of disruption to the supply chain can include both of these activities. Traditional risk management focuses on identifiable risks, analysing vulnerability and defining responses to known risky events that might occur. Then BCM gives a backup, showing how to deal with any events that were not anticipated and may even have been unknowable. You can imagine this as having risk management dealing with routine planning, and then BCM doing the repairs when the planning fails.

Tien-Shu Kowloon Ltd

Tien-Shu has recently been expanding its international markets and is increasingly concerned at its ability to guarantee deliveries to distant locations. One of its concerns is at the start of its operations, where it relies on suppliers to deliver raw materials.

The company routinely does an ABC analysis of materials, with A items being the 10 per cent of expensive items that account for 70 per cent of purchasing costs, and C items being the least expensive 70 per cent of items that account for 10 per cent of purchasing costs. But it is not just the value of purchases that is important, as suppliers of A items are generally the most critical, there are fewer alternative suppliers, and switching to another supplier gives significant costs. So the suppliers of these items are the key ones that Tien-Shu relies on.

The company does vendor rating and analysis to identify significant risks, but it is not accustomed to working closely with suppliers and realizes that it cannot identify all of the risks. Instead, it considers the consequences of failure of each key supplier, and ensures that it has plans to allow continuing operations in an emergency, or at least to resume operations after as short a break as possible. These plans include safety stock to give short-term cover, and alternative suppliers for longer-term problems. However, Tien-Shu also insists that its key suppliers use BCM to minimize the chance of breakdowns in their own operations, including policies for reserve stocks, spare parts, equipment maintenance and so on. Tien-Shu considers this an essential part of its own emergency plans, and hopes to develop more collaborative risk management in the future.

Use of BCM

BCM focuses on plans that allow an organization to continue working, or recover quickly, after a damaging event. Its essential features are:

■ analyses of a supply chain, identifying the elements that might be subject to disruption and the likely consequences of a breakdown;
■ design of plans to show what to do when an element is disrupted – especially how to ensure that key processes continue working normally or recover from any disruption as quickly as possible;
■ monitoring of operations to identify a crisis or trigger for the emergency plans;
■ activation of rehearsed plans to deal with the emergency;
■ when things have returned to normal, analyses of events to see what happened, learn lessons for the future and revise the emergency plans.

This is such a basic idea that you might imagine that it is a fairly standard procedure in supply chains, but a survey by Computer Sciences Corporation (2004) found that only 38 per cent of respondents had a written contingency plan to deal with a significant disruption. Of the remainder, 42 per cent did not have a written plan and 20 per cent did not know. However, there are signs that it is becoming more common, and a related survey (Chartered Management Institute, 2005) found that, in 2005, 51 per cent of firms had some kind of BCM plans to cover critical business activities, compared with 47 per cent in 2004, 46 per cent in 2003 and 45 per cent in 2002.

Not surprisingly, disruption of IT systems is a common theme for BCM, with 78 per cent of managers saying that losing IT systems was their greatest fear, and 74 per cent of contingency plans addressing this problem (Institute of Management, 1999). Presumably the banking and finance systems that are needed to keep organizations functioning are included in this general heading of IT. And Ginn (1989) was an early voice saying that disaster recovery was not just about computer systems, but was a broader subject that included all kinds of threats. This is recognized to a growing extent, but the 1999 survey still suggested that BCM plans were not necessarily addressing managers' main concerns. There were apparently marked differences between the perceived threats to operations and the problems that continuity management addresses. Notably, disruptions to the supply were recognized as posing a considerable threat to organizations' continuing performance, particularly with just-in-time operations, but only 32 per cent of BCM plans involved purchasing and logistics. When the survey was repeated in 2000, 93 per cent of managers reported that their businesses had been disrupted by the recent fuel crisis, and 64 per cent reported that heavy flooding in many areas of the UK had disrupted their businesses. They had struggled to get staff into work and materials to move into and out of their firms, as few had any contingency plans to deal with damage to transport and logistics facilities. Despite this, there were surprisingly few plans to extend BCM to the supply chain.

A brief survey (Scarborough, 2007) suggests that managers are most commonly concerned with the following types of disruption:

■ loss of information technology systems (76 per cent);
■ loss of telecommunication systems (67 per cent);
■ fire damage to facilities (52 per cent);
■ damage to the corporate image (47 per cent);
■ loss of skilled staff (42 per cent);
■ employee health and safety (41 per cent);
■ supply chain disruption (39 per cent);
■ access to facilities (32 per cent);
■ an environmental incident (31 per cent);
■ severe weather (27 per cent);
■ product safety (16 per cent);
■ terrorist damage (14 per cent).

It is clearly more difficult to make contingency plans for some of these concerns than others. For instance, it is fairly easy to back up data and have duplicate facilities at remote locations to deal with failure of information and telecommunications systems. But it is much more difficult to prepare for something as nebulous as damage to the corporate image. This makes people suggest that BCM is often aimed at areas that are easiest to manage, rather than those that are potentially most damaging. This may be the reason that, say, access to the site is often included in BCM, but damage to the corporate image is not. Only six types of emergency seem to be covered by most BCM plans (Chartered Management Institute, 2005):

■ loss of information technology capacity (82 per cent);
■ loss of telecommunications (73 per cent);
■ fire (70 per cent);
■ access to the site (68 per cent);
■ interruption of utilities (58 per cent);
■ terrorist damage (54 per cent).

Features of a disaster

BCM essentially prepares for disaster recovery, and you can imagine this in terms of a natural disaster such as an earthquake, fire or severe weather. Natural disasters occur completely unexpectedly, the risks are inherently unknowable in advance, and firms want to return to normal operations as soon as possible. Bosman (2006) makes the point that we quickly forget or underestimate how damaging these events can be. The 1995 earthquake in Kobe, Japan, killed more than 6,400 people, destroyed 100,000 buildings, closed Japan's largest port for two months, caused widespread disruption to industry, and caused more than US$100 billion in damage.

But for any single organization a disaster can be something as minor as a lost customer, a bad debt, industrial action, failure of an information system or loss of a key supplier. If you consider IT systems, most failures are not caused by catastrophic natural events or real emergencies, but are more likely to arise from poorly managed system upgrades or loss of staff with key skills (Jüttner, 2005). Similarly, loss of a facility is most likely to follow a physical network reconfiguration (Peck, 2003), while routine maintenance is a major cause of subsequent equipment failure. And indiscriminate introduction of new methods – including lean operations, outsourcing, JIT or relocation of operations – causes many system failures. Unfortunately, we have to recognize that many failures actually stem from management mistakes that could have been avoided, rather than the effects of real emergencies that were unknowable in advance.

Whatever the cause, the two essential features of a disaster are that: 1) events are very rare, with such a low probability of occurrence that they do not even register as anticipated risks; and 2) there are very severe consequences when an event occurs.

Dealing with disasters

The fact that disasters are very unlikely to happen is the reason why so many organizations do no adequate planning. If you calculate the expected value of a disaster it is low, simply because of the very low probability of it occurring. This suggests that BCM deserves little attention, which is the reason that managers often seem reluctant to accept that their companies are vulnerable to disasters and prefer to take the attitude that 'It will never happen to us.' Of course, even rare events happen sometimes, and without BCM organizations are ill prepared and unable to respond at critical times, when they face a complete breakdown of operations. Deloitte (2005) found that many of the greatest losses in market capitalization were attributable to events that were considered extremely unlikely and for which companies had apparently failed to plan. Affected companies lost more than 20 per cent of their market value in the month after a major event, and it often took more than a year before their shares returned to the previous levels.

The combination of low probability and high consequences gives emergencies a low expected value, but they are of considerable importance. This suggests that they should not be managed by the usual tools of risk management. The argument is that an organization cannot run the risk of complete failure – however unlikely this is – and it should make generic plans to allow continuing operations in any emergency. This view is similar in spirit to very high levels of quality management, where standard procedures are used to monitor operations and make sure that things are working normally. At the same time people are looking for ways of continuously improving performance, with the ultimate goal of perfect quality – or at least 'six sigma' quality, which corresponds to two or three defects per million units. Here quality management is looking for ways of avoiding the very rare defects that can affect product quality, in the way that BCM is preparing for the very rare events that threaten operations.

This rarity raises other problems, as managers base most of their planning on information and experience of past events – we know what did and did not work in the past and can design plans based on this information to make the best decisions for the future. But, by definition, disasters are so rare that few of us have close experience of, say, a major fire let alone an earthquake or hurricane. So we lack the body of experience that is the basis of most of our decisions.

Requirements of BCM

For supply chains, the basic requirement of BCM is that the flow of materials is not interrupted by any disaster hitting the chain, or that it is able to return to normal as quickly as possible. This means that there must be available:

■ enough people with the necessary expertise and skills to activate and manage the BCM process;
■ people to keep key functions working in the organization – with acceptable levels of safety, rewards, welfare and accommodation;
■ the various facilities and resources needed to allow business processes to keep functioning;
■ critical IT and communications systems, records and infrastructure;
■ the ability to procure, move and manage material flows;
■ the capability to establish communications with all staff and other concerned bodies – which is important, as many emergencies involve a broader group of stakeholders, including media, public sector regulators, police, pressure groups, etc;
■ records to allow learning from the experience.

As usual, an organization cannot ensure these requirements by simply waiting until an emergency occurs and then organizing its response, but to react in a reasonable time it must make plans for generic emergencies in advance. In most cases, operations can be restored without a full complement of staff, systems and facilities, so BCM is concerned with managing the available resources as effectively as possible. There may only be limited resources, but with careful planning these should be enough to maintain customer service. Often this means that there are two real objectives of recovery plans. The first is to get operations up to the level of giving an acceptable minimum service. This is a clear priority that managers want to achieve as quickly as possible. Then when a reasonable level of service has been restored, there is some more time to work on less pressing problems. The second objective is to restore full operations to normal working. Although speed is also important here, there can be more flexibility.

In practice, we can extend this idea of emergency plans working in phases and say that the first priority is really to ensure the safety of everyone concerned. Then we can suggest a rough outline for emergency plans, requiring them to:

1. *Ensure the physical safety of employees, customers, visitors and everyone else associated with the operations.* Taking steps to ensure the health and welfare of all stakeholders must be the primary concern of any emergency plans.
2. *Protect business facilities and assets.* When people's safety is ensured, the next consideration is usually to protect the organization's facilities, so that it has the resources needed for a quick recovery.
3. *Implement the procedures for returning a minimum acceptable level of service.* The purpose here is to work internally and ensure that key processes can deliver some level of service as quickly as possible and preferably without supply chain partners being affected.
4. *Work with supply chain partners to restore appropriate services.* Having done the work to get internal operations working (at least to some extent), managers can work with partners to see if they are affected, the specific services they need, and how these can best be provided. The aim here is to work externally and get operations in the broader supply chain functioning.
5. *Restore full operations in a timely and cost-effective way.* Ideally, this should be done as quickly as possible, but when an acceptable service is restored the pressure is somewhat removed and managers can start focusing on timetables and budgets. As always, there is a balance between getting things back to normal quickly and the costs involved.

Benefits of BCM

BCM prepares an organization for any emergency, with rapid, planned and practised responses. These aim at maintaining or restoring an organization's essential operations, so the basic benefit of BCM is that it helps an organization survive an emergency.

■ The fundamental aim of BCM is to help an organization survive and recover from an emergency.

Some more immediate benefits include:

- survival, even when hit by a major crisis;
- careful management that reduces the impact of an emergency and allows a faster recovery;
- better emergency plans, based on more careful analysis and flexible responses to emergencies;
- a competitive advantage over organizations that are not so well prepared;
- meeting the requirements of an increasing number of trading partners for adequate emergency plans;
- working together with trading partners to build sound BCM plans, encouraging further collaboration and improving the retention of suppliers and customers;
- improved – and guaranteed – service levels, making it easier to win and retain customers;
- demonstration of commitment to recovery, giving better rates and conditions for insurance;
- meeting statutory requirements for BCM – which exist in, say, financial institutions.

Volvo

Volvo, the Swedish automobile manufacturer (now a subsidiary of Ford), manages disturbances in the supply chain with the help of two planning documents (Svensson, 2000):

1. A logistics assurance document file (LADF), which describes the firm's intention of avoiding disruptions and its methods for achieving this. The file contains documents, procedures and policies aimed at preventing disruptions to the physical flow of materials from subcontractors in the supply chain. The documents contain steps, reports, guidelines and checklists for both Volvo and its suppliers to assure continuing logistics flows. The procedures apply to both Volvo and its suppliers and include areas such as logistics objectives, time schedules, a list of planning team members, EDI contracts, analyses of the effects of logistics failure, flexibility, capacity plans and logistics assurance plans.

2. A quality assurance document file (QADF), which is similar to the LADF in its overall structure and intention, but addresses quality assurance of the components and materials. Therefore, the procedural steps include quality targets, quality assurance plans, experiences from quality planning, quality output, quality risks and potential for improvement.

Volvo says that these two documents help to minimize its exposure to risks in the supply chain.

Steps in business continuity management

The basis of business continuity management is to identify the key operations in a process (here key elements of a supply chain), study the consequences if these parts are, for any reason, not available and then design plans to make sure that key operations can continue through any circumstances, even the most damaging. These plans are contained in a business continuity plan – which is alternatively known as a business recovery plan, disaster plan, disaster recovery plan, contingency plan or other similar name.

BCM runs along similar lines to traditional risk management, so we can describe similar steps in its development. In particular, we will consider six main steps, running from initiating the BCM process through to monitoring and controlling its working:

1. *Initiate the process of BCM.* This covers the usual initial stages of recognizing that a need exists, getting a sponsor, getting senior management support, forming a BCM team, getting a budget, acquiring resources, getting approvals, and so on.
2. *Define the requirements of BCM and develop a strategy to achieve them.* This gives the foundation for BCM and includes the long-term aims and how these fit in with other business strategies. At the core of this strategy is the way that the organization views risk, and the options for balancing risk reduction and recovery.
3. *Assess the risks.* For this we can use a variation of the traditional identify, analyse and respond steps:
   - Identify vulnerable operations. This starts by considering all elements of the supply chain, and identifying the ones that are critical to normal working. BCM accepts that it is impossible to identify all possible risks, as some are inherently unidentifiable, but we can identify the parts of the supply chain that must continue working for sustainable operations.

- Analyse the impact when a key operation is no longer available. This step, often described as 'business impact analysis', analyses the consequences for the organization of any kind of failure in a key operation. Ideally, managers might be able to assign some kind of probability that the key operation will fail, but the essence of BCM is that it is impossible to find realistic probabilities and there is no point in calculating expected values.
- Design options for dealing with the emergency (meaning that the key operation is not working). Generally, the options are the same as with normal risk management, including acceptance, avoidance, transfer and so on.

4. *Prepare the business continuity plan.* At this point managers have a clear picture of the key operations that are vulnerable to unspecified risks and that are best dealt with by BCM. And they know how to deal with a failure in these key areas. All details of the procedures for BCM are now presented in a business continuity plan. Essentially, this plan shows how an organization will respond to a disaster and how it will resume its business, so it must contain all information needed to help the organization restore normal working. The contents vary, but typically include:

   - statements of when the BCM procedures will be activated – in other words a description of the events that constitute an emergency severe enough to trigger the BCM response;
   - organizational roles and responsibilities for activities, including succession if initial responsibilities are untenable;
   - procedures for assessing the scope and actual impact of an emergency;
   - organization and routeing of communications during the crisis;
   - procedures for activating the recovery team, or perhaps one recovery team for each critical business activity;
   - procedures for managing the emergency, including responses, jobs undertaken by the recovery team, salvage, public relations, retrieval of backup data, installation of emergency communications, the possible move of operations to a secure location, emergency sourcing of materials, etc;
   - procedures to ensure the safety and health of all staff and visitors, including food, water, shelter, clean air, security and medical support;
   - descriptions of the roles of all support functions, such as finance, IT systems, telecommunications, security, personnel, finance, etc;
   - procedures for evacuation and shelter, including non-employees such as visitors, customers, suppliers and contractors who are on-site;
   - arrangements for secure backup, normally at a remote site, of key business systems and data.

5. *Implement the business continuity plan.* When the business continuity plan has been designed and agreed, it is time for implementation (meaning

implementing the plans and not activation of the actual disaster recovery procedures). This involves the usual procedures for introducing new plans, including communication, discussion, training and so on. Activation comes when a crisis is identified, and then the emergency procedures identified in the plan are started. So implementation makes the organization ready to deal with an emergency, and activation uses the planned procedures to deal with the emergency in earnest.

An important point is that an organization can only be confident that its business continuity plan will work quickly and effectively if it periodically practises the response. You see this in fire drills, where the business continuity plan specifies evacuation procedures, and these are practised through routine drills. So as well as designing the plans, there should be tests to make sure that the plans work. For these tests, different types of emergency are suggested, and the procedures are gone through to make sure that they have the desired results. These tests highlight any weaknesses and problems with the plans, they show procedures that can be improved, they raise awareness for the need and importance of BCM, and they give the organization confidence that it can recover from a crisis.

The tests should aim at testing some specific aspect of procedures, and there should be measurable results to see if the results are satisfactory. For instance, a fire drill might check that a building can be evacuated within 15 minutes. This can be done by either theoretical exercises (simulating crises and recovery procedures) or practical trials (using real procedures to test the operations in earnest). You see how these alternatives work with emergency evacuation of aeroplanes. Business continuity plans describe procedures for getting passengers from planes; computer simulations test procedures to see if these will work in theory; trial evacuations with real passengers (or at least volunteer substitutes) test whether the plans work in practice. The full technical tests should replicate crisis conditions as closely as possible, using actual procedures and involving external parties. And the principle underlying all tests is that procedures are more efficient when practised, rehearsed and well tested.

6. *After the plans are implemented they should not be left, but continually monitored and tested, with adjustments to allow for changing conditions.* The aim is to ensure that the strategy, facilities and procedures are maintained as part of day-to-day business activities. This can involve different activities, including periodic reviews, reinforcing awareness, training and education, and change management. Although the reviews should be done continually, they are particularly important when introducing new products, processes, equipment, facilities, sites, suppliers, trading partners or any other significant change.

Pulitzer-Brand-Heimleich Inc

Pulitzer-Brand-Heimleich (PBH) is a small chemical company in lower Saxony, Germany, with other production facilities in Slovakia and Georgia. Chemical processes often involve risk, and the company take its management very seriously. It has well-developed risk strategies and crisis plans to ensure rapid recovery from emergencies. Although these cover the usual areas of IT failure, supply chain failure, etc, their main emphasis is on dealing with accidents during chemical processes.

Part of the plans include a series of procedure manuals – usually described less formally as 'crib sheets' – that show what each team involved in emergency procedures should do. A typical crib sheet contains:

- a review of the company's attitudes towards risk and its risk strategies;
- a description of the types of emergency covered by the team;
- a statement of the membership of the team and contact details;
- general responsibilities of the team and its individual members;
- circumstances that trigger actions by the team;
- details of the actions the team will take in different circumstances, ranging from minor adjustments to operations for minor incidents through to closure of plants and associated actions for major crises;
- facilities, resources and funds available for the team;
- assembly points, recovery sites and incident control centres and details of how to get there;
- timetables for both restoring a minimum level of operations and returning to full working;
- useful contacts;
- the names of the people who designed the plan and updated it.

Types of response

In practice, crisis management often involves informal arrangements and rules of thumb that have evolved through experience or trials. So a simple rule might go along the lines of 'When the IT systems fail, switch to the remote backup system', 'When a facility is unavailable, use a designated and tested subcontractor' or 'When a key delivery is delayed, switch from road to air transport.' Another guideline is that all supply chain partners need not be treated equally. For instance, when deliveries are disrupted it makes sense to prioritize customers and give preferential treatment to those in strategic alliances, the largest, the most profitable, those with long-term contracts or others that deserve special treatment. Unfortunately, this has the disadvantage of moving resources away from customers that have no claim to special treatment. And, of course, this can harm relationships with customers that are currently small but have potential for growth and increasing long-term benefits. In reality, if an organization is open and fair, communicates with customers and restores normal operations quickly, this kind of preferential treatment might not cause too much damage.

In the same way, an organization need not treat all its suppliers equally. Managers should be most concerned with sole sources of key materials and give them preferential treatment. Of course the drawback is that suppliers of less important items are treated less well, but these are generally less important and can be replaced without a significant impact on operations.

One other point about responses is that they need not be immediate but can develop over some period. This happens when emergencies do not suddenly occur but grow over time – in the way that political, economic or industrial crises often tend to develop fairly slowly. This suggests two important facts. First, by monitoring conditions managers have more time to prepare and adjust their response. For instance, managers may detect a move towards disastrous industrial action. By monitoring the details they can make fine adjustments to their continuity plan to ensure the best response. Second, managers may have to decide when an emergency exists and they have to activate the continuity plan. Of course, this is obvious with an earthquake or fire, but the effects of a serious fraud might become more apparent over time, and at some point managers have to make a positive decision that action is needed. Both of these effects suggest the importance of careful monitoring to see if conditions are changing.

Monitoring and control

All organizations work with continuous change, so the threats they face and the most appropriate actions also change. At the very least, managers responsible for emergency planning should do periodic reviews to identify significant changes to:

■ internal operations, products, systems, employees, finances, etc;
■ identifiable risks facing the supply chain and its vulnerabilities to unidentifiable threats;
■ the impacts of failure of different parts of the supply chain;
■ the procedures for dealing with crises.

Some organizations prefer to do such reviews periodically, say annually, while others review procedures whenever there are major changes to the supply chain, organization or environment. Within these major reviews, adjustments can be made for less important changes, such as new personnel, results from tests and practices, and responses to normal day-to-day changes.

But if BCM needs continuing changes, we enter the area of change management. Many organizations have formal change management procedures, and then it becomes relatively straightforward to include BCM in these, giving an established mechanism for revising the systems and procedures of crisis management. This link to change management also ensures that the broad span of changes within the organization and its environment are routinely fed back to risk managers. In this sense, change management complements BCM and highlights issues that might otherwise be overlooked.

Education and awareness also come within the scope of monitoring and control, ensuring that everyone is familiar with BCM procedures, their roles and responsibilities, and what they are expected to do in an emergency, in other words that people are familiar with the business continuity plan. The training can take many forms, starting with simple activities, such as knowing how to evacuate a building and move to assembly points when there is a fire. And the training can move up to more sophisticated actions, such as medical assistance, IT staff restoring systems, trauma counselling or any of the many possible specialized functions. With proper training, everyone should know their role in dealing with any emergency that hits their organization.

Department of Trade and Industry – 10-point plan

The UK's Department of Trade and Industry (2006) – in association with the Business Continuity Institute and the Disaster Recovery Institute International – summarizes the business continuity management process. This is phrased in terms of a 10-point plan for running a project to implement BCM:

1. *Project initiation and management.* Identify a business continuity manager, get support and sponsorship from senior managers and establish a management structure.
2. *Risk evaluation and control.* Do a risk assessment and identify procedures for reducing and mitigating risk.
3. *Business impact analysis.* Identify critical business processes, assess the impact of their loss and consider the interdependencies between operations.
4. *Developing business continuity strategies.* Consider both recovery and risk reduction, set timetables for business recovery, and consider related strategies and support for operations.

5. *Emergency response and operations.* Establish a crisis management process for responding to emergencies, and ensure that all team members are aware of their responsibilities.
6. *Developing and implementing business continuity plans.* Design business continuity plans to support the strategy, and ensure their ownership and management.
7. *Awareness and training plans.* Make sure that all staff are aware of business continuity management and that this is promoted as an ongoing initiative, train recovery teams in their roles and responsibilities, and ensure that IT and other specialist groups are aware of their responses and can provide the necessary support.
8. *Maintaining and exercising business continuity plans.* Assign responsibilities for maintaining the plans, ensure that they are regularly maintained and tested, and update the plans to reflect changes in business operations.
9. *Public relations and crisis coordination.* Include both internal and external communications in the business continuity plans and ensure that procedures are in place to keep all stakeholders informed of the current status.
10. *Coordination with public authorities.* Inform local authorities and emergency services about the plans and ensure that procedures and policies comply with statutes and regulations.

As you can imagine from the Department of Trade and Industry's 10-point plan, when an organization does not already have procedures in place for continuity planning it can be a major effort to introduce them. But remember that everything does not have to be done at once, and managers can make progress over some period. However, there are always different views of how this should be done, and the following example gives an alternative.

Expecting the unexpected

The National Counter Terrorism Security Office (2006), London First and the Business Continuity Institute produced a booklet, *Expecting the Unexpected*, that summarizes five steps needed to develop a business continuity plan. These steps are described as:

1. *Analyse your business.* Working with the support of senior management, understand your business and the way it works, including identification of the functions that are essential and where vulnerabilities lie.

2. *Assess the risks.* Understand the emergencies that might affect your business and the impacts they could have. By focusing on impacts rather than causes, your plan will be broad enough to deal effectively with an incident, no matter what the source.

3. *Develop your strategy.* Agree with senior management the organization's overall view of risk. You can then decide which risks can be accepted, which risks can be reduced and which risks should be managed using BCM.

4. *Develop your plan.* Develop BCM plans covering the agreed areas. All plans look different, but they should be clear about roles and responsibilities, easy to understand and open for consultation and review around your organization.

5. *Rehearse your plan.* This helps to confirm that your plans will work and be robust enough if ever they are needed. Rehearsals are also a good way of training staff who have BCM responsibilities. Lessons from exercises can be used to refine your decisions in steps 1 to 4.

In summary

Risk management is based on the three core activities of identifying, analysing and responding to risks. But often there is no way of identifying risks in advance – especially the category of inherently unknowable risks. Then another approach is needed, and this is provided by business continuity management.

BCM is known by a number of titles, and it describes an approach to dealing with unexpected emergencies. The characteristic of BCM is that it does not analyse risks, but instead considers the elements of a supply chain, sees what happens when an element is unavailable, and makes plans to restore the flows of materials when the element is unavailable. In other words, it does not look for the causes of problems, but concentrates on dealing with the effects. So supply chain managers might use traditional risk management for identifiable risks, with BCM giving a backup for dealing with events that could not be anticipated.

Surveys suggest that BCM is becoming more widely used, but they also raise doubts about whether the issues faced are the most important. Problems with supply chain security still appear in surprisingly few BCM plans.

BCM typically prepares for disasters, which are very rare events that can have devastating consequences. The expected values of disasters are low, but they still deserve attention, suggesting that they cannot fit into normal risk management procedures. For supply chains, the basic requirement of BCM is that the flow of materials is not interrupted by any disaster hitting the chain, or that it is able to return to normal as quickly as possible.

The process for BCM is similar to that for risk management, and we described it in six steps, ranging from preparation for BCM through to monitoring and control. As usual, there are different views of the steps needed.

12

Review

Risk and the supply chain

In this book we have developed the idea of supply chain risk management. Unfortunately, when you collect any group of managers and ask them to discuss risk in the supply chain, they will rarely agree on the meaning of either 'risk' or 'the supply chain'. So our initial problem is to make sure that we are all talking about the same thing. For this, the early chapters review the underlying principles of risk and supply chain management.

In general, risk is viewed as the potential harm from unforeseen events. As we cannot say with certainty what will happen in the future, there is risk in all operations. We can develop analyses for this based on the standard features of decisions. In particular, we can categorize the doubts about future events as certainty, uncertainty, risk and ignorance. With certainty we know exactly which event will occur; with uncertainty we can list possible events but not give them probabilities; with risk we can add probabilities; with ignorance we cannot even list the possible events. In reality, 'risk' is generally used to suggest any level of doubt.

Supply chain management

Logistics, or supply chain management, is responsible for the movement and storage of materials. We take a broad view with materials as everything that moves, including both tangible goods and intangible services; and a supply chain is a series of activities and organizations that materials move through on their way from initial suppliers to final customers. Each product has its own supply chain, and these can form very long and complicated webs of inter-acting parts.

The aim of SCM is to move materials along the supply chain efficiently enough to give both high customer satisfaction and low costs. To achieve these, managers must design both the structure of the supply chain and the methods of controlling the flow of materials.

The broad function of SCM integrates several different activities ranging from procurement through to physical distribution. The cost of these activities varies widely, but is typically around 15–20 per cent of revenue. This means that SCM is in the awkward position of being both essential and expensive. Any disruption to the supply chain can be very damaging to the whole organization and the broader supply chain. This recognition is encouraging more logistics managers to introduce formal methods for supply chain risk management (SCRM).

The complex and diverse nature of supply chains makes them particularly vulnerable to risk. Some of these risks are external to the supply chain and outside managers' control; others are internal the organization and to some extent under the managers' control. Because they link a large number of disparate members, risks in one area are transmitted to other members – and a small event in one remote area can grow into major consequences for another area.

SCM is evolving quickly, with managers under continuing pressure to find better ways of organizing their logistics. These improvements are changing both the activities that are done in logistics and the way that they are done. Managers generally aim at lower costs (corresponding to a strategy of cost leadership) or better customer service (corresponding to product differentiation). A worrying trend is that new methods aimed at achieving these goals are inadvertently increasing risk.

We can illustrate this effect with several trends. For instance, organizations are moving toward greater integration of their supply chains. This brings many benefits, but it also increases some risks through, say, greater reliance on fewer trading partners. In the same way, an emphasis on cost reduction can remove all slack from the supply chain, increasing vulnerability to unexpected events; agility emphasizes customer service, but increases the risks of reduced financial and operational performance; improved communications are essential, but they make the supply chain vulnerable to any problem in the network of systems; globalization continues to grow, but increases risks from working in distant and unfamiliar locations; outsourcing should improve performance, but increases the risks from lost control and reliance on external partners. The message is clear, that SCM is an inherently risky function, and the risks are inadvertently drifting upwards.

Risk

Risk is generally viewed as the chance that an unexpected event will harm an organization. In principle, risk only suggests uncertainty, so it can also be beneficial, but managers tend to be pessimistic and focus on the negative impact. In practice, there are many types of risk to the supply chain, ranging from minor inconveniences through to the complete destruction of the chain. The idea of positively managing these risks is new, even though logistics managers have traditionally used standard methods to mitigate the most obvious effects (such as high stocks and spare capacity). More usually, managers tend to ignore risks to the supply chain, and take reactive action when an unforeseen event actually occurs. Unfortunately, this reactive approach is too slow, and a lot of harm can be done before it begins to have an effect. A better approach to risk management is proactive, analysing likely events before they occur and planning steps to mitigate their effects.

Risk management has a long history, originally developing through gambling, insurance and actuarial studies. But this role has expanded into a core element of general management, and has spread into separate functions. The context for risk management is laid by the organization's broad strategies, particularly its risk strategy, which is passed on to the separate functions and forms the basis of their own risk management. Specifically, SCRM is responsible for risk management in logistics, and its overall aim is to ensure uninterrupted flows of materials. The context for SCRM is given in a supply chain risk strategy, which is designed by a mixture of top-down design and bottom-up emerging.

Supply chain risk management

Because circumstances vary so widely, we cannot describe precise procedures for SCRM, but there are some general principles, such as the need to balance operational efficiency and risk, take a proactive approach to risk management, share information, and so on. These lead to three core activities of SCRM, of risk identification, analysis and response. Around these three core activities is a series of other tasks, starting with preparation for SCRM and ending with monitoring and control of risks. These steps do not give a recipe for SCRM, but they outline a continuing process that evolves over time.

Identifying risks in the supply chain is notoriously difficult, as there are a huge number of possible risks and forms in which they appear. It is best to focus on the most significant types of risk, and to help with this we can define different categories of risk. A standard classification describes risks as affecting the internal operations of the supply chain members, within the supply chain itself, or coming from the external environment.

The usual approach to identifying risks breaks the overall supply chain process into a series of activities, systematically examines each of these in turn and identifies the risks in each. Many tools have been developed to help with this, and they work in three ways – by analysing past events, collecting opinions or directly analysing operations.

Risk identification leads to a register of significant risks to the supply chain. But there can always be problems – such as the difficulty of identifying risk, managers' reluctance to accept that risks exist, and inherently unknowable risks.

After compiling a register of the most significant risks, managers can analyse each to assess its potential impact. The usual way of doing this uses a quantitative approach that is based on two key factors – the likelihood of a risky event occurring and the consequences when it does occur. Multiplying these together gives an expected value. Managers generally give risks with the highest expected values the most attention. Unfortunately, both the probability and the consequences can be difficult to evaluate, so we often have to use broad estimates, subjective values or agreed categories. Several tools can help with these analyses, such as risk maps, probability–impact matrices and systematic searches of operations.

The risk analysis stage gives an ordered list of risks and their potential impact. Now managers have to design appropriate responses. These depend on circumstances, with the usual alternatives being to ignore the risk, reduce its likelihood, reduce its consequences, transfer the risk, make contingency plans, adapt to it, oppose it or move to another environment. After deciding the most appropriate type of response, managers have to translate this into specific actions. For example, when managers decide to reduce the likely consequences of a risk, they might keep more stocks, add spare capacity, increase agility, improve forecasts and planning, increase collaboration, make to order and so on. Many models can help with such decisions, and we illustrated them by systematic analysis and decision trees.

After designing the response, the next task is to implement it. This has two parts: implementation (to prepare for a risky event) and activation (which actually does the required activities). Often a critical event causes activation, but it can be difficult to identify a specific trigger.

Integrated SCRM

SCRM often seems to focus on the risks within a particular organization, but we know that each member of a supply chain occupies a unique position. Then risks to any single member can be transmitted and expanded into risks to the whole chain. The best way of dealing with these joint risks is not to work in isolation but to have all members cooperating and working together to reduce the level of risk to the whole chain. Although this seems a sensible idea, it is new to most organizations and little real progress has been made. There are many practical reasons for this, ranging from unclear responsibilities through to communication problems.

In principle, integrated SCRM is similar to organizational risk management. Then the core activities are risk identification, analysis and response – with preparation needed before this and monitoring and control afterwards. But now the process is much more complicated, as it needs cooperation between organizations with widely different operations, aims and views. Realistically this limits the amount of likely progress.

We can describe some general principles for integrated SCRM, such as visibility and cooperation – but the most important point is to design a resilient supply chain in the first place. A number of standard principles apply to the design of resilient supply chains, such as starting within individual organizations, taking a strategic view, really understanding the concept of supply chain risk, design chains with risk in mind, always looking for collaborative solutions, and so on.

There are some common features of resilient supply chains. Some of these are essentially physical features, with a resilient supply chain being short, wide and agile, with spare capacity, and so on. Other features refer to relationships, with a resilient chain having collaboration, confidence in partners, visibility, process integration, etc, to allow the joint solution of mutual problems.

Business continuity management

Even the best risk management has unexpected events, and when these are severe they create emergencies. Business continuity management gives a general way of dealing with emergencies. Its characteristic approach is not to analyse risks but instead to consider the elements of a supply chain, see what happens when an element is unavailable, and make plans to restore the flows of materials when the element is unavailable. In other words, it does not look for the causes of problems, but concentrates on dealing with the effects.

For supply chains, the basic requirement of BCM is that the flow of materials is not interrupted by any disaster hitting the chain, or that it is able to return to normal as quickly as possible. The process for organizing this is similar to that for risk management, and we described it in six steps, ranging from preparation for BCM through to monitoring and control.

Surveys suggest that BCM is becoming more widely used, but they also raise doubts about whether the issues faced are the most important. Problems with supply chain security still appear in surprisingly few BCM plans.

Sources of information

Useful websites

Supply chain risk is a new topic, so there is no standard textbook. Of course, there is a lot of material about risk management and a lot more about supply chains – but no text has really brought the two ideas together. There are a growing number of papers in academic and professional journals, and the following references suggest useful places to start looking. Other sources are related websites.

Associations

www.airmic.com – The Association of Insurance and Risk Managers
www.aria.org – the American Risk and Insurance Association
www.ifrima.org – International Federation of Risk and Insurance Management Associations
www.rims.org – the Risk and Insurance Management Society
www.thebci.org – the Business Continuity Institute
www.theirm.org – the Institute of Risk Management

Some other useful websites

www.disasterplan.com
www.genevaassociation.org
www.globalcontinuity.com
www.riskinfo.com

References

Adams, J (1999) *Risky Business*, Adam Smith Institute, London

Ansell, J and Wharton, F (1995) *Risk: Analysis, assessment and management*, John Wiley, Chichester

Bosman, R (2006) *The New Supply Chain Challenge: Risk management in a global economy*, FM Global, Johnston, RI (and at www.fmglobal.com)

Bowman, C and Ash, D (1987) *Strategic Management*, Macmillan, London

Braithwaite, A and Hall, D (1999a) Risky business? Critical decisions in supply chain management (Part 1), *Supply Chain Practice*, **1** (2), pp 40–57

Braithwaite, A and Hall, D (1999b) Risky business? Critical decisions in supply chain management (Part 2), *Supply Chain Practice*, **1** (3), pp 44–58

British Standards Institute (2006) *PAS 56: Guide to business continuity management*, BSI, London

Buehler, K and Pritsch, G (2003) Running with risk, *McKinsey Quarterly*, **3**

Cadbury, J (1992) *Report of the Corporate Governance Working Party*, Gee Professional Publishing, London

Cavinato, JL (2004) Supply chain logistics risks, *International Journal of Physical Distribution and Logistics Management*, **34** (5), pp 383–87

Chapman, CB and Ward, SC (1997) *Project Risk Management*, John Wiley, Chichester

Chapman, P *et al* (2002) Identifying and managing supply chain vulnerability, *Journal of the Institute of Logistics and Transport*, **4** (4), May, pp 59–64

Chapman, R (1998) The effectiveness of working group risk identification and assessment techniques, *International Journal of Project Management*, **16** (6), p 337

Chartered Management Institute (2005) *Business Continuity Management*, CMI, London

Childerley, A (1980) The importance of logistics in the UK economy, *International Journal of Physical Distribution and Materials Management*, **10** (8)

Christopher, M (1986) *The Strategy of Distribution Management*, Heinemann, Oxford

Christopher, M (1998) *Logistics and Supply Chain Management*, 2nd edn, Financial Times Prentice Hall, Harlow

Christopher, M (1999) Global logistics: the role of agility, *Logistics and Transport Focus*, **1** (1)

Christopher, M and Lee, H (2004) Mitigating supply chain risk through improved confidence, *International Journal of Physical Distribution and Logistics Management*, **34** (5), pp 388–96

Christopher, M *et al* (2002) *Supply Chain Vulnerability: Final report on behalf of DTLR, DTI and Home Office*, School of Management, Cranfield University, Cranfield, Bedford

Combined Code on Corporate Governance (2003) Financial Reporting Council, CCH, July

Commercial Motor (2000) Top hauliers are making less, 17 February, p 8, Reed Business Information, Sutton

Computer Sciences Corporation (2004) *Global Survey of Supply Chain Progress*, CSC, Waltham, MA

Cooper, MC, Lambert, DM and Pagh, JD (1997) Supply chain management, *International Journal of Logistics Management*, **8** (1), p 2

Corbett, K (2005) Red scare, *Checkout*, July

Countryman and McDaniel (2007) International vessel casualties and pirates database for year 2006, Law offices of Countryman and McDaniel, Los Angeles, CA (and online at www.cargolaw.com)

Datamonitor (2004) *European Logistics Market Maps 2004*, Datamonitor, London

Decker, H and van Goor, A (1998) Applying activity-based costing to supply chain management, Proceedings of the 1998 Logistics Research Network Conference, Cranfield University

Deloitte (2005) *Disarming the Value Killers: A risk management study*, Deloitte Development, London

Department of Trade and Industry (2006) *Information Security: Understanding business continuity management*, Stationery Office, London

Department for Transport (2005) *Transport Statistics Great Britain*, Stationery Office, London

DETR (1998) *Improving Distribution Efficiency through Supply Chain Co-operation: Energy efficiency best practice programme*, General Information Leaflet 47, Department for the Environment, Transport and the Regions, Harwell

Diekmann, JE, Sewester, EF and Taher, K (1988) *Risk Management in Capital Projects*, Construction Industry Institute, Austin, TX

Drucker, P (1962) The economy's dark continent, *Fortune*, **4**, April, p 103

Economist (2005) Editorial, 29 October, p 71

Economist Intelligence Unit (2001) *Enterprise Risk Management: Implementing new solutions*, Economist Intelligence Unit, London

Evans, B and Powell, M (2000) Synergistic thinking: a pragmatic view of 'lean' and 'agile', *Logistics and Transport Focus*, **2** (10), pp 26–32

Evans, JR and Olson, D (2002) *Introduction to Simulation and Risk Analysis*, Pearson Education, Reading, NJ

Eye for Transport (2005) *Survey of Outsourcing: The latest trends in using 3PL providers*, www.eyefortransport.com

Factor, R (1996) Logistics trends, *Materials Management and Distribution*, June, pp 17–21

Flanagan, R and Norman, G (1993) *Risk Management and Construction*, Blackwell, Oxford

Forrester (2006) *Report on eBusiness*, Research Paper, Forrester, Cambridge, MA

Forrester, JW (1958) Industrial dynamics: a major breakthrough for decision makers, *Harvard Business Review*, **38**, July–August, pp 37–66

Forrester, JW (1961) *Industrial Dynamics*, MIT Press, Boston, MA

Fraser, BW (2003) Managing risk proactively, *Strategic Finance*, **84** (10), pp 36–40

Gartner (2006) *Worldwide B2B Internet Commerce*, Gartner Group, Stamford, CT

Ginn, R (1989) *Continuity Planning*, Elsevier, Amsterdam

Goodwin, P and Wright, G (1998) *Decision Analysis for Management Judgment*, 2nd edn, John Wiley, Chichester

Hammer, M and Champy, J (1993) *Reengineering the Corporation*, Harper Collins, New York

Handfield, RB and Nichols, EL (1999) *Introduction to Supply Chain Management*, Pearson, Upper Saddle River, NJ

Handfield, RB and Nichols, EL (2002) *Supply Chain Redesign: Transforming supply chains into integrated value systems*, Prentice Hall, Upper Saddle River, NJ

Handy, C (1999) *Beyond Certainty*, Harvard Business School Press, Boston, MA

Harrington, L (1996) Untapped savings abound, *Industry Week*, **245** (14), pp 53–58

Hendricks, KB and Singhal, VR (2003) The effect of supply chain glitches on shareholder wealth, *Journal of Operation Management*, **21** (5), pp 501–23

Hetland, PW (2003) Uncertainty management, in *Appraisal, Risk and Uncertainty*, ed NJ Smith, Thomas Telford, London

Hill, GV (1994) Assessing the cost of customer service, in *Logistics and Distribution Planning*, 2nd edn, ed J Cooper, Kogan Page, London

Hunt, B (2001) Issue of the moment, in *Mastering Risk*, vol 1: *Concepts*, ed J Pickford, Pearson Education, Harlow

Hunt, P (2006) Sensible risk and the law, Presentation to Health and Safety Executive Conference on Safe Schools, Healthy Schools, March, London

IBM (2005) *The GMA 2005 Logistics Survey*, IBM Consulting Services, Somers, NY

Imai, M (1986) *Kaizen: The key to Japan's competitive success*, McGraw-Hill, New York

Institute of Directors (1995) *Standards for the Board*, Institute of Directors, London

Institute of Logistics (1998) *Members' Directory*, Institute of Logistics and Transport, Corby

Institute of Management (1999) *Business Continuity Management*, Institute of Management, London

Ishikawa, K *et al* (1988) *What is Total Quality Control?*, Prentice Hall, Englewood Cliffs, NJ

Julius, DA (1990) *Global Companies and Public Policy*, Royal Institute of International Affairs, London

Jüttner, U (2005) Supply chain risk management, *International Journal of Logistics Management*, **16** (1), pp 120–41

Kajüter, P (2003) Risk management in supply chains, in *Strategy and Organization in Supply Chains*, ed SA Seuring *et al*, Springer Verlag, Heidelberg

Kendall, R (1998) *Risk Management for Executives*, FT Prentice Hall, London

Kleindorfer, PR and Saad, GH (2005) Managing disruption risks in supply chains, *Production and Operations Management*, **14** (1), pp 53–68

Kleindorfer, PR *et al* (2003) Accident epidemiology and the US chemical industry, *Risk Analysis*, **23** (5), pp 865–81

Knight, F (1921) *Risk, Uncertainty and Profit*, Harper & Row, New York

Knight, RF and Petty, DJ (2001) Philosophies of risk, shareholder value and the CEO, in *Mastering Risk*, vol 1: *Concepts*, ed J Pickford, Pearson Education, Harlow

Kunreuther, H and Heal, G (2004) Interdependent security: the case of identical agents, *Journal of Risk and Uncertainty*, **23** (2), pp 103–20

Lamming, R (1993) *Beyond Partnership: Strategies for innovation and lean supply*, Prentice Hall, London

Larson, PD and Halldorsson, A (2004) Logistics versus supply chain management: an international survey, *International Journal of Logistics: Research and applications*, **7** (1), pp 17–31

Latour, A (2001) Trial by fire, *Wall Street Journal*, 29 January

Lawless, J (1998) Challenges of going global, *Sunday Times*, 26 April

Lee, H (2004) The triple-A supply chain, *Harvard Business Review*, October, pp 102–12

Lennox, RB (1995) Customer service reigns supreme, *Materials Management and Distribution*, January, pp 17–22

Leontiades, JE (1985) *Multinational Business Strategy*, DC Heath & Co, Lexington, MA

Logistics Institute (2006) *Annual Report on Third-Party Logistics Providers*, Georgia Institute of Technology, Atlanta, GA

MacCrimmon, KR and Wehrung, DA (1986) *Taking Risks: The management of uncertainty*, Free Press, New York

McKinnon, AC (1999) Benchmarking vehicle utilisation and energy efficiency in the food supply chain, School of Management, Heriot-Watt University, Edinburgh

McKinnon, A (2006) Road transport optimisation, in *Global Logistics*, 5th edn, ed D Waters, Kogan Page, London

Malone, R (2006a) *Growing Supply Chain Risks*, www.Forbes.com

Malone, R (2006b) *Worst Supply Chain Risks*, www.Forbes.com

Manktelow, B (2006) Why does outsourcing not deliver?, *Logistics and Transport Focus*, **8** (9), pp 42–45

March, JG and Shapira, Z (1987) Managerial perspectives on risk and risk taking, *Management Science*, **33** (11), pp 1404–18

Mason-Jones, R and Towill, D (1998) Shrinking the supply chain uncertainty cycle, *Control*, September, pp 17–22

Merna, A and Smith, NJ (1999) Privately financed infrastructure for the 21st century, *Proceedings of the Institution of Civil Engineers*, **132**, pp 166–73

Merna, T and Al-Thani, FF (2005) *Corporate Risk Management*, John Wiley, Chichester

Michaels, JV (1996) *Technical Risk Management*, Prentice Hall, Upper Saddle River, NJ

Minahan, TA (2005) *The Supply Risk Benchmark Report*, Aberdeen Group, Boston, MA

MRO (2001) *Supplying the Goods*, MRO Software, London

Murphy, PR and Hall, PK (1995) The relative importance of cost and service in freight transportation choice before and after deregulation: an update, *Transportation Journal*, **35** (1)

National Audit Office (2000) *Supporting Innovation: Managing risk in government departments*, Report by the Comptroller and Auditor General, 17 August, Stationery Office, London

National Counter Terrorism Security Office (2006) *Expecting the Unexpected*, NaCTSO, London

Nelson, D, Mayo, R and Moody, P (1998) *Powered by Honda: Developing excellence in the global enterprise*, John Wiley, New York

Norman, A and Jansson, U (2004) Ericsson's proactive supply chain risk management, *International Journal of Physical Distribution and Logistics Management*, **34** (5), pp 434–56

Office of National Statistics (2006) *Annual Abstract of Statistics*, HMSO, London

Ohmae, K (1985) *Triad Power: The coming shape of global competition*, Free Press, New York

Pauchant, TC and Mitroff, II (1992) *Transforming the Crisis-Prone Organization*, Jossey-Bass, San Francisco, CA

P-E Consulting (1997) *Efficient Customer Response: Supply chain management for the new millennium?*, P-E Consulting, Surrey

Peck, H (2003) *Creating Resilient Supply Chains: A practical guide*, School of Management, Cranfield University, Cranfield, Bedford

Peck, H (2004) Resilience: surviving the unthinkable, *Logistics Manager*, March, pp 16–18

Peck, H (2006) Supply chain vulnerability, risk and resilience, in *Global Logistics*, 5th edn, ed D Waters, Kogan Page, London

Poirier, CC and Quinn, FJ (2003) A survey of supply chain progress, *Supply Chain Management Review*, September/October

Porter, ME (1985) *Competitive Advantage*, Free Press, New York

Porter, ME (1996) What is strategy?, *Harvard Business Review*, November–December, pp 61–79

Prahalad, CK and Hamel, G (1990) The core competencies of the corporation, *Harvard Business Review*, May–June, pp 79–91

Project Management Institute (2004) *A Guide to the Project Management Body of Knowledge*, 3rd edn, PMI, Newton Square, PA

Rawlinson, J (1986) *Creative Thinking and Brainstorming*, Gower, London

Rice, J *et al* (2003) *Supply Chain Response to Terrorism*, August, MIT Center for Transportation and Logistics, Cambridge, MA

Richards, G (2006) *Client Satisfaction with 3PL Suppliers*, Burman Group, London

Richmond and Associates (2007) European logistics, Presentation to the Logistics Round Table, Strasbourg

Road Haulage Association (2000) *Fair Play on Fuel 2000*, RHA, Weybridge

Road Transport Association (2004) *Security Survey Results*, RTA, London

Royal Society (1983) *Risk Assessment: A study group report*, Royal Society, London

Royal Society (1992) *Risk Analysis Perception and Management*, Royal Society, London

Scarborough, J (2007) *Risks during Transportation*, RPW Reports, London

Security Service (2006) *Security Advice: Business continuity*, HMSO, London (and website at www.mi5.gov.uk)

Shapiro, RD and Heskett, JL (1985) *Logistics Strategy*, West Publishing, St Paul, MN

Sheffi, Y (2002) Supply chain management under threat of international terrorism, *International Journal of Logistics Management*, **12** (2), pp 1–11

Smith, N (1995) *Engineering Project Management*, Blackwell, Oxford

Stemmler, L (2006) Risk in the supply chain, in *Global Logistics*, 5th edn, ed D Waters, Kogan Page, London

Supply Chain Digest (2006) Logistics cost survey, Online newsletter, 16 March, www.scdigest.com

Svensson, G (2000) A conceptual framework for the analysis of vulnerability in supply chains, *International Journal of Physical Distribution and Logistics Management*, **30** (9)

Szymankiewicz, J (1997) Efficient customer response: supply chain management for the new millennium?, *Logistics Focus*, **5** (9), pp 16–22

Taguchi, G (1986) *Introduction to Quality Engineering*, Asian Productivity Association, Tokyo

Turnbull (1999) *Internal Control* (Turnbull Report), Institute of Chartered Accountants in England and Wales, London

Wall Street Journal (2003) Oil markets have less margin of error than in last Iraq war, 11 March, A1

Waters, D (1998) *A Practical Introduction to Management Science*, 2nd edn, Addison Wesley Longman, Harlow

Waters, D (2002) *Operations Management*, 2nd edn, Financial Times Prentice Hall, Harlow

Waters, D (2003a) *Inventory Control and Management*, 2nd edn, John Wiley, Chichester

Waters, D (2003b) *Logistics: An introduction to supply chain management*, Palgrave Macmillan, Basingstoke

Waters, D (2006) Trends in the supply chain, in *Global Logistics*, 5th edn, ed D Waters, Kogan Page, London

White, D (1995) Applications of systems thinking to risk management: a review of the literature, *Management Decision*, **33** (10), pp 35–45

Wilding, R and Bernon, M (1999) Millennium fear becomes millennium folly, *Logistics Solutions*, **4**

Wright, G and Goodwin, P (1998) *Forecasting with Judgment*, John Wiley, Chichester

World Trade Organization (2005) *International Trade Statistics*, WTO, Geneva

Index of company examples

Index

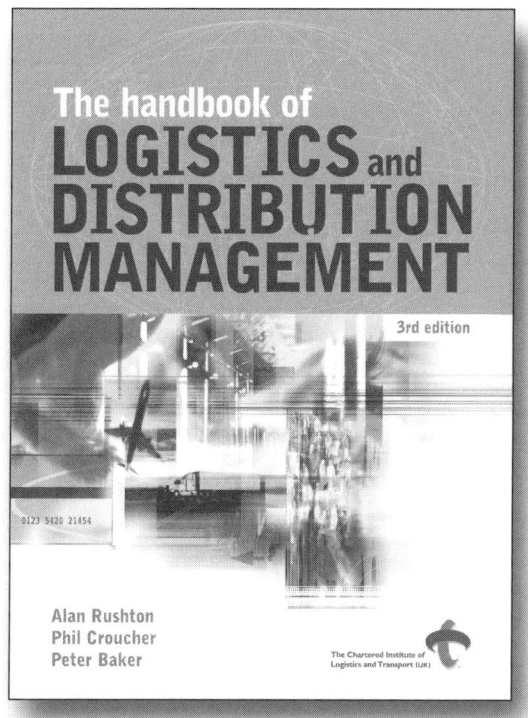